TIME
LIFE ®
BOOKS

Other Publications:

*This volume is one of a series that explains and demonstrates
how to prepare various types of food, and that offers in each
book an international anthology of great recipes.*

Snacks & Sandwiches

BY
THE EDITORS OF TIME-LIFE BOOKS

TIME-LIFE BOOKS/ALEXANDRIA, VIRGINIA

Cover: A composite loaf formed from layers of diverse ingredients yields a vividly patterned slice. To create the cross-sectional geometry, a whole sandwich loaf was sliced horizontally, then bound together by wine-flavored butter studded with pistachios, parboiled asparagus, strips of ham and baked mushrooms *(pages 44-45).*

Time-Life Books Inc.
is a wholly owned subsidiary of

TIME INCORPORATED

Founder: Henry R. Luce 1898-1967

Editor-in-Chief: Henry Anatole Grunwald
President: J. Richard Munro
Chairman of the Board: Ralph P. Davidson
Executive Vice President: Clifford J. Grum
Editorial Director: Ralph Graves
Group Vice President, Books: Joan D. Manley

TIME-LIFE BOOKS INC.

Editor: George Constable
Executive Editor: George Daniels
Director of Design: Louis Klein
Board of Editors: Dale M. Brown, Thomas A. Lewis, Robert G. Mason, Gerry Schremp, Gerald Simons, Rosalind Stubenberg, Kit van Tulleken
Director of Administration: David L. Harrison
Director of Research: Carolyn L. Sackett
Director of Photography: John Conrad Weiser

President: Reginald K. Brack Jr.
Senior Vice President: William Henry
Vice Presidents: George Artandi, Stephen L. Bair, Peter G. Barnes, Robert A. Ellis, Christopher T. Linen, James L. Mercer, Joanne A. Pello, Paul R. Stewart

THE GOOD COOK

Staff for *Snacks & Sandwiches*
Editor: Gerry Schremp
Assistant Editor: Ellen Phillips
Designer: Ellen Robling
Chief Researcher: Juanita T. James
Picture Editor: Adrian Allen
Text Editor: Robert Menaker
Staff Writer: Carol Dana
Researchers: Pamela Gould (principal), Cécile Ablack, Christine Bowie Dove, Patricia Kim, Ann Ready, Maria Zacharias
Assistant Designer: Peg Hosier Schreiber
Copy Coordinators: Allan Fallow, Tonna Gibert, Brian Miller, Ricki Tarlow
Art Assistant: Robert K. Herndon
Picture Coordinator: Alvin Ferrell
Editorial Assistant: Audrey P. Keir
Special Contributors: Susan Feller, Randy Houk, Mark Kauffman (text)

Editorial Operations
Design: Anne B. Landry (art coordinator);
James J. Cox (quality control)
Research: Phyllis K. Wise (assistant director),
Louise D. Forstall
Copy Room: Diane Ullius (director), Celia Beattie
Production: Gordon E. Buck, Peter Inchauteguiz

CHIEF SERIES CONSULTANT

Richard Olney, an American, is a regular contributor to gastronomic magazines in France and in the United States, and is the author of *The French Menu Cookbook* and the award-winning *Simple French Food.* He has conducted cooking courses in France and the United States, and is a member of several renowned gastronomic societies, including La Confrérie des Chevaliers du Tastevin, La Commanderie du Bontemps de Médoc et des Graves and Les Amitiés Gastronomiques Internationales. Although he is chief consultant for the series, this volume was prepared under the guidance of American consultants.

CHIEF AMERICAN CONSULTANT
Carol Cutler is the author of a number of cookbooks, including the award-winning *The Six-Minute Soufflé and Other Culinary Delights.* During the 12 years she lived in France, she studied at the Cordon Bleu and the École des Trois Gourmandes, and with private chefs. She is a member of the Cercle des Gourmettes, a long-established French food society limited to just 50 members, and a charter member of Les Dames d'Escoffier, Washington Chapter.

SPECIAL CONSULTANT
François Dionot, a graduate of L'Ecole des Hôteliers de Lausanne in Switzerland, has worked as a chef, hotel general manager and restaurant manager in the United States and in France. He now conducts his own cooking school in Maryland. He has been largely responsible for the step-by-step photographic sequences in this volume.

PHOTOGRAPHER
Aldo Tutino, a native of Italy, has worked in Milan, New York City and Washington, D.C. He has won a number of awards for his photographs from the New York Advertising Club.

INTERNATIONAL CONSULTANTS
THE UNITED STATES: *Julie Dannenbaum,* director of a cooking school in Philadelphia, Pennsylvania, also conducts cooking classes at the Gritti Palace in Venice, Italy, and at The Greenbrier in White Sulphur Springs, West Virginia. She is the author of two cookbooks and numerous magazine articles. *Judith Olney,* author of *Comforting Food* and *Summer Food,* received her culinary training in England and France. In addition to conducting cooking classes, she regularly contributes articles to gastronomic magazines. *Robert Shoffner,* wine and food editor of *The Washingtonian* magazine, has written many articles on food and wine. GREAT BRITAIN: *Jane Grigson* has written a number of books about food and is cookery correspondent for the London *Observer. Alan Davidson,* a former member of the British Diplomatic Service, is the author of four cookbooks. FRANCE: *Michel Lemonnier,* cofounder and vice president of Les Amitiés Gastronomiques Internationales, is a frequent lecturer on wine. GERMANY: *Jochen Kuchenbecker* was trained as a chef, but has worked for 10 years as a food photographer in several European countries. *Anne Brakemeier* is the co-author of a number of cookbooks. ITALY: *Massimo Alberini,* the author of many cookbooks, is particularly interested in culinary history. THE NETHERLANDS: *Hugh Jans* has published cookbooks, and his recipes appear in a number of Dutch magazines.

Correspondents: Elisabeth Kraemer (Bonn); Margot Hapgood, Dorothy Bacon (London); Miriam Hsia, Lucy T. Voulgaris (New York); Maria Vincenza Aloisi, Josephine du Brusle (Paris); Ann Natanson (Rome).
Valuable assistance was also provided by: Jeanne Buys (Amsterdam); Hans-Heinrich Wellmann, Gertraud Bellon (Hamburg); Judy Aspinall (London); Diane Asselin (Los Angeles); Bona Schmid, Maria Teresa Marenco (Milan); Carolyn T. Chubet, Christina Lieberman (New York); Michèle le Baube (Paris); Mimi Murphy (Rome).

CONTENTS

Convivial Fare

As is so often the case in culinary matters, the French have the best term for snacks: *amuse-gueule*—that which amuses the palate. The clear implication is that sustenance takes second place; these are savory treats to be eaten not as part of a meal but purely for pleasure.

Almost any food in any form can conceivably serve in this role, but some dishes seem especially designed for snacking. The sandwich is the paradigm. Supposedly named for a gambling Earl of Sandwich who ate his meat between two slices of bread in order not to interrupt his play, a sandwich is an assembly—an easily handled platform or container that may be covered or filled with any of dozens of spreads, sauces or stuffings. Other snacks, which employ vegetables or pastry as containers or platforms, call for particularly delicate fillings, but the principle remains the same.

How to form these assemblies is the subject of this book. The following 12 pages introduce the basic components of snacks: the doughs that become breads and buns; the pastries that make puffs, miniature tart shells and other containers; and the flavored butters, sauces and saucelike dips that serve as fillings, spreads and condiments.

After this introductory section, a series of chapters deals with particular types of assemblies. The first chapter focuses on assemblies whose foundations come ready-made: vegetables that can be hollowed out and filled, eggs that can be hard-boiled and stuffed, and cheeses that can be blended with flavorings, molded into various shapes and coated with spices and herbs or made into appealing packages with wrappers of green leaves.

A chapter devoted to sandwiches deals with traditional American assemblies such as the cheeseburger, but it also includes sandwiches that are fried, broiled or baked. In this chapter you will also learn how to mass-produce canapés, how to garnish sandwiches most appealingly, how to make the fanciful concoctions served at tea parties, and even how to stuff whole loaves of bread with savory sandwich fillings.

A chapter concerning pastry snacks teaches how to shape folded packages and miniature shells from simple short-crust pastry and explores ways to handle other pastries. Among these are French *choux* paste, paper-thin phyllo from the Middle East and the delicate flour or wheat-starch wrappers of China. A final chapter demonstrates how to make the apparently exotic snacks founded on dough or batter—among them, Italian pizza, Russian blini and Mexican tortillas.

Once you have mastered the principles of assembling these snacks, you will be able to improvise countless arrangements and combinations to suit your own fancy. As inspiration, the second half of this book offers an anthology of more than 200 recipes, selected from the cookbooks of 21 countries.

Matching food and drink

Sausages wrapped in crisp pastry, eggs stuffed with Roquefort cheese and herbs, and small, yeasty pancakes coated with sour cream and caviar are delightful frivolities best appreciated when shared with friends. Like all snacks, these lend themselves to sociable eating—and drinking. In fact, it is the beverage that frequently determines the atmosphere of the gathering and the snack assemblies appropriate to it.

Beer, for instance, calls for hearty snacks that complement its robust taste: hot dogs, pizza, or any of the spicy combinations based on tortillas. The subtler flavor of tea, in contrast, is traditionally set off by mild, buttery sandwiches or—in the Chinese manner—by the delicate steamed pastries and buns known as *dim sum,* or "heart's delight."

When the beverage is assertively alcoholic and the group of friends is large, snacks usually increase in number and variety for the entertainment of the guests. This ritualized form of snacking, known in the United States as the cocktail party, has counterparts in almost every country. In Spain, for instance, as many as 30 different snacks may be presented to accompany chilled dry sherry. Served late in the evening, the snacks are known as *tapas,* or "lids," after the bread slices that once were laid on top of wineglasses to discourage flies. Greeks serve a similar variety of light foods with ouzo, a sweet, anise-flavored liqueur; the Greek assortment is known as *orektika,* or "sampling." The Russian version of a snack table is called *zakuski*—"small bites." Not surprisingly, the drink that accompanies the food is vodka, and the table is dominated by caviar.

The making of snacks

As a rule, snacks are founded on simple ingredients and cooking techniques. It is the cook's imaginative, lighthearted approach to the combinations and shaping of ingredients—and to their presentation—that turns the food into a culinary diversion, whether the occasion is a cocktail party for a hundred people, a gathering of a few good friends or tea for two. The humble cheese sandwich, for instance, becomes a tempting golden package when it is deep fried to make *mozzarella in carrozza (pages 54-55).* Similarly, raw vegetables sliced for dipping in a rich sauce such as garlic mayonnaise acquire immeasurable appeal when they are cut so that they may be reassembled as the edible still life shown on page 21. The object of all such creations is to delight the curious appetite—to amuse the palate.

A Breadmaking Primer

Sandwiches, pizza *(pages 86-87)*, Chinese pork buns *(pages 84-85)* and innumerable other snacks all begin with flour, liquid and yeast. Correctly handled, these ingredients produce breads—nourishing, sweet-smelling, and at once both light and substantial.

The initial steps in forming bread—demonstrated at right, top, with a basic dough *(recipe, page 164)*—are designed to promote leavening by the yeast, a fungus that is grown commercially and sold either as dry granules or as fresh cakes. To activate the yeast and ensure its even distribution in the dough, it must be dissolved—the granules in 85° F. [30° C.] water, the cake in 110° F. [45° C.] water. The yeast is then combined with flour, more water, and salt for flavor.

The next step is kneading, which disperses water through the flour, activating flour proteins called gluten. Gluten forms a microscopic three-dimensional mesh that holds the dough together. At the same time, kneading distributes the yeast, a necessity if the bread is to have an even texture.

After it is kneaded, the dough must be left to rest so that the yeast can grow. Feeding on the starch in the flour, the organisms give off the carbon dioxide gas that expands the dough. To break the gas bubbles down into tiny units and spread them more evenly, thus producing a finer texture, the risen dough is punched down *(Step 4, top),* kneaded again and left to rise, after which it may be formed into a ball or cylinder and baked to make a hearty, crisp-crusted loaf.

Although these basic steps remain the same for any bread dough, elaborations and variations are legion. For example, sandwich bread *(bottom demonstration; recipe, page 165)* includes butter and milk to make it moist and rich. To produce a close-grained, fine-textured bread that may be sliced very thin, the dough receives additional punchings down and kneadings. And to give it the requisite rectangular shape and keep it from forming a thick crust in the dry oven heat, the loaf is baked in a covered pan. The pan shown here is a lidded one, available at kitchen-equipment shops; a loaf pan can be used instead, if covered with buttered foil, a baking sheet and a weight.

Producing a Basic Dough

1 **Mixing yeast and flour.** In a large bowl, combine the yeast with tepid water. Stir briefly, then allow the mixture to rest in a warm place (80° F. [25° C.] is ideal) for 10 to 15 minutes, until it is frothy. Stir in the flour and salt.

2 **Blending ingredients.** Using a wooden spoon, stir in additional tepid water until the mixture becomes a stiff, shaggy dough. Squeeze the dough with your hands *(above)* to mix the ingredients more thoroughly. Then gather the sticky mass into a ball.

Shaping a Sandwich Loaf

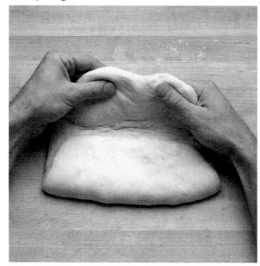

1 **Folding the dough.** Make sandwich-bread dough as in Steps 1 through 4 above. Then place the dough on a floured surface and knead it for three or four minutes. Flatten it into a rectangle about 12 inches [30 cm.] long and 10 inches [25 cm.] wide. Fold the rectangle into thirds across its length, overlapping the three layers *(above)*.

2 **Folding again.** Place the folded dough in an oiled bowl, cover and let it rise for about 45 minutes, until it has doubled in volume. Punch down the dough, transfer it to a floured surface, knead for three or four minutes and flatten it again into a rectangle. Fold the rectangle in half and pinch the edges together to seal them.

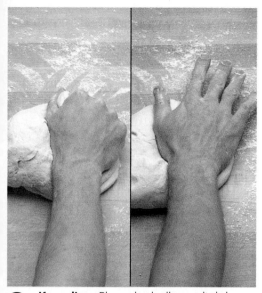

3 **Kneading.** Place the ball on a lightly floured work surface. Flatten the dough with the heel of your hand, fold it toward yourself, turn it so that the fold is at one side, and push it down and away *(above, left)*. Fold, turn and push until the dough is smooth and elastic *(right)* — about 10 to 15 minutes.

4 **Punching down.** Ball up the dough and place it in a clean, oiled bowl. Cover and put it in a warm, draft-free place. After about one and a half hours, when the dough has doubled in volume, lightly press it; the dent you make should close slowly. Plunge your fist into the dough with one stroke to deflate it.

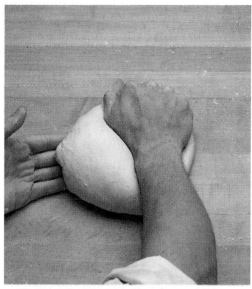

5 **Kneading again.** Place the dough on a lightly floured surface and knead as before, working for three or four minutes, until the dough is satiny. If you are making a basic bread, flatten the dough with the heel of your hand, then roll it into a ball or cylinder and let it rise for about one hour before baking it.

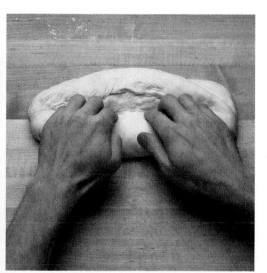

3 **Shaping a loaf.** Roll the dough toward yourself until the long sealed edge is on top. Push your finger tips down into the dough along this edge to form a deep crease. Fold the dough in half along the crease to form a cylinder.

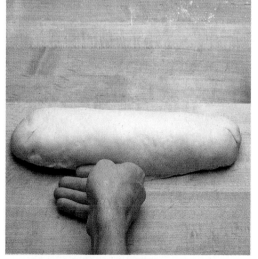

4 **Sealing the dough.** With your finger tips, pinch together the edges of the cylinder to seal them. Then roll the cylinder forward so that the long sealed seam is underneath it.

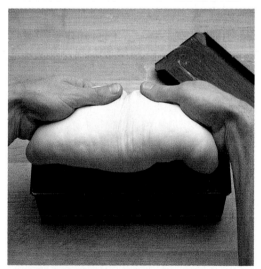

5 **Baking.** Fit the dough, seam side down, into a buttered sandwich-bread pan. Let the dough rise, uncovered, until it doubles in size — about 45 minutes. Butter the pan lid, slide it on, and place the pan in an oven preheated to 400° F. [200° C.]. Reduce the heat at once to 375° F. [190° C.], and bake for about 45 minutes.

A Pair of Versatile Pastries

Two forms of pastry, *choux* paste and short crust, give rise to a broad spectrum of snacks ranging from tiny puffs to tarts and turnovers. Both types are based on flour, water and butter, but the ingredients are handled differently to give each pastry its distinctive character.

Choux paste *(top; recipe, page 163)* is made by cooking large quantities of water together with flour and butter, then enriching the mixture with eggs. The result is a stiff, sticky paste that must be piped from a pastry bag or spooned onto a baking sheet. During baking, the water becomes steam, forcing the paste to puff into airy, hollow mounds.

Short crust *(below; recipe, page 164)* is made with an absolute minimum of water—only enough to activate the gluten in the flour so that the pastry will cohere and can be rolled into thin sheets. Too much water will cause the gluten to become overdeveloped, producing tough, rubbery pastry. Too little, on the other

hand, will result in underdeveloped gluten and mealy pastry.

Butter helps to control development of gluten in short crust. The butter is cut into the flour—distributed throughout in small bits—before water is added, and it acts as waterproofing, preventing water from reaching more flour particles than necessary to make the pastry cohere. For the short crust to be crisp and flaky, both butter and water must be ice-cold: If the butter softens, it will spread and coat too many flour particles.

To prevent warm hands from softening the butter as you form the pastry, handle it as little as possible. Some softening is inevitable, of course; to firm the butter, chill the pastry before you roll it out.

The pastry may be simply rolled into a thin sheet to make short crust, which may be used as it is, or transformed by repeated rolling and folding *(Steps 5 and 6, opposite)* into the many-layered pastry known as rough puff.

Choux: An Egg-rich Paste

1 **Adding flour.** In a heavy saucepan, bring water and diced butter to a rolling boil. When the butter has completely melted, reduce the heat to medium, and pour in flour all at once, stirring steadily with a wooden spoon.

Short Crust: A Butter-flecked Sheet

1 **Cutting in butter.** Place the flour and salt in a mixing bowl. Cut chilled unsalted butter into small pieces and drop them into the bowl. Rapidly cut the butter into tiny bits in the flour, using two knives in a crossed slicing motion.

2 **Binding with water.** When the butter pieces are the size of peas and well coated with flour, use a fork to stir in ice water—a little at a time. Add just enough water to make the pastry cling together in a mass.

3 **Chilling the pastry.** Quickly gather up the pastry with both hands and lightly press it into a ball. Flatten the ball into a thick cake, enclose it in plastic wrap, and chill it in the refrigerator for two to three hours.

2 **Blending ingredients.** Cook the mixture over medium heat, beating steadily with the spoon to blend the flour and liquid together. The mixture will be lumpy at first *(above)*, but it will smooth out within a minute or so.

3 **Finishing cooking.** As soon as the mixture pulls away from the sides of the pan in a smooth mass *(above)* remove the pan from the heat. Let the mixture cool for about two minutes.

4 **Enriching with eggs.** Beat whole eggs, one at a time, into the cooled mixture, making sure that each is thoroughly incorporated before adding the next. When all of the eggs are incorporated, the *choux* paste will be smooth and shiny and ready for use.

4 **Rolling short crust.** Place the chilled pastry on a lightly floured work surface. Smack it with a rolling pin to soften it slightly. Working from the center in short, light strokes, roll out the pastry into a long narrow rectangle no more than ¼ inch [6 mm.] thick. It now may be used as short crust or folded to make rough puff pastry.

5 **Starting rough puff pastry.** On a lightly floured surface, fold one end of the rectangle at a time toward the center of the dough. The two ends should meet or overlap slightly in the center.

6 **Finishing rough puff.** Brush excess flour from the pastry. Then fold the dough in half lengthwise to make a package four layers thick. Starting from the narrow end of the package, roll the dough into a rectangle. Repeat the folding, enclose the dough in plastic wrap and refrigerate it for 30 minutes. Repeat the rolling, folding and chilling three times.

Varying the Character of Butter

Butter is indispensable in assembling most sandwiches and snacks. Used plain (and in unsalted form for the finest flavor), it adds richness and seals bread against sogginess. Made into a compound butter by the addition of herbs, vegetables, meat or seafood, it transforms the blandest bread or vegetable into a snack of distinction.

To produce compound butters, you will need butter that is soft enough to amalgamate with the flavoring ingredients. Warming the butter to soften it would also make it greasy; instead, the butter should be chilled, then creamed—pounded with a rolling pin to make it pliable, and beaten with a spoon to aerate it. The result is *beurre en pommade* (creamed butter), the foundation of all classic compound butters.

Almost any food, properly prepared, can be used to flavor the *beurre en pommade (recipes, page 163)*. Mild-flavored ingredients such as herbs *(box, below, right)* or sautéed mushrooms are simply chopped and beaten into the prepared butter. The mixture is then sieved to ensure a smooth texture.

If the flavoring is an assertive ingredient such as horseradish or anchovies *(opposite, top)* you must add it in precisely gauged amounts. For the best results, the flavorings should be puréed or grated, then sieved before they are added to the butter. This way, you can incorporate small quantities, tasting after each addition to be sure the mixture does not become too pungent.

Puréeing and sieving perform extra functions for butters that are flavored and colored by the crushed shells and meat of cooked shrimp, lobster, crab or crayfish. To extract their essences, the shells and flesh must be pounded together vigorously with the butter. The purée mixture is then carefully sieved, not only to refine its texture, but also to remove every particle of shell.

Compound butters can be applied in a variety of ways. They may be simply spread on bread or bland vegetables such as zucchini *(page 23)*. Or, for particularly attractive effects, the butters can be piped through a pastry bag *(pages 26-27)* or chilled and cut into appealing shapes for garnishes *(page 39)*.

1 **Softening the butter.** Chill two ¼-pound [125-g.] sticks of unsalted butter until they are hard. Beat each stick with a rolling pin to flatten and soften it, folding it over from time to time with a spatula. With the spatula, transfer the butter to a chilled bowl.

2 **Creaming the butter.** With a sturdy wooden spoon or whisk, vigorously beat the softened butter for about five minutes, until it is light and fluffy. It is now ready to be flavored.

A Mild Herbal Blend

1 **Chopping herbs.** Blanch 2 cups [½ liter] of fresh herbs to brighten their colors; watercress, parsley, chervil and chives are used here. Dry the herbs on paper towels. Mound handfuls of herbs and rock the blade of a knife over them to chop them fine. Stir the chopped herbs into creamed butter.

2 **Smoothing the butter.** Use a rubber spatula or wooden spoon to force the herb-butter mixture through a fine-meshed sieve into a bowl. Cover the bowl and refrigerate the butter until you are ready to use it.

A Bold Partnership with Anchovies

1 **Pounding the anchovies.** Drain eight or nine oil-packed anchovy fillets. Transfer the fillets to a mortar and pound them with a pestle until they are reduced to a rough paste. Alternatively, purée the fillets in a food processor.

2 **Sieving.** Transfer a few spoonfuls of the anchovy paste to a fine-meshed sieve and, with a wooden spoon, sieve the paste onto creamed butter.

3 **Blending the butter.** Stir, then taste the butter: It should have a distinct but not overwhelming anchovy flavor. If it is too mild, sieve in more anchovy paste, stir to incorporate it, and taste again. When the flavor satisfies you, cover the bowl and chill the butter until you are ready to serve it.

The Essence of Shellfish

1 **Pounding the shellfish.** Poach fresh, unpeeled shellfish — shrimp are used in this demonstration. Drain the shellfish, chop them coarse — without separating the meat from the shells. A handful at a time, crush the shellfish to a rough paste, using either a mortar and pestle, as here, or a food processor.

2 **Blending in butter.** A spoonful at a time, pound the creamed butter into the crushed shellfish. Continue pounding until you have a fairly smooth paste.

3 **Straining out shell.** Force spoonfuls of the shellfish-and-butter paste through a fine-meshed sieve — the drum sieve shown makes the job easier. Scrape off and discard the bits of shell and cartilage that collect on the mesh as each spoonful is sieved. Cover the mixture and chill it until serving time.

Two Ways to Make Mayonnaise

The sauce most widely employed in making snacks and sandwiches is mayonnaise. Its basic formulation could hardly be simpler: Egg yolks, oil and flavorings are whipped into a creamy emulsion by hand, or whole eggs, oil and flavoring are whirled in a blender or food processor.

Mayonnaise will form successfully if two rules are followed: First, the eggs, oil, and the vinegar or lemon-juice flavoring must be at room temperature; chilled ingredients will not emulsify. Second, the oil must be beaten into the eggs very gradually. Begin adding drops of oil, beating until no oil is visible on the surface of the mixture. When the mayonnaise begins to form, the oil may be added in a thin stream. (In all, you will need about ½ cup [125 ml.] of oil for each yolk, or, if using a machine, each whole egg.) Never add large amounts of oil at a time—the egg will not be able to absorb it, and the mayonnaise will separate and liquefy, a mishap known as breaking.

Even if the mayonnaise does break, it can be salvaged: Beat an egg yolk in a clean bowl, then gradually whisk the liquefied mayonnaise into it.

Breaking is less apt to occur when mayonnaise is made in a blender or a processor, because the machine combines the ingredients rapidly and thoroughly. Mayonnaise made in a machine, however, will thicken into a heavy mass in the time it takes to add the oil unless egg white is included to thin it. The result is a mayonnaise less rich in flavor and less silky in texture than that made by hand.

Any basic mayonnaise tastes mainly of egg and oil, with a hint of acidity from the vinegar or lemon juice. The oil may be olive, which makes the mayonnaise very strong flavored. Many cooks replace part or all of the olive oil with mild-flavored vegetable oil. And the basic mixture may be varied by the addition of other ingredients *(recipes, page 166)*. You may, for instance, add chopped sour gherkins, scallions and herbs to produce remoulade sauce; or you can make green mayonnaise by including chopped herbs and leaves such as watercress and spinach.

Making mayonnaise by hand. Place a bowl on a damp towel to prevent slipping and put in it egg yolks, salt, pepper and vinegar *(above, left)* or lemon juice. Whisk the mixture until it is foamy, then add drops of oil, whisking steadily so that each drop is absorbed. When the mixture thickens *(center)*, whisk in oil in a thin stream. Finished mayonnaise is yellow and thick enough to hold its shape in the whisk *(right)*. If the mayonnaise is too thick, thin it by whisking in drops of vinegar or lemon juice.

Making mayonnaise in a blender. In a blender jar, combine an egg with vinegar or lemon juice, salt and pepper, and blend at high speed for 30 seconds. While you continue to blend, pour in the oil in a thin stream *(above, left)*. Add a few drops of vinegar if the mixture becomes stiff. The finished mayonnaise will be soft and cream-colored *(right)*.

Cream-Cheese Transformations

Cream cheese has a mild, tart flavor that makes it a fine foundation for spreads, fillings and dips. However, cream cheese is too stiff for use as a spread or a filling unless it is first mashed to a paste, then thinned with sour cream and lightened with whipped heavy cream. For a dipping sauce, it is necessary to thin the cream cheese even further—this time using un-whipped light cream *(Steps 3 and 4)*.

To give any such mixture a more assertive flavor, mash the cream cheese together with a pungent cheese such as Roquefort *(box, bottom right)* or Gorgonzola before thinning it. If you want contrasts in color and taste, add chopped ingredients to the basic whipped cream cheese. In the demonstration on pages 24-25, for instance, a filling for mushrooms is produced by adding Roquefort cheese and chopped pistachio nuts to cream cheese. Other possible additions to thinned cream cheese are chopped green pepper, white radish, scallions or cucumber. Dips based on cream cheese might include chopped clams, smoked salmon, fines herbes or liver paste.

1 Whipping the cream. Pour chilled heavy cream into a chilled bowl. Whisk the cream slowly at first, then more vigorously as it begins to foam. When the cream thickens, whisk slowly again. Beat until the cream forms soft peaks when the whisk is lifted *(above)*.

2 Blending ingredients for a spread. Let cream cheese soften at room temperature for one hour, until it is malleable; then mash it with a fork until it is soft and pasty. Add sour cream, blending with a whisk *(above, left)*. Whisk in whipped cream until the mixture is smooth and holds its shape when lifted *(right)*. The mixture now may be flavored and used as a spread or filling.

3 Thinning with cream. To make a dip, pour light cream into the thick, whipped cheese mixture, adding only small amounts at a time and whisking after each addition so that the cream is thoroughly incorporated.

4 Testing the dip. Continue whisking in light cream until the cream-cheese mixture, when lifted with the whisk, falls back onto the surface in the form of a slowly dissolving ribbon. The cream cheese is then liquid enough for a dip.

Adding a Sharp Note

Blending two cheeses. When using a strong cheese such as Roquefort to season a cream-cheese spread or dip, first allow both cheeses to come to room temperature, then mash them together with a fork *(above)*. Thin the mixture as shown above and left.

A Multiplicity of Dips

Dips—highly seasoned, saucelike mixtures used as condiments for crackers, bread and vegetables—can be prepared with many different kinds of equipment: a heavy chopping knife, a grater, a mortar and pestle, a blender or, as shown here, a food processor. In choosing tools, consider the ingredients of the dip and the texture it is meant to have *(recipes, pages 92-106)*.

The most saucelike dips are puréed vegetables or fish thinned with oil, vinegar or lemon juice, and brightened with distinctive seasonings. French *tapenade (top)*, for instance, is a purée of ripe olives and anchovies—in this case salt anchovies, which have a more robust taste than oil-packed fillets. Greek *hummus (bottom, near right)* consists mainly of puréed chick-peas, flavored and enriched with *tahini*, or sesame-seed paste.

Other Mediterranean puréed dips include *baba ghanoush*, an eggplant purée flavored with garlic *(bottom, far right)*; *taramosalata*, made of *tarama*, or mullet roe, available at Greek markets *(page 16)*; and *skordalia*, a blend of potatoes, garlic and pine nuts *(page 16)*.

Any of these dips may be puréed with hand tools, but the work goes more quickly and the dip will be smoother if a food processor is used. However, if garlic is included, mash it to a paste with a mortar and pestle before combining it with other ingredients. A processor would chop garlic into fragments and roughen the dip.

A processor may be used to prepare ingredients for dips that feature textural contrast, but not for the final blending. A Middle Eastern *tzatziki (page 17)*, for instance, is made from grated cucumber—salted and drained to prevent wateriness—and yogurt. The cucumber may be grated in the processor, but it should be mixed with the yogurt by hand so that the pieces remain distinct: The processor would reduce the ingredients to a purée.

Relish-like dips—mixtures of roughly chopped elements—should be handmade. Cypriot relish *(recipe, page 102)*, made mainly of green olives and garlic, is a dip of this type, as is Mexican *guacamole*—mashed avocado with chopped onion, chilies and tomatoes *(page 17)*.

Tapenade

1 **Pitting the olives.** With a small, sharp knife cut a deep, lengthwise slit to the pit of each olive. Split each olive open with your thumbs *(above)*; prize out the pit and discard it.

2 **Boning the anchovies.** Soak salt anchovies in cold water for about 30 minutes, to reduce their saltiness. With your thumbnail, split each anchovy along its belly from head to tail. Pull the halves apart to expose the backbone; pull out the backbone. Or bone the anchovies while they are still firm, then soak them. Dry the fillets on a towel.

Hummus

1 **Assembling ingredients.** Soak dried chick-peas in water overnight, then boil them until tender — about one hour. Drain them, reserving the liquid. Pound salt and peeled garlic cloves to a paste; stir in lemon juice. Pour the chick-peas into a food processor. To enrich the purée, add up to one part *tahini* for every four parts chick-peas.

2 **Adding oil.** Process the chick-peas and *tahini* for a few seconds to form a coarse purée. Add the garlic paste and process to blend. Moisten with a little cooking liquid and process for a few seconds more; repeat until smooth. Spread the *hummus* on a dish and dress it with olive oil *(above)*. Garnish it with paprika and chopped parsley.

3 **Puréeing the ingredients.** After fitting the steel chopping blade into the food processor, put the olives and the anchovies into the processor bowl. Add dry mustard, capers *(above)*, Cognac, lemon juice and freshly ground pepper.

4 **Adding oil.** Start the processor. To ensure a smooth paste, stop the machine every few seconds and scrape down the sides of the bowl. When the purée is smooth, stop the machine and dribble in olive oil *(above)*. Process the purée for a few seconds more. Continue to add oil and to process briefly until the mixture becomes creamy and moist.

5 **Storing the tapenade.** Spoon the *tapenade* into a jar. Shake the jar to settle the contents, and smooth the surface of the *tapenade*. To seal the surface, dribble in a thin layer of olive oil, then close the jar. Refrigerated, the *tapenade* will keep for several months; after each use, smooth its surface and cover it with a new film of oil.

Baba Ghanoush

1 **Puréeing eggplant.** Prick eggplants and bake them at 350° F. [180° C.] for about an hour, until their stem ends can be pierced easily. Cool the eggplants, halve them, scoop out their flesh *(above)* and process it. If the purée seems too moist, add fresh white bread crumbs.

2 **Flavoring the purée.** Pound together salt and peeled garlic with a mortar and pestle *(left)*; stir in lemon juice. Add the flavorings to the processor or, as here, stir the eggplant purée into the mortar. Dribble in a little olive oil *(center)* and stir with the pestle; continue to stir in oil until the mixture is rich and smooth *(right)*.

Taramosalata

1 **Puréeing the roe.** Trim the crusts from firm, homemade-type white bread and soak the bread in water briefly. With a mortar and pestle, pound the *tarama*, then pound in grated onion and olive oil until a smooth paste forms.

2 **Thickening the dip.** Transfer the *tarama* paste to a mixing bowl. Squeeze the bread pieces one by one to extract as much moisture as possible. Then, bit by bit, whisk the bread into the paste.

3 **Seasoning.** Beat freshly squeezed lemon juice into the purée. Then whisk in small amounts of olive oil until the *taramosalata* is the consistency of a thick mayonnaise. Cover the bowl and keep it refrigerated until serving time.

Skordalia

1 **Pounding the flavorings.** Boil potatoes until they are tender. Drain, peel and mash them, and let them cool. Combine pine nuts, peeled garlic cloves and salt in a mortar and, with a pestle, pound them to a thick paste.

2 **Seasoning the mixture.** Scrape the nut paste onto the mashed potatoes. Rinse the mortar with fresh lemon juice and pour the juice onto the potatoes.

3 **Forming the dip.** Mix the ingredients together, using an electric mixer set at medium speed, as here, or a sturdy spoon. Stir in olive oil to thin the mixture to the consistency of a very thick mayonnaise, then beat in an egg to enrich the dip. Cover the *skordalia* and refrigerate it until serving time.

Guacamole

1 **Seeding chilies.** Peel and seed tomatoes; chop them into coarse pieces. Chop coriander leaves and onion into fine bits. Halve ripe avocados; remove the pits. Slice open fresh green serrano chilies and scoop out the seeds with your thumbs; to keep the oils from irritating your skin, wash your hands.

2 **Pounding the seasonings.** Put the onion, coriander, chilies and salt in a mortar and pound them to a thick paste. Transfer the paste to a bowl.

3 **Blending.** Scoop out the avocado flesh and add it to the seasoning paste. Mash the avocado with a fork, blending it with the paste, then fold in the tomatoes. Garnish with chopped onion and coriander sprigs and serve immediately to prevent discoloration.

Tzatziki

1 **Extracting excess liquid.** Peel cucumbers, halve them and scoop out the seeds, then grate the flesh and salt it. Put the cucumber flesh in a strainer set over a bowl to drain for at least 30 minutes. Press the cucumber in the strainer with the back of a spoon to force out liquid. Peel and crush garlic cloves fine; chop fresh mint leaves.

2 **Mixing ingredients.** Add the drained cucumber, the mint leaves and the garlic to yogurt. Sprinkle on a little salt and freshly ground pepper.

3 **Finishing the dip.** Stir the ingredients gently with a spoon to blend them thoroughly. Season to taste and, if you are not going to serve the dip immediately, cover it and chill it in the refrigerator until serving time.

1
Small Treats
Exploring the Potential of Everyday Foods

Sectioning raw vegetables
How to stuff mushroom caps
The handling of a pastry bag
Rolling up an egg sponge
Ways to mold softened cheeses

With the addition of a tiny heart of Bibb lettuce, this platterful of fresh raw vegetables is ready to partner a tangy hot or cold dip. To capture both the beauty and the bounty of the garden, the vegetables are presented unpeeled, and the largest have been sliced only partway to preserve their natural shapes.

Any small, sturdy snack that can be eaten from the hand, without the aid of a fork or the support of a plate, qualifies as finger food. Examples of such fare range from packaged, ready-to-eat morsels—chips and nuts and such—to painstakingly assembled canapés *(pages 36-45)* and miniature pastries *(pages 60-77)*. Between these extremes is a host of easily prepared but imaginative creations that the cook can make from scratch with three kitchen staples: vegetables, eggs and cheeses.

Vegetables, for instance, can simply be presented raw, accompanied by a dipping sauce *(pages 20-21)*. Small vegetables such as mushrooms or green beans need only be cleaned to be eaten whole. Large vegetables can be sliced into sticks or rounds or, in a less conventional approach, sectioned partially *(page 21)* to produce a natural-looking market basket or centerpiece *(left)*. With a bit more artifice, vegetables also can be hollowed or sculpted to form edible containers for flavored butters or cheese mixtures. Tender vegetables such as zucchini and green peppers may be used for this purpose in their raw state *(pages 22-23)*; dense-fleshed vegetables such as beets and new potatoes require only minimal precooking to make them ready for transformation into containers *(pages 24-25)*.

Eggs are as versatile a finger food as vegetables. Stuffed hard-boiled eggs, for example, produce a variegated display when the yolk mixture is tinted with herbs, puréed tomato or sorrel, or pounded anchovies or shrimp. With a pastry bag, the yolk can be piped into the hollows of halved egg whites *(pages 26-27)* in swirls and spirals of the cook's choosing. To ring a change on the egg theme, beaten eggs that are thickened with cream sauce and baked in a jelly-roll pan will yield a delicate, spongy sheet, suitable for spreading with mousses and purées. The sheet is then rolled into a sausage shape and sliced *(pages 28-29)*.

Flavored cheeses served with crackers or rounds of dark bread form yet another important genre of finger food. The basic formula calls for softened cream cheese *(page 13)* enriched with seasonings, molded into a log or ball, and coated with nuts, herbs, peppercorns or paprika. The same techniques also can be applied to shredded scraps of hard cheeses such as Cheddar or Gouda, or to underripe Camembert or Brie that has been soaked in wine—a process the English call sousing—drained, and then mashed to a paste.

An Artful Cornucopia

Raw vegetables, fresh from the garden or the greengrocer, make the most colorful of finger foods. Small vegetables can be presented whole, unaltered except for basic cleaning and trimming. Large ones must be separated into sections, florets or leaves for eating, but if they are cut as demonstrated here, they can be reassembled and displayed as if they, too, had been newly picked.

Depending on the cook's taste, this splendid array—known as *crudités* in France—may be accompanied by one or more of myriad dips or sauces based on mayonnaise, cream cheese, puréed vegetables, sour cream or yogurt *(demonstrations, pages 20-21; recipes, pages 92-106)*. The dipping sauce used here is an assertive blend of anchovies and garlic called *bagna cauda,* meaning "hot bath" in Italian. Because it is served warm, rather than at room temperature as are most dips, it contrasts pleasantly with the cool vegetables.

Whatever the sauce chosen, the vegetables themselves remain the chief attraction. For maximum appeal to eye and palate, they must be unflawed and of absolute freshness: Wilted or blemished specimens cannot be disguised in this sort of presentation. The vegetables may be prepared in advance and kept refrigerated in perforated plastic bags—or in a bowl of ice water, in the case of roots—for up to three hours. However, the chilled vegetables should be brought to room temperature before serving; otherwise, their flavors will be muted.

Numerous vegetables are tender and tasty enough to serve raw. The arrangement at right features carrots, turnips, zucchini, yellow crookneck squash, red and green peppers, cauliflower florets, mushrooms, spinach and Belgian endive leaves, and Boston lettuce hearts. Other candidates include celery ribs, parsnips, cucumbers, asparagus, cabbage leaves, radishes, scallions and cherry tomatoes.

1 **Slicing carrots.** Insert a knife tip about ½ inch [1 cm.] from the base of each peeled carrot, and slice lengthwise through the tip. Make slices at ¼-inch [6-mm.] intervals until the carrot is cut into thin strips attached at the base. Bind the strips with string to prevent curling. Immerse the carrots in ice water to keep them crisp.

2 **Slicing turnips.** Scrub and trim turnips and slice them from top to bottom into thin disks, cutting them all the way through. Bind the pieces together with string to keep each turnip assembled. Immerse the tied vegetables in ice water to keep them crisp and to prevent their flesh from discoloring.

Bagna Cauda: A Pungent Counterpoint

1 **Preparing anchovies.** Drain oil-packed anchovy fillets. On a cutting board, stack together a few fillets at a time and chop them fine. Transfer the anchovies to a bowl. Combine butter, olive oil and finely chopped garlic in the top of a double boiler; cook over simmering water, stirring continuously until the butter has melted.

2 **Finishing the sauce.** Remove the double boiler from the stove. Add the anchovies to the garlic mixture and stir for 15 minutes, or until the anchovy fillets have melted and the sauce has become thick and smooth. If the bottom of the double boiler becomes cool to the touch, remove the top and reheat the water to a simmer.

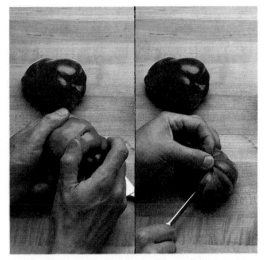

3 **Slicing zucchini.** Rinse the zucchini and trim off the woody ends. Slice the vegetables crosswise at ¼-inch [6-mm.] intervals, cutting down to within ¼ inch of the bottoms. Immerse the vegetables briefly in cold water to rid them of stickiness, but do not soak them; dry and refrigerate them.

4 **Preparing cauliflower.** Tear off the outer leaves of a cauliflower head, cut off the stem end, and remove the core by cutting diagonally around it. Pull off the remaining leaves, then cut through the stem of each floret to separate it from the cauliflower head. Rinse the florets, dry them with paper towels and refrigerate them.

5 **Preparing peppers.** Slice off the stem end of each pepper, and pull away the stem and the seeds clinging to it *(above, left)*. Trim the ridges of membrane inside the pepper and brush out stray seeds. Turn the pepper over and slice down at ¼-inch [6-mm.] intervals to within ¼ inch of the stem end *(above)*. Refrigerate.

6 **Presenting the vegetables.** Clean whole mushrooms with a damp paper towel. Wash spinach leaves in cold water and pat them dry. Quarter the hearts of Bibb lettuces, wash them in cold water and dry. Untie and dry the carrots and turnips. Arrange all of the vegetables, reassembling the cauliflower to simulate a head. To serve *bagna cauda*, transfer the warm sauce to a heatproof container and set it over a portable heat source to keep it warm; stir occasionally.

Devising Containers from Raw Vegetables

Firm-textured raw vegetables can provide a surprising range of sturdy, edible containers for fillings. The natural concavities of celery ribs, mushroom caps and Belgian endive leaves make these vegetables popular choices for such use. Cherry tomatoes are easily hollowed out to produce bite-sized vessels. And with a little imaginative cutting, other less obviously suitable vegetables can become equally attractive vehicles.

For example, slices of cucumbers or summer squashes yield cups when they are cut thick and hollowed out *(below, top demonstration)*; or they can be cut thin and used in pairs to form sandwiches *(opposite, top)*. The thick, empty shells of peppers invite filling—and when sliced crosswise, the shells frame their contents with scalloped rings *(below, bottom demonstration)*. Containers can even be fashioned from carrots or parsnips: The vegetables are slivered, coiled and chilled to produce rigid curls *(opposite, bottom)*.

The fillings suitable for raw vegetable containers vary with the shapes created. Cups can be filled safely with soft mixtures based on cream cheese, yogurt, sour cream or mayonnaise. Rings and sandwiches require a filling that will firm up when chilled: a flavored butter, for example, or a cheese blend. Curls will hold either a firm mixture or, if stoppered with a fragment of lettuce leaf as shown, a soft dip or spread.

Cucumber Cups

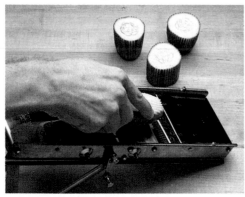

1 **Fluting cucumbers.** For a large receptacle, score cucumbers lengthwise with a fork or, as here, with a mandolin. Slice thick segments crosswise.

2 **Hollowing out cups.** Use a melon baller or a serrated spoon *(above)* to scoop out the cucumber flesh, leaving shells about ¼ inch [6 mm.] thick.

3 **Filling.** Salt the cups. Invert them on a rack to drain briefly. Add filling—in this case, yogurt dip *(recipe, page 99)*—and garnish; mint is used here.

Green-Pepper Rings

1 **Preparing peppers.** Cut around the top edge of each pepper and remove the stem along with the seeds clinging to its underside. Trim the membranous ribs and wipe out all loose seeds.

2 **Stuffing peppers.** Pack a firm filling—a blend of Roquefort, pistachio and cream cheese is shown—into the peppers. Wrap in foil and refrigerate for two hours to harden the filling.

3 **Slicing the peppers.** Place each chilled pepper on its side and cut it into slices about ¼ inch [6 mm.] thick, dipping the knife into warm water to make the cutting easier.

Zucchini Sandwiches

1 **Preparing zucchini.** Cut zucchini crosswise into slices ¼ inch [6 mm.] thick. Using a biscuit cutter slightly smaller than the diameter of the slices, or a small, sharp knife, remove the zucchini peel to create uniform rounds.

2 **Spreading the filling.** Place a spoonful of the filling — a compound butter flavored with herbs is used in this instance — on a slice and spread it evenly with a narrow-bladed spatula. Top the filling with a second slice to make a miniature sandwich.

3 **Garnishing the edges.** On one platter spread mayonnaise (recipe, page 166), and on another spread chopped nuts or herbs — parsley is used in this demonstration. Roll the edges of the sandwiches first in the mayonnaise, then in the nuts or herbs.

Carrot Coils

1 **Shaping curls.** Peel large, young carrots, then cut them lengthwise into broad strips ⅛ inch [3 mm.] thick. Coil each strip around your finger, slide it off, and secure the curl with a wooden pick. Immerse the curls in cold water, and refrigerate them for at least an hour before removing the picks.

2 **Lining the curls.** If the curls unwind, drain them, reinsert the picks, and refrigerate the curls in perforated plastic bags for several hours. Prepare the filling —tapenade (recipe, page 166) is shown. To make the curls suitable for such a soft filling, press a piece of lettuce inside each of them to form a cup.

3 **Filling the curls.** Spoon the filling into the lettuce-lined curls, mounding the filling slightly. Arrange the curls on a platter. If the curls are not to be served at once, cover them with an inverted bowl or domed lid that will not touch the filling, and refrigerate. Warm to room temperature before serving.

Miniature Vessels from Cooked Vegetables

For an interesting change in texture, vegetables such as zucchini and mushrooms may be cooked before they are formed into shells. Cooking also makes possible the use of vegetables too firm to be eaten raw. The cooking is done in two ways—baking or boiling—but always for the briefest time needed to tenderize a vegetable. To form sturdy containers, the vegetables should offer a bit of resistance when pierced with a knife or pinched.

Baking is the method of choice for moist or soft-textured vegetables such as dwarf eggplants, tiny new zucchini, or the mushrooms shown at right. A short spell in the oven will develop their succulence without making them soggy.

Mushroom caps need only be parted from their stems to become cups. Small eggplants or zucchini should be halved lengthwise before baking, then hollowed with a sharp-tipped spoon or a grapefruit knife when they emerge from the oven. If they were hollowed out before baking, the heat might distort their shapes.

Boiling is the fastest way to soften firm or dense-textured vegetables. New beets or potatoes, boiling onions or Brussels sprouts can be cooked whole, then hollowed with a knife or melon baller as shown below. Before boiling large, firm vegetables such as celeriac, rutabagas or turnips, reduce them to bite-sized balls or ovals with a knife so that they will cook more quickly; scoop out the centers of the presculpted shapes after they have cooked and drained.

The cook's options for fillings vary as widely as the flavors of the vegetables. The mushroom caps used on these pages are stuffed with a nut-studded blend of cheeses, while the beets and Brussels sprouts hold the garlicky potato dip demonstrated on page 101. Herbed butter or cream cheese complements almost any vegetable: Dill is a particularly felicitous choice for potatoes, basil for zucchini, and savory for onions. Piquant horseradish marries well with sweet roots such as celeriac; anchovies suit assertive turnips.

Baking Mushroom Caps

1 **Stemming mushrooms.** Clean mushrooms with a damp cloth, then twist off the stems. (Reserve the stems for fillings or spreads.) Place the caps, hollow sides up, on an ungreased baking sheet. Cook in a preheated 425° F. [220° C.] oven for about 10 minutes, or until the caps fill with their own juices and yield slightly when pinched.

Hollowing Natural Spheres

1 **Preparing Brussels sprouts.** Peel the outer leaves off the largest Brussels sprouts so they all will be about the same size and will cook at the same rate. Trim the stems to give each vegetable a flat base. Boil them five to seven minutes, plunge them into cold water to avoid further softening and drain at once.

2 **Hollowing Brussels sprouts.** With the tip of a sharp paring knife, cut diagonally down into the tightly packed center leaves in the top of each sprout to hollow out a small cavity.

3 **Preparing the beets.** Rinse but do not scrub or peel small beets—none more than 2 inches [5 cm.] in diameter. Boil for 30 minutes, or until just tender. Drain and cool them, then peel them and trim the stems. Cut a slice off the bottom of each beet so it stands up. Hollow the top with a melon baller (above).

2 **Emptying the caps.** Remove the mushrooms from the oven. After about two minutes — when the mushrooms are cool enough to handle but before they reabsorb any of their juices — pour off the liquid from each cap into a bowl. (The juices can be refrigerated and used in stocks and sauces.) Let the caps cool to room temperature.

3 **Filling the caps.** Prepare the filling — in this case a mixture of Roquefort and cream cheeses *(page 13)* with chopped pistachios — and spoon it into each cap. To shape the top of a firm filling into a cone, hold a small knife or spatula against it, as above, and rotate the cap. For a decorative flourish, dip the tips of the cheese cones into a small amount of paprika.

4 **Filling the vegetables.** Prepare the filling — in this demonstration, a mashed-potato-and-garlic dip *(page 101)*. Spoon the filling into the hollowed Brussels sprouts and beets and arrange them on a platter. Serve the vegetables at once, if possible. However, covered with an inverted bowl and refrigerated, the vegetables can be safely kept for up to three hours, but they must be brought to room temperature before serving.

Fancy Twists for Filled Eggs

Like a hollowed-out raw or cooked vegetable, the white of a halved, hard-boiled egg is a natural container that invites colorful fillings. By using a pastry bag fitted with a decorative tube, a cook can transform the fillings—three mixtures based on egg yolk are shown—into a variety of artful swirls and spirals.

The best egg for hard-boiling is about a week old. A new-laid egg is impossible to peel smoothly because the two membranes that cover the white are tightly attached to the shell. After about four or five days, however, enough air will have seeped through the microscopic pores in the shell to form a layer between the membranes, ensuring easy peeling. The seepage of air into the egg makes possible an easy test for age. Drop the egg into a pan of water: A new-laid egg will sink to the bottom, where it will lie flat. A week-old egg will tilt in the water because of an air pocket at the round end.

Hard-boiling should be done gently. If eggs are cooked too long or at too high a temperature, the white will become rubbery and the surface of the yolk will turn green as the hydrogen sulfide and iron of the white are drawn to it by the heat. Cover the eggs with cold water, bring it to a boil, then immediately turn off the heat, cover, and let the eggs stand for 15 minutes. Then, to stop their cooking, immerse the eggs in cold water.

To peel an egg quickly and easily, roll it on a flat surface to crack the shell, then roll it between your palms to loosen the membranes from the white. Run cold water over the egg for a few seconds: The shell sections should slide right off.

The fillings in this demonstration are made by ricing the egg yolks through a strainer to fluff them, then dividing them into batches for coloring and flavoring. Adding mayonnaise to one batch moistens the yolks and keeps them golden; compound butters flavored with Roquefort and herbs and with liver paté give the other batches pale green and tan hues, respectively. Other possible additions include chopped ham or smoked salmon, puréed sorrel or chopped mushrooms, *tapenade* or even caviar.

1 Ricing the yolks. Halve hard-boiled eggs and remove the yolks. Use a wooden spoon to press the yolks through a strainer set over a bowl, then divide the riced yolks into thirds. Mix one third with enough mayonnaise to make a paste. Mix one third with soft butter, herbs and Roquefort cheese, and the final third with butter and liver paté.

2 Preparing a pastry bag. Cut a slice off the bottom of each egg-white half to steady it. Slide a ¼-inch [6-mm.] open-star pastry tube over your forefinger as if it were a thimble. Push the tube through the pastry bag and out the opening at the bottom. Squeeze the bag around the wide top of the tube to force it into place.

6 Piping designs. Moving the tube in various directions produces all the designs above. From left, they are a double shell, made by overlapping consecutive bands at the center of the hollow; a single shell, made with one sweep; a braid, made with figure-8 loops; a spiral, made with the bag held level; and a twist, made by lifting the tube as you pipe filling.

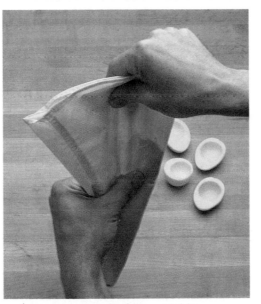

3 **Filling the bag.** Fold the top half of the pastry bag into a cuff over the hand holding the tube. Spoon in the filling, packing it down lightly as you work. If the filling is of the proper consistency, it will not ooze out of the bag; if filling does escape, return the mixture to a bowl and thicken it with more egg yolks. When the bag is half-full, unfold the cuff.

4 **Compacting the filling.** Holding the end of the bag in one hand, place the thumb and forefinger of your other hand on opposite sides of the bag. Then, beginning near the top, move your fingers downward, gently forcing the filling into the bottom of the bag. Do not press so hard that the filling is forced from the tube. Twist the bag shut.

5 **Holding the bag.** Cradle the bag in the palm of one hand so that the twisted top of the bag rests between your thumb and forefinger. Keep the bag closed by tightening your thumb against the twist. To force out the filling, apply pressure with the hand holding the bag, guiding the tube with the other hand.

7 **Serving the eggs.** Repeat the piped designs with each of the filling mixtures to produce a multicolored array. Arrange the eggs on a platter and decorate them. Parsley sprigs are used here, but you could substitute watercress leaves, small, diamond-shaped pieces of pimientos, chopped pistachios or sliced olives.

A Decorative Rim of Green

Decorating whites. Before stuffing hard-boiled egg whites, you can garnish their rims for an extra dash of color and flavor. Dip each rim in mayonnaise to make its surface sticky, then dip it in finely chopped fresh herbs such as chives, rosemary, savory, chervil or, as above, parsley. Instead of herbs, you could use slivered almonds or finely chopped walnuts.

The Ultimate Egg Roll

Baking eggs into the airy sponge called a souffléed omelet and then rolling the omelet into the shape of a cylinder produces a delicious and eye-catching case for just about any filling that is soft enough to spread. As its name suggests, a souffléed omelet *(recipe, page 129)* must be both light and firm. The egg yolks are blended with a simple white sauce—milk thickened with a butter-and-flour roux—to give the omelet enough substance so that it can be rolled without breaking. And the whites are beaten to a stiff foam before mixing them with the yolks and sauce, ensuring that the omelet puffs delicately in the oven.

For a sponge sheet large enough to form a roll of respectable size, the omelet is baked in a jelly-roll pan. To simplify the process of unmolding the sheet intact, line the pan with parchment or wax paper, oiled so that it peels off easily after the omelet is baked.

The secret of shaping a souffléed omelet into a cylinder that will not unwind is to roll it up while it is still hot from the oven. If the filling itself is a hot one, the omelet can be spread and rolled as soon as it is baked, then served immediately. But if the filling is a cold one that would turn runny on a hot base and ooze out the sides, roll up the omelet in a towel, as shown here, and let it cool on its seam while wrapped. This initial rolling will keep the omelet pliable enough to be safely unrolled, spread with the cold filling and rolled again.

The best fillings for a rolled omelet are thick spreads based on cream cheese, sour cream or purées. The souffléed omelet here is spread with a double layer of filling: softened cream cheese *(page 13)* that has been flavored with dill, and puréed smoked salmon that has been bound with a bit of the cream-cheese mixture. Other possibilities include creamed spinach, caviar blended with softened cream cheese, chopped, sautéed mushrooms, and ground ham or chicken moistened with sour cream.

1 Making the white sauce. Melt butter in a saucepan and whisk in flour a little at a time. Stirring constantly, cook for two or three minutes until the mixture is foamy. Gradually whisk in milk, then add salt and pepper. Simmer for two minutes, stirring, to thicken the sauce to the consistency of heavy cream. Remove the pan from the heat.

2 Adding the yolks. Separate an egg and place the yolk in one bowl, the white in another—in this case, the whites go into a bowl made of copper that will interact with the egg albumen to help the beaten whites retain their puff. Whisk the yolk into the white sauce. Repeat until all of the yolks are incorporated in the sauce.

6 Rolling the omelet. Fold the edge of the towel over one of the long sides of the souffléed omelet *(top)*. Slowly and carefully roll up the omelet with the towel *(bottom)*. Set the rolled omelet aside to cool to room temperature.

7 Filling the omelet. Prepare the fillings—here, a dill-flavored cream cheese and puréed smoked salmon with cream cheese. Unroll the cooled omelet. Using a long spatula, spread the omelet with the salmon mixture, then the dilled cream cheese, and top with snipped dill and grated lemon peel.

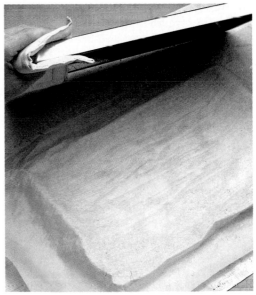

3 **Incorporating the whites.** Using a clean whisk, beat the whites until they form soft peaks. With a spatula, stir about a quarter of the whites into the yolk-sauce mixture to lighten its texture. Add all of the remaining whites, and fold gently until the mixture is a pale yellow with no streaks of white.

4 **Baking the omelet.** Brush a jelly-roll pan with oil and line it with parchment paper oiled on its upper surface and large enough to extend over the sides of the pan. Then pour the omelet mixture into the pan and spread it even *(above)*. Bake the omelet at 400° F. [200° C.] for 15 to 20 minutes, or until it is puffed and golden and feels springy.

5 **Turning out the omelet.** Quickly invert the jelly-roll pan on a towel that has been sprinkled with grated cheese or fine bread crumbs to prevent the cloth from sticking to the souffléed omelet. Lift off the pan *(above)*. Peel off the parchment paper and trim away any dry or irregular edges from the omelet.

8 **Serving the omelet.** Roll up the filled souffléed omelet *(above)*. If the omelet is not to be served right away, it can be tightly enclosed in plastic wrap and refrigerated for up to three hours, then returned to room temperature for serving. To serve the omelet, cut it into slices ¾ inch [2 cm.] thick *(right)*; arrange the slices on a bed of watercress.

New Incarnations for Humble Cheeses

For centuries, frugal cooks have been preserving, improving on and extending cheeses by mashing them with butter or cream, brandy or wine, and putting them up in pots. These potted cheeses are the prototypes for a plethora of spreads that begin with scraps of firm cheese or with chunks of bland or underripe soft cheese and end in imaginatively flavored coated or wrapped molds such as the array shown below and demonstrated on the following pages.

The method of preparation varies with the cheese. Firm cheeses such as Cheddar, Gouda or Gruyère must be shredded or grated before they can be mashed into a pliable paste with butter or whipped cream cheese *(demonstration, page 31; recipe, page 95)*. Cream cheese and its less fatty relative, Neufchâtel, need only be softened, beaten to a paste, and augmented with cream, cottage or farmer cheese and wine, brandy or liqueur in any combination *(demonstrations, right and page 13; recipe, page 95)*. Soft Brie, Pont-l'Évêque and Camembert often are found to be underripe—as evidenced by a hard, chalky core—when they are cut open. These cheeses can be rescued by being peeled, sectioned, marinated in wine to develop their taste, then mashed *(demonstration, page 32; recipe, page 93)*.

Depending on its natural flavor and on the cook's predilections, the mashed cheese can be flavored with anything from assertive garlic or pickles to mild lemon peel or celery seeds. As a rule, bland cheeses are receptive to strong or delicate additions; hearty cheeses marry best with pungent accents.

The mashed, flavored cheese can readily be shaped in a mold or with a spatula or your fingers, as shown at right. However, the shapes chosen should be simple ones—cylinders, disks or blocks, for example—that are sturdy and easy to coat with chopped herbs or nuts, crushed peppercorns or bright paprika. Soft cheeses will not hold the designs of ornate molds or intricate sculptures.

An assemblage of embellished cheeses. The home-flavored spreads grouped above, which should be served cool but not cold for the best taste and consistency, illustrate the varied effects that can be achieved with different shaping and coating techniques. Clockwise from top left are a paprika-coated log of cream and cottage cheeses, an herb-coated Cheddar-and-cream-cheese block, a round of lemon-flavored whipped cream cheese coated with crushed peppercorns, an herbed cream cheese wrapped in grapevine leaves, and a wine-soaked Camembert blanketed with pistachios and toasted bread crumbs.

A Paprika-coated Cylinder

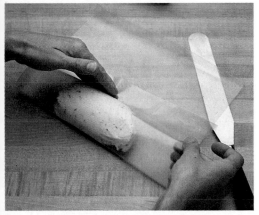
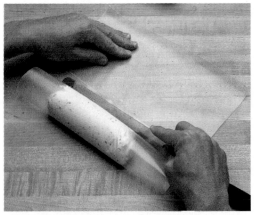

1 **Preparing the cheese.** Blend the cheese — in this case a sharp Liptauer based on cream and cottage cheeses *(recipe, page 95)*. Center the cheese on a long strip of wax paper. Lift the near end of the paper over the cheese, fold that end back on itself and tuck the fold under the far side of the cheese.

2 **Compressing the cheese.** Place a long spatula in the fold with the blade flat against the cheese. Then, holding the paper in place with one hand, pull the spatula toward you to compress the cheese into a log. Roll up the log in the paper, pinch the ends shut, and refrigerate for at least three hours.

3 **Coating the cheese.** Unroll the chilled cheese and smooth out any rough spots in the log with the spatula. Using a fine-meshed sieve for even sifting, sprinkle sweet Hungarian paprika along the log, rolling it until it is evenly coated *(left)*. Use a small pastry brush to dust off the excess paprika *(right)*.

An Herb-covered Block

1 **Preparing the cheese.** Use a box grater to grate or shred Cheddar cheese into a bowl. With a wooden spoon, blend the cheese with enough whipped cream cheese *(page 95)* to bind them into a smooth mass, and flavor it as desired — in this case, Madeira, crushed garlic and celery seeds are used. Thoroughly mix the ingredients.

2 **Shaping the cheese.** Place the cheese mixture on a square of wax paper and cover it with a second piece of wax paper. With your hands, pat the cheese into a block *(above)*, then remove the top sheet of paper and smooth the block with a spatula. Wrap the cheese in wax paper and refrigerate it for three hours, or until it is firm.

3 **Coating the cheese.** Chop fresh herbs fine — parsley, savory and rosemary are shown — and spread them on a work surface. Unwrap the cheese onto the herbs. Lift the herbs onto the sides and top of the cheese and pat them in place. Invert the block and serve the cheese at once, or rewrap it and refrigerate until serving time.

A Wine-drenched Disk Dressed in Nuts

1 **Flavoring the cheese.** Cut the rind from a chilled underripe Brie or, as here, Camembert cheese. Quarter the cheese and put the pieces in a nonreactive glass or ceramic bowl. Cover the cheese with dry white wine, then cover the bowl and marinate at room temperature for 12 hours or overnight.

2 **Draining the cheese.** Remove a stick of unsalted butter from the refrigerator and set it aside to soften. Transfer the wine-soaked cheese quarters to paper towels to drain. Pat the top and sides of the cheese dry.

3 **Combining the ingredients.** Mash the cheese with the softened butter, adding a little of the marinating liquid to the mixture as you work. Flavor the mixture to taste — brandy, salt and cayenne pepper are used here.

A Peppery Crust for a Mild Mixture

1 **Preparing the cheese.** Make a mild-flavored cheese mixture — in this case, a blend of cream cheese, sour cream and grated lemon peel. Line a ramekin or other small, round mold with wax paper or foil, and fill it with the cheese. Pack the mixture firmly, fold the wax paper over it, and refrigerate for three to four hours, or until firm.

2 **Unmolding the cheese.** Spread half a cup [125 ml.] of whole black peppercorns on a work surface and crush them by pressing and twisting a heavy skillet into them. Or wrap the peppercorns in a towel and crush them with a rolling pin. Spread the crushed peppercorns on a plate. Remove the cheese from its mold.

3 **Coating the cheese.** Unwrap the cheese and set it on top of the peppercorns. With a spatula, lift the peppercorns up onto the sides and top of the cheese, using your finger tips to press the peppercorns into the cheese. Turn the cheese over to coat the other side. Serve immediately, or wrap and refrigerate until serving time.

4 **Preparing the mold.** Line a small, round mold — in this case, the container in which the Camembert was packed — with foil or wax paper. Shell enough natural (not red-dyed) pistachios to produce 1 cup [¼ liter], or shell and chop a like amount of walnuts, pecans or hazelnuts.

5 **Filling the mold.** Spoon half of the cheese mixture into the mold and top it with half of the nuts. Add the rest of the cheese *(above)* and smooth the top with a spatula. Fold the foil or wax paper over the top of the cheese and chill the mixture until firm, about three hours.

6 **Coating the cheese.** Chop the remaining nuts fine and spread them on a plate. On another plate, spread crumbs made from bread cubes toasted in a 400° F. [200° C.] oven for five minutes. Unwrap the cheese and roll the edges in the nuts *(above)*. Pat the crumbs over the top and bottom.

A Vine-Leaf Wrapping for a Garlicky Blend

1 **Preparing leaves.** Mold and chill a cheese mixture *(opposite, bottom)* — here, cream cheese flavored with garlic and herbs *(page 13)*. Rinse brine-packed vine leaves, or wash and dry fresh ones. Overlap the leaves in a circle on a length of raffia string. Unmold the cheese onto the leaves.

2 **Wrapping the cheese.** Fold up the leaves one by one over the cheese, overlapping their edges as you wrap. When the cheese is wrapped, place another leaf on top to cover the spaces between leaves, and curl it down over the sides and under the cheese.

3 **Tying the leaves.** Twist the ends of the string around the cheese to form a cross, turn the cheese over, and loop the string diagonally across it *(above)*. Repeat this step until the leaves are held firmly, then knot the string and trim the ends. To serve, cut the string and open the leaves as a natural platter.

2
Bread Bases and Cases
A Profusion of Possibilities

A coat of clear aspic is spooned over French *gourmandises* made with ham and roast beef and garnished with small vegetables, chives and hard-boiled egg white *(pages 40-41)*. Chilled until firm, the aspic will provide a shining surface for the open-faced sandwiches, and will hold the elaborate garnishes in place.

Many people think of a sandwich as two slices of bread with a filling between them. In fact, the term encompasses dozens of culinary creations, from bite-sized open-faced canapés to hearty double-decker club sandwiches, and it even includes whole stuffed loaves that are served as wedges or slices. The finished product depends as much on the bread chosen as on the way it is sliced, shaped, topped, filled or garnished.

In open-faced sandwiches and canapés, for instance, bread serves as a display platform for other ingredients. The bread may be toasted or plain, it may be cut into circles or other shapes, and usually it is coated with butter to prevent sogginess and provide an adhesive for toppings. The most versatile platform is a close-grained sandwich loaf, which is firm enough to be sliced thin *(pages 36-37)*. This basic bread, however, may be replaced by firm loaves flavored with whole wheat, rye or pumpernickel flour, or by flat bread—an unleavened product that is similar to a thick cracker.

The exposed toppings and garnish ingredients give open-faced sandwiches instant appeal. Toppings may be as simple as shredded cheese, broiled to a bubbling blanket *(page 53)*. Or they can be as elaborate as the sculptured collages of meats, seafood, vegetables and eggs—carefully balanced and anchored by butter or sauce—that characterize a Danish *smorrebrod (pages 46-49)*. Similarly, the garniture may vary from sprinklings of chopped herbs *(page 38)* to pipings of colorful compound butter *(page 36)*. And for the ultimate in elegance, the topping can even be glazed with glittery aspic *(opposite)* or coated with a rich compound of aspic and cream *(pages 42-43)*.

When sandwiches employ breads as envelopes rather than as platforms, the selection expands to embrace rustic rounds, French or Italian cylindrical loaves, and buns and rolls of endless variety. These, too, should be firm-textured if the bread is to be sliced. But if the roll or loaf is to be hollowed, a more important characteristic is a thick crust that will form a sturdy shell. Fillings may be layers of contrasting ingredients—bacon, lettuce and tomato, for instance—or homogeneous mixtures such as ground meat or vegetable purées. Because the filling is securely enclosed, it can be a hot food such as a cheeseburger, or it may be fried *(pages 54-55)* or baked *(pages 52 and 57)* inside the sandwich.

A Practical Approach to Canapés

When the dainty, open-faced sandwiches known as canapés are constructed on bread or toast bases, the loaf used must be a sturdy, close-grained sandwich variety *(recipe, page 165)* that will not crumble if sliced very thin. For best results, let a freshly baked loaf stand unwrapped at room temperature for a day so that it stales slightly and becomes even firmer.

The fastest way to produce large numbers of small bread-based canapés is to cut the loaf into thin, lengthwise slices *(Step 1, top)*. The slices can then be coated on an assembly-line basis before being cut into the desired shapes; for triangles and rectangles, some decorating can be done before cutting *(Steps 2 and 3, top)*.

Melba toast appropriate for canapés requires uniformly thin slices that will bake evenly. These are produced most easily if you make the lengthwise cuts horizontally *(Step 1, below)*, using a pair of skewers as a guide for keeping the knife blade level. Assembly-line production is out of the question: The bread will be too brittle to cut after baking, and it must be sliced into individual canapés beforehand. Shape is a matter of cook's preference, but a round is least likely to curl at the edges. In all cases, the toasting should be done gently, in an oven set no higher than 250° F. [120° C.].

Melba toast, like plain bread canapé bases, can be topped with any coating that spreads easily but is not runny. Softened compound butter, cheese spread, whipped cream cheese, flavored mayonnaise, tartar steak and caviar are some of the possibilities. Both kinds of canapés may be decorated and garnished as fancifully as desired *(opposite and pages 38-39)*. With bread-based canapés, however, the topping must be applied as soon as the loaf is sliced to prevent surfaces from drying out. When the topping or piping is compound butter, as shown here, the canapés should be chilled briefly to let it harden. Prompt serving is best, but bread canapés can be kept refrigerated under a domed cover for about two hours.

Melba toast can be shaped and baked in advance and safely kept in a tightly covered container for seven or eight days. However, the topping chosen should be spread at the last possible moment so that the canapé does not become soggy.

An Efficient Scheme for Cutting

1 **Slicing.** Prepare compound butters —in this case, shrimp and herb *(pages 10-11)*. On a cutting board, remove the crust from one side of a sandwich loaf, using a serrated bread knife to cut straight down with a sawing motion. Slice the loaf lengthwise at ¼-inch [6-mm.] intervals. Trim the remaining crusts.

2 **Buttering.** Spread each slice with softened compound butter. Fit a pastry bag with a tube—a star tube is shown—and fill it with butter. Pipe borders along the sides of each slice. If you are using two butters, as here, wash the bag before refilling it. Chill the slices for 30 minutes to firm the butter.

Fashioning Uniform Melba Rounds

1 **Slicing.** Place a pair of long, flat-sided skewers against the long sides of the loaf. Slice the bread horizontally by sliding a bread knife along the skewers. Remove the bottom crust, reposition the skewers, and repeat the procedure until the loaf is cut into slices ⅛ inch [3 mm.] thick.

2 **Cutting bread rounds.** With a biscuit cutter or the rim of a glass, stamp out rounds from each slice of bread. Cut the rounds as close together as possible to minimize waste. The leftover bread, like the crusts, may be saved for making bread crumbs.

3 **Cutting and garnishing.** When the butter is firm, cut the slices into rectangles or triangles, as above. Garnish the canapés just before serving them. Cooked shrimp — halved lengthwise — and thin radish slices are used here to decorate the shrimp-butter canapés. The herb-butter canapés are topped with violet petals and radish cones dotted with capers. To form the cones, cut from the center to the edge of a radish slice, then overlap the cut edges.

3 **Toasting the rounds.** Place the rounds on an ungreased baking sheet and toast them in a preheated 250° F. [120° C.] oven. After an hour or so, turn each round over with your fingers or with wooden tongs (left). Continue baking the rounds for about one hour longer, or until they are a pale gold and feel hard to the touch (right). Cool the rounds on wire racks before using them.

4 **Topping the canapés.** Prepare a compound butter or other thick spread — in this demonstration, a green mayonnaise made with chopped watercress and flavored with grated onion is used. Just before serving time, butter the rounds or spoon a spread onto them, shaping the spread into mounds with a spatula (above). Serve the canapés immediately.

Ingenious Tactics for Garnishing

Most canapé garnishes perform a dual role, contributing decorative notes of color and texture while adding a counterpoint of flavor to the assemblage. Almost any food in the larder can furnish the makings of a patterned garnish. How the garnish is applied will depend on the basic topping for the canapé.

A soft topping such as a cheese spread, a flavored meat or fish paste, or a compound butter will have a sticky surface that can hold chopped or sieved garnish ingredients in place. Fresh herbs, hard-boiled eggs or yolks, firm vegetables, pickles, anchovies and capers can all be used in this form.

To be appealing as garnishes, however, these tiny morsels should be applied in broad bands, large circles or other clear-cut geometric conformations, using templates as guides. Suitable templates are easy to improvise, using materials that are already on hand *(box, right)*. Spatulas or dough scrapers, cookie or biscuit cutters, even strips of wax paper or pieces of cardboard can serve the purpose.

Firm toppings such as sliced meat or fish, on the other hand, call for large, flat garnishes that will balance on them securely. Strips or thin slices of raw or cooked vegetables will fit those requirements; so will the naturally narrow asparagus stalks shown on the opposite page at bottom.

In some cases, large garnishes may have to be anchored with dabs of mayonnaise. One exception to that rule is the cut butter garnish shown on the opposite page in the top demonstration; as it softens at room temperature, the butter cements itself to the canapé.

A Range of Improvised Templates

Decorating a triangle. Spread bread triangles with topping—caviar, in this case. Use a spatula or dough scraper to mask most of each triangle. Along the exposed edges sprinkle fine morsels such as sieved egg yolk. Move the mask, press it down to imprint its pattern, then sprinkle chopped onion within this smaller triangle.

Decorating a circle. Use a cookie cutter or biscuit cutter or the rim of a glass to cut bread into rounds. Spread each round with a topping—caviar is shown. Place a smaller circular biscuit or cookie cutter in the center of the round and fill it with finely chopped morsels—in this case, onion *(above)*. Gently lift off the cutter.

Decorating a rectangle. Cut a lengthwise slice from a loaf *(page 36)* and spread it with topping—horseradish butter, here. With folded wax paper, mask all but a thin strip down the center of the slice. Sprinkle the exposed area with finely chopped morsels—in this case, parsley *(below)*. Cut the bread in strips *(inset)*.

Stamping Decorations from a Sheet of Butter

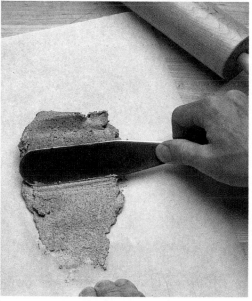  

1 **Spreading the butter.** Prepare a compound butter; this one is made with herbs *(page 10)*. Spread the butter on wax or parchment paper. Cover it with another piece of paper, and use a pin to roll the butter into a sheet ¼ inch [6 mm.] thick. Chill until firm, about an hour.

2 **Cutting the butter.** Peel off the top piece of paper. Shape the butter with small cutters, dipping them in hot water as you work so that the butter does not stick. Lift out the cut designs with the tip of a knife, and put them in a bowl of ice water so they will stay firm.

3 **Applying the designs.** Cover slices of buttered bread with thin slices of meat or fish — roast beef, ham and smoked salmon are shown. Cut the bread into small rectangles. Lift one butter shape at a time on a knife, drain it on a paper towel, then apply it to a canapé.

Emphasizing Linear Shapes

1 **Cutting the asparagus.** Align stalks of cooked asparagus beside a square of bread topped with sliced fish or meat — in this case, ham. Trim the tips and stems, using the edges of the bread as a guide. Reserve the tips. Place the asparagus on the meat, reversing alternate stalks to allow for their taper.

2 **Cutting triangles.** Holding the asparagus firmly in place, slice each square diagonally from corner to corner to form two triangles. Then halve the two triangles, as above, to form bite-sized canapés. (Because of the moistness of the asparagus, even tiny pieces will adhere naturally to the meat.)

3 **Completing the canapés.** Top each canapé with a dab of mayonnaise and garnish with two of the reserved asparagus tips. For variety, place the tips parallel to the asparagus stalks on some of the canapés; on others, place the tips across the stalks.

A Lustrous Finish of Aspic

Aspic adds gloss to cold canapés and to other such open-faced sandwiches as the hearty French *gourmandises* shown here. Applied as a syrupy liquid *(Steps 7 and 8)*, the aspic sets into a smooth jelly that unites the flavors of toppings and garnishes while keeping their surfaces fresh. Almost any firm topping or garnish—sliced meat or fish, for example, or liver paté—can be glazed with aspic. Do not, however, glaze mayonnaise-based toppings (which would soak up the liquid), fine-cut garnishes (which would float away), or compound butters (which would be too slippery to hold the aspic).

Depending on the cook's taste and the topping selected, the aspic may be made from any meat or fish stock. Ideally, a meat stock becomes crystal clear when it is strained, and its natural content of gelatin—produced by including calf's or pig's feet or pork rind among the stock meats—will set it into a firm aspic *(recipe, page 161)*. Clarity is achieved by skimming off all the protein scum that rises to the surface as the stock first comes to a boil, and by subsequently keeping the stock at the gentlest simmer, with the pot lid ajar.

A fish fumet *(recipe, page 162)* always requires extra steps. The fish bones yield little gelatin, and the protein they produce dissolves poorly so that it cannot be skimmed away. To remedy the lack of natural gelatin, commercial gelatin is added. And clarification is accomplished with the aid of egg whites and crushed shells, which bond with the impurities and can then be strained out. Stir in a raw egg white and crushed shell for each quart of liquid, bring the fumet to a boil, and let it rest off the heat for 10 minutes; repeat two more times before straining.

In some cases, these same measures must be applied to meat stock. If the stock is cloudy after straining, clarify it as you would a fish fumet. And if the finished stock does not set to a firm jell when a sample is tested *(Step 4)*, enrich it with powdered gelatin softened in cold water so that it will dissolve readily. To avoid producing rubbery aspic, add the gelatin in small amounts—starting with 1 tablespoon [15 ml.] of gelatin and ¼ cup [50 ml.] of water to each quart of stock—and test the aspic after each addition.

1 **Preparing the stock.** Cover meaty veal bones and a split calf's foot with cold water and bring to a boil over low heat — this takes about an hour. Skim off scum that rises to the surface. When the liquid reaches a boil, add cold water to encourage more scum to form. Skim and repeat until no more scum appears.

2 **Adding the flavorings.** To the stock add carrots, two peeled onions (one stuck with cloves), a leek, celery rib, peeled garlic clove and bouquet garni. Salt lightly and skim off any fresh scum that appears as the liquid returns to a boil. Then partly cover the pan, reduce the heat if necessary, and simmer the stock slowly for five hours.

5 **Jelling.** Pour the stock into a bowl set over ice. Stir until it cools and thickens to the syrupy consistency shown above. If it begins to thicken so that it will not flow smoothly — now or as you apply it — remove the aspic from the ice, warm it slightly and chill it again.

6 **Preparing sandwiches.** Cut bread into slices ½ inch [1 cm.] thick. Spread the bread with butter to form a seal, then top it with slices of cold poultry or meat, such as the ham and roast beef shown above, or with paté. With scissors, trim the meat to fit the bread.

3 **Straining the stock.** Line a colander with a double layer of dampened cheesecloth and set it over a large bowl or pot. Strain the stock through the colander and discard the solids. Let the stock cool to room temperature, then use folded paper towels to blot up fat from the surface.

4 **Testing the stock.** Ladle some of the cooled stock into a shallow bowl to a depth of about ¼ inch [6 mm.] *(above)* and refrigerate it for 10 to 15 minutes. The jelled stock should feel firm and cling to the bowl when it is tipped *(inset)*. If not, warm all of the stock over low heat, then stiffen it with a little powdered gelatin softened in water or wine. Cool the stock and test it again.

7 **Applying aspic.** Place the sandwiches on a wire rack set over a shallow tray to catch drippings. With a well-chilled ladle, spoon a thin coating of aspic over the meat. The aspic should begin to jell on contact with the cold meat. Chill the sandwiches five to 10 minutes, until the aspic has firmly set.

8 **Decorating.** Apply chilled garnishes, first coating large ones with aspic. Here, the ham is decorated with slices of radish, pickle, egg white and olive; the beef with pea-filled baked mushroom caps and cheese-filled snow peas. Finally, apply thin coats of aspic, chilling each one, until the glaze is ⅛ inch [3 mm.] thick.

A Silken Coat of Jellied Cream

When aspic is combined with aromatic vegetables, herbs and heavy cream, the result is a sauce of incomparable delicacy *(recipe, page 162)*. Applied in a thin layer, it hardens into a silken coating suited—because it is so rich—to the plainest meat-, fish- or poultry-topped canapés and other open-faced sandwiches.

The French call this aspic cream a *sauce chaud-froid,* or hot-cold, since it must be heated to thicken it and concentrate its flavor, then cooled before it is spooned over food. The aspic base for the cream should be mild in flavor; veal or chicken stock or fish fumet are all appropriate *(recipes, pages 161 and 162)*.

When the aspic cream has been reduced to the proper consistency *(Step 2, right)*, it must be strained to remove bits of seasonings and chilled to begin its setting—two processes that can be combined readily by straining the cream over ice. After that, the aspic cream can be applied to already topped canapés in the same way plain aspic is *(page 41, Steps 7 and 8)*. Or, for the neatest coating, it can be spooned onto the toppings before the canapés are assembled *(Step 5)*.

The natural color of aspic cream is a pleasing ivory tint, but for variety you may wish to alter the hue of all or part of the mixture. Adding puréed herbs to the aspic cream just before it is strained will produce a green color; tomato sauce yields a rosy pink, and egg yolks will turn the sauce yellow. Yolks require special handling to prevent them from coagulating: Add a little of the simmering sauce to the yolks to warm them before they are added to the mixture, and remove the aspic cream from the heat as soon as the warmed yolks have been stirred in.

1 **Combining ingredients.** Prepare an aspic—in this case, one based on veal stock *(page 161)*. In a saucepan, combine the aspic with aromatic flavorings: Sliced onion, diced carrot and thyme are shown. Add heavy cream and stir to blend the ingredients.

2 **Reducing the mixture.** Bring the mixture to a boil over medium heat, stirring frequently. Then, without covering the pan, simmer the mixture over low heat for about 20 minutes, or until it has been reduced to about half of its original volume. Season the mixture with salt and white pepper.

Coloring with Herbs

1 **Preparing herbs.** Plunge fresh herbs—parsley and thyme are used above—into boiling water and blanch them for one minute. Drain the herbs, squeeze them dry and chop them fine. Add the herbs to the reduced aspic cream *(Step 2, above)*.

2 **Blending the mixture.** Stir the herbs into the aspic cream and simmer for a minute or two, until the mixture is pale green. Strain the aspic cream through a double layer of dampened cheesecloth *(Step 3, above)*.

3 **Straining the aspic cream.** Line a fine-meshed strainer with a double thickness of dampened cheesecloth, and place the strainer over a bowl set in ice. Ladle the aspic cream a little at a time into the strainer, and let it drip through.

4 **Testing the consistency.** Stir the aspic cream over the ice until it begins to cool and thicken. After about five minutes, it should be thick enough to coat the back of a metal spoon heavily *(above)*. Remove the aspic cream from the ice so that it does not set too quickly while you are using it. (If the sauce should become too firm to spoon, rewarm it briefly and then chill it again.)

5 **Decorating.** Slice chilled fish or meat — chicken, here — to top canapés *(page 40, Step 6)*, and place the slices on a rack set above a pan. Quickly spread aspic cream over the toppings *(above)*, and refrigerate them until the cream sets — about five minutes. Set the coated toppings on bread bases and garnish the canapés. The designs at right were made from chive and scallion stems, and eggplant, tomato and zucchini peels cut with a knife, aspic cutters or the tip of a pastry-bag tube.

A Play of Geometry

The most inventively structured sandwiches consist of multiple layers of bread cemented together by spreads that harden when they are chilled: compound butter *(pages 10-11)*, whipped cream cheese *(page 13)*, or flavored cheese *(pages 30-33)*. All such assemblies begin the same way, with a rectangular loaf of firm, fine-textured bread, trimmed of its crust and sliced horizontally by the method demonstrated on page 36. The slices are spread with softened filling, stacked one on top of another, and refrigerated until the filling hardens and seals the sandwich together. Just before serving, the loaf is sliced into ribboned cross sections.

Particularly striking assemblies can be formed by using two or more kinds of bread: In the sandwich at right, for instance, contrasting layers of white and pumpernickel bread are joined with a green herb butter. You can create a similar effect by joining layers of one bread with two or more bright spreads—red-tomato and orange-paprika butters, perhaps, or cream-cheese mixtures colored by herbs and red peppers. The sandwiches may consist of layers stacked on top of one another so that a ribbon effect is created when the loaves are sliced in cross sections, or the cross sections may be restacked, then sliced again to form a checkerboard *(Steps 2 and 3, top)*.

Garnishes may help generate complex patterns as well. In the sandwich demonstrated at right, bottom, vegetables, nuts and meat are embedded in layers of golden *beurre fermière*—farmer's wife butter—flavored with wine and egg yolks *(recipe, page 92)*. When the assembly is sliced, the garnishes are revealed in mosaic-like cross sections. In this case, green pistachios, pink ham, brown mushrooms and green asparagus are shown. But countless other garnishes, ranging from smoked salmon julienne to green grapes, may be used; the only requisite is that they be firm enough to hold their shape but soft enough for slicing.

A Two-Bread Checkerboard

1 **Assembling.** Trim the crusts from two rectangular loaves—in this case, pumpernickel and white bread. Cut the loaves horizontally into ½-inch [1-cm.] slices. Starting with white bread, butter and stack the slices, alternating colors and ending with pumpernickel. Leave the top slice unbuttered.

2 **Slicing the loaf.** Cover the stacked loaf with plastic wrap and refrigerate it for at least one hour to firm the butter. Then, using a serrated bread knife, slice the loaf at ½-inch [1-cm.] intervals to form ribbon sandwiches.

A Ribboned Showcase for Garnishes

1 **Assembling ingredients.** Bake mushroom caps *(pages 24-25)* and cool them. Boil asparagus, shell and peel pistachios, and julienne boiled ham. Trim a whole-wheat loaf and cut it into ¼-inch [6-mm.] horizontal slices. Butter one slice and press the mushrooms into it.

2 **Adding ham.** Butter a second bread slice and set it, buttered side down, on top of the mushrooms. Butter the top of the slice and arrange the ham strips on it in rows. Between the strips place rows of pistachios.

3 **Creating a checkerboard.** Spread a ribboned slice with a thick layer of herb butter, and on it lay a second slice, turned so that the pumpernickel strips rest on top of the white strips. Layer and butter the remaining slices in this fashion (above). Wrap the loaf and chill it again for one hour to firm the butter. Unwrap the loaf and slice it, halving each slice diagonally (right) to produce triangles.

3 **Adding asparagus.** Butter the third bread slice and set it, buttered side down, over the ham. Butter the top of the bread and lay the asparagus spears on it in rows, alternating directions so that the spears fit neatly together.

 Completing the assembly. Butter the remaining slice and place it, buttered side down, on the asparagus. Coat the sides of the loaf with a thin layer of butter (above). Chill the loaf — unwrapped because plastic would stick to the butter coating — for one hour, until it is firm. To serve, slice the loaf into thin cross sections, and halve or third each slice (right).

The Sandwich as a Still Life

No nation has explored the possibilities of open-faced sandwiches with more enthusiasm or greater artistry than Denmark. The diversity of Danish *smorrebrod,* as these sandwiches are called, seems boundless: One restaurant in Copenhagen lists 178 varieties on its menu.

The essence of making *smorrebrod* is creativity. No two sandwiches need ever be exactly alike. But each sandwich—as evidenced by the array shown below and demonstrated on the following pages—must be composed with the kind of care a painter would lavish on a still life. Ingredients may range from leftover meats and vegetables to poached shrimp and

fresh caviar. A lettuce leaf usually serves as a frame of sorts, perched on the sandwich and held in place by other ingredients. Fresh dill or tomatoes, tucked into crevices, furnish color accents. Slices of hard-boiled egg or rings of onion, propped up on one another, contribute a three-dimensional aspect to the composition.

To taste their best, all the ingredients must be brought to room temperature ahead of time, and the sandwich must be put together at the last possible moment so that its elements do not dry out. The assembly usually starts with spreading softened butter over a slice of bread: sour rye, pumpernickel, trimmed white bread or toast, or crisp flat bread. Butter brings

a rich taste while sealing the surface of the bread or toast; however, mayonnaise may be substituted where its tangy flavor would better complement a topping.

Because the bread is sliced wafer-thin and the topping is a multilevel affair, pieces of *smorrebrod* are customarily eaten with knife and fork. One notable exception is the traditional combination of caviar and a shell-cupped raw egg yolk presented on flat bread *(below, bottom left).* The diner picks up the bread, pours the yolk into the hollow made by the eggshell, then eats the sandwich by hand. And he may wash it down, as the Danes do, with cold beer or chilled aquavit.

A smorrebrod sampler. The common denominator of these open-faced sandwiches — prepared on the following pages — is the artistic arrangement of the toppings. Clockwise from top left are prune-stuffed pork with red cabbage, shrimp salad with red caviar, pork paté with diced aspic, herring with beet salad and egg slices, shrimp with dill, roast beef with fried onions, hard-boiled egg with Scandinavian sprats, dill-marinated salmon, and black caviar with raw-onion rings and an egg yolk.

46

Stuffed Pork with Red Cabbage

1 **Stuffing pork.** With a scoured sharpening steel, pierce a boned pork loin. Stuff it with prunes; roast at 325° F. [160° C.] for 30 minutes a pound [½ kg.].

2 **Buttering bread.** Cool, then slice the pork. Butter trimmed white bread. At one end, mound red cabbage cooked with apples *(recipe, page 110)*.

3 **Completing the sandwich.** Prop overlapped slices of pork against the mound of cabbage. Garnish with a sprig of fresh parsley.

Shrimp Salad with Caviar

1 **Spooning on caviar.** Cover buttered toast with a mixture of diced cooked shrimp and mayonnaise. Place red caviar on the center.

2 **Making a lemon twist.** Cut a lemon slice halfway through and twist the halves in opposite directions. Place the twist at one edge of the sandwich.

3 **Garnishing the sandwich.** Lay a sprig of fresh dill opposite the twist of lemon, and serve the shrimp-and-caviar sandwich immediately.

Pork-Liver Paté with Beef Aspic

1 **Slicing paté.** Cut uniform slices of pork-liver paté *(recipe, page 110)*. As you work, dip the knife blade into hot water to keep it from sticking to the meat.

2 **Dicing aspic.** Set a paté slice on buttered bread, tuck lettuce and tomato under it, and garnish. Unmold and dice beef aspic *(recipe, page 161)*.

3 **Finishing the sandwich.** With a spatula, transfer a generous amount of aspic to the sandwich, positioning it around the paté, opposite the lettuce.

Beets, Herring and Hard-boiled Egg

1 **Spreading the salad.** Prepare a salad with diced herring and beets *(recipe, page 111)*; slice a herring fillet. Set a lettuce leaf on buttered pumpernickel; spoon the salad onto it.

2 **Piping sour cream.** Arrange the herring slices across the salad. Then pipe a swirl of sour cream onto the lettuce. For extra color, the sour cream may be tinted with beet juice.

3 **Adding garnishes.** Prop two slices of hard-boiled egg alongside the sliced herring. Tuck a sprig of fresh dill into the lettuce to set off the sour cream.

A Pinwheel of Shrimp with Dill

1 **Preparing shrimp.** Poach shrimp until pink; drain, peel and devein them. Spread mayonnaise *(recipe, page 166)* on toast. Arrange the shrimp in a ring.

2 **Adding the garnish.** Fill in the center of the ring with additional shrimp. Tuck some sprigs of fresh dill into the crevices between the shrimp.

3 **Seasoning the sandwich.** Grind a generous amount of fresh black pepper over the shrimp. Squeeze fresh lemon juice over the sandwich.

Roast Beef with Sweet Mayonnaise

1 **Making the mayonnaise.** Prepare a mayonnaise *(demonstration, page 12; recipe, page 166)*, flavoring the yolks with a pinch of mustard and some sugar before adding the oil. Flavor with dill.

2 **Preparing the topping.** Brown thinly sliced onion rings in butter or oil, then drain them. Slice rare roast beef, and cut a tomato in wedges. Butter a slice of pumpernickel.

3 **Arranging the sandwich.** Place a lettuce leaf, tomato wedge and parsley sprig on a corner of the bread. Fold roast beef slices to fit, add mayonnaise and garnish with the onion rings.

An Egg-and-Fish Assemblage

1 Shaping bread. Assemble the toppings: drained Scandinavian sprats, sliced egg, tomato wedges, lettuce and dill. Cut a circle of bread with a biscuit cutter or a glass, as shown, and butter it.

2 Arranging the egg slices. Place a leaf of lettuce on the circle of bread, and spread the hard-boiled egg slices across it, overlapping the slices.

3 Adding the sprats. Cross a pair of sprats over the egg slices. Tuck a tomato wedge behind the eggs, and garnish the assembly with fresh dill.

Salmon Marinated in Dill

1 Slicing salmon. Pack boned fresh salmon with dill and seasonings (recipe, page 111), and chill for 24 hours. Wipe it and cut it in thin diagonal slices.

2 Arranging the salmon. Place lettuce at one end of a slice of buttered bread. Lay salmon slices on it, folding the tips to weigh down the lettuce.

3 Adding sauce. Garnish the sandwich with a lemon twist and dill. Spoon sweetened mayonnaise (recipe, page 166) onto the fish; grind pepper over it.

A Caviar Bed for a Cupped Egg Yolk

1 Buttering flat bread. Assemble the toppings: black caviar, lettuce, onion rings and a raw egg. Butter a piece of flat bread and put a lettuce leaf on one end.

2 Spreading the caviar. Smooth a generous portion of caviar over the flat bread, covering part of the lettuce in order to anchor it. Spread the caviar lightly to avoid damaging it.

3 Breaking the egg. Overlap fresh onion rings on top of the caviar. Break a small egg and stand the half of the shell that holds the yolk beside the lettuce leaf, settling it in the caviar.

An Array of American Favorites

The plenteous combinations of meats, cheeses and vegetables that Americans cram into rolls or pack between slices of bread form the most robust sandwiches of all. Those shown here represent six favorites: a vegetarian sandwich, a hero, a club sandwich, a cheeseburger, a chili dog and a Reuben. But the possibilities are almost endless: The only real rule is that the filling must be securely enclosed so the sandwich can be eaten by hand.

The vegetarian sandwich, for example, is a kind of portable salad that can incorporate almost any collection of raw vegetables and fruits. Most include broad leaves of spinach, as here, or lettuce to cup smaller ingredients. To keep the assembly together, the dressing should be thick—mayonnaise *(recipe, page 166)*, perhaps, or the yogurt blend shown below *(recipe, page 101)*.

Any kind of firm-textured bread, dark or white, may hold a vegetarian sandwich. A hero, however, is Italian in origin, and tradition demands a cylindrical Italian loaf split lengthwise *(recipes, page 120)*. Whether known as a hero or as a submarine, grinder, poor boy or hoagy, the sandwich always boasts layers of thin-sliced salami, mortadella, bologna, ham, provolone cheese, and vegetables such as tomatoes, onions and peppers. To moisten the filling and unite its flavors, the inside of the loaf should be sprinkled in advance with vinaigrette *(recipe, page 165)*, flavored here with basil.

A more sedate stacked sandwich is the club, often made with three or more slices of toast, and filled as the cook chooses. The one at right contains bacon, lettuce and tomato—a popular combination in itself—with turkey and cheese *(recipe, page 117)*. To prevent slipping, the bread must be hot from toasting, and the tomato slices lightly coated with mayonnaise.

The bun for a burger also should be freshly toasted so that meat juices do not soak it. The hamburger or cheeseburger *(opposite, top right)* may be broiled, barbecued or pan fried *(recipe, page 119)*. Its quality depends on the beef, which should be fresh ground and have a fat content of about 15 per cent; more fat will make the burger shrink too much, less fat will make it dry. For extra flavor, the hamburger can be topped with condiments ranging from relishes and pickles to onion slices and tomatoes or lettuce.

Hot dogs, too, can be cooked by many methods—broiling, pan frying, barbecuing or boiling—and topped with various condiments. Because of its shape, however, a hot dog requires soft or fine-chopped toppings, such as the chili *(recipe, page 118)* and raw onions shown at right, to cover the meat evenly—and a steamed or toasted bun to keep it warm.

A Reuben, on the other hand, is sautéed after it is assembled, a process that browns the bread and melts the cheese inside to bind the filling. Here the filling includes corned beef, turkey, Swiss cheese and sauerkraut *(recipe, page 116)*. Pastrami may replace the corned beef, and coleslaw topped with Russian dressing could substitute for the sauerkraut.

Vegetarian sandwich. Clean spinach and bean sprouts, slice mushrooms and tomatoes, shred red cabbage and grate carrots*(inset)*. Cover a slice of whole-wheat bread with the spinach and add the other vegetables, plus nuts, raisins and yogurt dressing *(above)*.

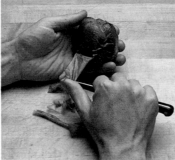

Hero sandwich. Broil peppers until they char, then peel them *(inset)*. Halve an Italian loaf lengthwise and sprinkle the cut surfaces with herb vinaigrette. Cover the bottom slice with layers of tomato, zucchini, mortadella, provolone, red onion, salami and pepper *(above)*.

Club sandwich. Score the rinds of bacon slices *(inset)* to prevent curling, then fry and drain them. Cut the crusts from three bread slices; toast them. Build the sandwich in two layers, filling each with lettuce, tomato, sliced turkey and bacon. Halve the sandwich *(above)*.

Cheeseburger. Shape ground beef into two patties and sandwich a slice of Cheddar cheese between them *(inset)*. Sear both sides, then cook slowly until the beef browns and the cheese melts. Set on a toasted bun and top with slices of onion and tomato *(above)*.

Reuben sandwich. Wash sauerkraut, then squeeze it dry *(inset)*. Layer the sauerkraut with turkey, corned beef and Swiss cheese on two or three slices of bread — rye, in this case. Brush the outside of the bread with butter, and fry until the bread browns and the cheese melts *(above)*.

Chili dog. Prepare ground-beef chili *(inset)*, omitting the beans. Plunge the hot dog into boiling water and set a wire rack over the pan to heat the opened bun. After about three minutes, place the hot dog in the bun, spoon chili over it and garnish with chopped onion *(above)*.

Toasted Shells for Creamy Sauces

Warm sandwich fillings and toppings call for equally warm bread or rolls that have been toasted to crispness so that they do not turn soggy. One such marriage is shown here: Hollowed, buttered and toasted rolls are packed with a blend of shallots, mushrooms, tongue, cream and egg yolks *(recipe, page 133)*, then baked until they are piping hot.

Because of their thickness, the roll shells are toasted for five minutes in the oven—in this case, one set at 450° F. [230° C.]. Thinner breads such as halved hamburger buns are best toasted for seven or eight minutes at 375° F. [190° C.]; so are bread slices, which must be turned after four minutes or so.

Because a preheated oven's warmth is relatively even, rolls and bread may be baked in any rack position, or on two racks if the number of pieces warrants it. The bread may be brushed with oil or melted butter before toasting or, if it is more convenient, afterward—providing the surfaces are still warm enough to absorb flavors.

1 Preparing the filling. In a skillet, sauté chopped shallots in butter for five minutes. Stir in finely chopped garlic and sliced mushrooms, cover, and cook over low heat for three or four minutes to soften the mushrooms. Season, then slowly add heavy cream and diced smoked tongue. Simmer for a few minutes to blend flavors.

2 Thickening the filling. Stir a little of the simmering sauce from the filling into lightly beaten egg yolks to raise their temperature so that they will not curdle. Blend the yolk-and-sauce mixture gradually into the filling and stir over low heat until the sauce just begins to bubble. Remove it immediately from the heat and adjust seasonings.

3 Toasting roll shells. Slice the tops off crusty rolls. Use a fork to pull out the centers, and form shells about ½ inch [1 cm.] thick. Brush the inner surfaces with melted butter. On a baking sheet, toast the shells in a 450° F. [230° C.] oven for five minutes, or until brown and crisp.

4 Filling the shells. Spoon the filling into the hot toasted shells, dividing the mixture evenly among them and mounding the filling slightly. Return the filled shells to the baking sheet.

5 Baking the shells. Bake the filled shells in the oven for five minutes, or until the tops are bubbly and lightly browned. Arrange the shells on a warm platter and serve them at once.

A Golden Blanket of Cheese

One of the simplest but most delectable of cooked open-faced sandwiches is made by spreading shreds of cheese over crisp bread and broiling the assemblage so that the cheese melts into a golden, molten mass. Close attention to the cooking is essential; the heat of a broiler is so intense that the cheese could quickly overcook and turn leathery.

The bread for the base should be sliced no more than ½ inch [1 cm.] thick, so that it heats through in the time that the cheese takes to melt. Because it is toasted in advance—either in a toaster or in the oven—the slice may be cut from any sort of loaf: French, sandwich, rye, pumpernickel or the potato bread shown here. To add extra flavor, the toast may be brushed with melted butter or with oil, or spread with a soft topping such as deviled ham or anchovy paste.

The range of suitable cheeses includes Cheddar (used in this demonstration) as well as Edam, Gouda, Swiss, Gruyère, Monterey Jack and Muenster. Scraps, of course, are an appropriate source.

1 Preparing the bread. Cut bread into slices ½ inch [1 cm.] thick. Toast the slices. While the slices are still warm and absorbent, spread them out on wax paper and brush the tops with olive oil. The oil used here has been flavored by steeping unpeeled garlic cloves in it for four to seven days.

2 Shredding the cheese. Using a box grater or, as above, a rotary grater, shred the cheese into fine strips. Or cut the cheese into small chunks and shred them in a food processor.

3 Making the sandwiches. With your fingers or a fork, sprinkle a thick layer of cheese over the toast *(left)*. Cover each slice to the edges so that the crusts will not burn when they are broiled. Place the sandwiches on a baking sheet and set them 4 inches [10 cm.] below the broiler. Broil for about five minutes, until the cheese melts and begins to bubble *(above)*.

Deep Frying to Meld Bread and Cheese

In the repertoire of nearly every country that produces cheeses, there is at least one robust fried sandwich—sautéed, pan fried or deep fried—in which cheese is the main element. These creations range from the traditional American grilled-cheese sandwich, made with Cheddar and bread buttered on the outside so that it can be sautéed on an ungreased stove-top griddle, to the French Gruyère-and-ham-filled *croque-monsieur,* moistened with egg and then pan fried in butter *(recipe, page 119).*

Among the heartiest of these pairings is *mozzarella in carrozza* (mozzarella in a carriage), the deep-fried cheese sandwich demonstrated here. Because the cheese is bland, this sandwich is usually served drenched with a warm olive-oil sauce, redolent of anchovies and garlic.

Like any sandwich that is dipped in egg before frying, *mozzarella in carrozza* should be made with a firm-textured bread that will not disintegrate as it soaks. The eggs, which bind and enrich the sandwich, help to hold an edging of bread crumbs that add a bit of crunch-iness while forming a seal to prevent the cheese from oozing out as it melts.

To absorb the eggs evenly, the bread crusts are removed. Here, both bread and cheese are cut into circles, but triangles or rectangles would do just as well.

The cheese for a classic *mozzarella in carrozza* should be a whole-milk mozzarella, bought from a market that sells it in bulk and regularly gets a fresh supply. Whole-milk mozzarella will melt more smoothly and has a richer flavor than the variety made partly with skim milk.

For other tastes, a cheese sandwich fried the same way can be made with any firm, sliceable cheese that melts readily. Muenster, Cheddar, Gouda, Edam, Jarlsberg, provolone, Emmentaler or Monterey Jack offer delicious variations.

1 **Shaping the bread and cheese.** Cut 12 slices from a loaf of sandwich bread and six ¼-inch [6-mm.] slices from a block of whole-milk mozzarella cheese. Using biscuit cutters or the rims of upturned glasses, shape the bread and cheese into circles, making the cheese rounds about ½ inch [1 cm.] smaller in diameter than the bread rounds. Place the mozzarella between the bread rounds to make six sandwiches.

2 **Soaking the sandwiches.** Prepare fine crumbs from day-old bread and set them aside. In a shallow dish, beat together two eggs, 1 teaspoon [5 ml.] of water and a pinch of salt. Holding a sandwich between your thumb and forefinger, dip it into the egg mixture and turn it to moisten the edges. Soak the sandwich in the egg mixture until the bread is uniformly moistened.

3 **Sealing the sandwich.** As soon as each sandwich is coated with the egg mixture, lift it out of the dish and roll it in the bread crumbs until the edges become thoroughly covered with crumbs. Set the mozzarella sandwiches aside on a platter.

4 **Frying the sandwiches.** In a skillet, heat 1 inch [2½ cm.] of olive oil until it is hot and bubbling but not smoking. Lower the sandwiches into the oil with a spatula and fry them for about one minute on each side, or until they are golden. Lift the sandwiches out of the oil with tongs or two spatulas. Drain the sandwiches on paper towels and transfer them to serving dishes.

5 **Making the sauce.** Pour ¼ cup [50 ml.] of fresh olive oil into a saucepan. Drain nine or 10 oil-packed flat anchovy fillets and chop them fine. Put them in a bowl with one finely chopped garlic clove. Stir in 1 tablespoon [15 ml.] of lemon juice. Heat the olive oil until it just bubbles, pour in the anchovy mixture *(left)*, and stir for 30 seconds. Remove from the heat and spoon or pour a little of the sauce over each sandwich *(below).*

A Sandwich Extravaganza

A whole loaf of crusty bread, hollowed and stuffed, produces a sort of super-sandwich that can be served in slices or wedges. Round or cylindrical loaves of French or Italian bread are particularly well suited to such treatment because their thick crusts form strong shells.

The hollowing process is straightforward. If the loaf is round, saw off the top with a serrated knife, then cut and scoop out the interior *(right)*. If the loaf is cylindrical, cut off the tips, then slice into it from both ends to free and remove the center. Before either kind of loaf is ready for stuffing, the inner surfaces must be sealed with butter or whipped cream cheese *(page 13)* so that the bread does not become soggy.

The ample cavity of a round loaf calls for a many-layered stuffing. All the ingredients must be firm enough to retain their separate identities. They should also be slightly moist, so that their flavors intermingle when the top cover is

set back on the loaf and the bread is chilled or, as in this case, when it is warmed before serving.

Here, the cavity is lined with slices of prosciutto that wrap around the other ingredients. Any meat that would provide large, thin slices—turkey, ham or rare roast beef, for example—could be used in its place. The stuffing itself is made up of layers of puréed spinach, ricotta and sautéed mushrooms; alternatives include other spreadable cheeses and such cooked vegetables as zucchini or peppers, sliced or julienned meats or sausages, and even flavored omelets.

A cylindrical loaf requires a malleable stuffing that can be packed into its narrow cavity with a spoon. And the stuffing should be based on a mixture of cheese, sausage or meat—such as the steak *tartare (recipe, page 106)* shown here—so that it will firm up when it is chilled and will not crumble or ooze out when the bread is sliced crosswise.

Filling a Round Loaf

1 **Hollowing the loaf.** With a serrated knife, slice the top off a round loaf of crusty bread. Set the top aside. Cut down around the loaf's edge about an inch [2½ cm.] inside the crust to within ½ inch [1 cm.] of the base. Use a fork and your fingers to pull out the interior.

Filling a Long Loaf

1 **Buttering the cavity.** With a serrated knife or a ham slicer, as here, slice off the tips of a long cylindrical loaf. Working from each end in turn, hollow out the bread, leaving a shell about ¼ inch [6 mm.] thick. With a narrow spatula, coat the cavity with softened butter. Chill the loaf until the butter firms—about 20 minutes.

2 **Stuffing the loaf.** With a spoon, push a thick but pliable stuffing—in this instance, steak *tartare*—into the cavity. Press the stuffing firmly so that there will be no air pockets. Wrap the loaf in foil and refrigerate it for several hours in order to set the filling.

3 **Serving the loaf.** Cut the chilled loaf into slices about ½ inch [1 cm.] thick *(left)*. Serve the slices at once, garnished, if you like, with sour cream and a sprinkling of black caviar *(right)*.

2 **Lining the cavity.** If you plan to serve the loaf hot, set it over sliced bacon on a baking sheet. Butter the cavity lightly, then line it with overlapping prosciutto slices arranged to radiate from the center of the loaf and cover its sides. Use a spatula to slather a thick layer of puréed spinach into the cavity.

3 **Completing the stuffing.** Spread a layer of softened cheese such as ricotta over the spinach, then cover it with another filling — in this case, mushrooms sautéed with garlic, onions and parsley and enriched with wine. When you have finished, the layers should reach almost to the top of the cavity.

4 **Closing the loaf.** Fold the ends of the prosciutto slices over the mushroom layer to cover the top of the stuffing as completely as possible. Set the reserved lid back in place on top of the loaf. The sandwich now may be wrapped in foil and chilled several hours to set the filling, or baked as shown in Step 5.

5 **Heating the loaf.** Brush a light coat of olive oil over the top and sides of the loaf *(below)*. Bake the loaf in a preheated 375° F. [190° C.] oven for 20 to 30 minutes to heat it through. As it warms, baste the loaf two or three times with the fat from the bacon. Slice the loaf into wedges *(right)* and serve.

3

Pastry

A Versatile Vehicle

Cutting and rolling crescents
Adding cream to filled pies
Two ways to blind-bake tarts
Creating puffs
How to produce Chinese specialties

Few snacks are more appealing than crisp pastry casings with savory fillings, and few offer so many opportunities for improvisation and invention. Basic short-crust or rough puff pastry *(pages 8-9)*, for instance, may be curled into crescents, folded into triangular, square or semicircular packages, or formed into miniature shells that are shaped in small molds or even over the bottoms of muffin pans. Paper-thin sheets of Middle Eastern phyllo *(left)* yield many-layered buttery packages of exceeding delicacy. Rich *choux* paste puffs up during the baking process into deliciously light, hollow containers. And packages made from the flour-and-water mixture used in China—the simplest pastry of all—can be fried until crisp or, for a uniquely tender result, steamed.

No matter what kind of pastry or how it is shaped, success depends upon brisk, deft handling. Short-crust pastry that is manipulated too long becomes sticky and unmanageable as the butter in it softens. The pastry is, of course, chilled in the refrigerator after it has been formed to firm the butter again, but chilling will not correct the other result of overhandling: toughness caused by the overdevelopment of the gluten in the flour. The only way you can be sure of getting light, crisp short crust is to work with chilled pastry—and to work quickly enough so that it remains chilled.

Phyllo or Chinese pastry requires speedy shaping for a different reason: These pastries contain no fat and therefore quickly become dry and brittle when exposed to the air. For protection, phyllo sheets are brushed with melted butter before they are shaped. Chinese pastries are divided into small quantities for shaping, and pastry that is not in use is covered with a dampened towel.

The fillings suitable for any of these pastries include meats, fish, vegetables, eggs, cheese and sauces, in whatever combinations strike the cook's fancy *(recipes, pages 134-150)*. All that need be remembered is to suit the consistency of the filling to the containers. Fillings to be cooked inside folded pastry packages should be dense ones such as cooked sausages or chopped meat and vegetables: Thin sauces or melting cheese will tend to ooze out as the packages bake. Sauced fillings such as snails bathed in garlic butter *(page 93)* are best reserved for prebaked shells, which serve as cups to hold the liquid.

Folded phyllo triangles *(pages 68-69)* emerge from the oven crisp and golden after their brief baking. Inside the buttery coils and triangles shown here is a rich and highly seasoned mixture of spinach and feta cheese.

Mass-producing Short-Crust Crescents

Short-crust or rough puff pastry can be readily wrapped around any of a variety of fillings to produce small, savory packages in the eye-catching form of crescents. If the crescents are to be properly crisp yet tender, care must be taken in handling the pastry, choosing the filling and baking the parcels.

The crescents begin with a sheet of chilled pastry, rolled out as described on page 9. To divide the sheet into portions, cut it into strips, then stack the strips and slice through the stack, forming triangles. For clean cutting, use a pastry wheel or a very sharp knife: A dull blade will pull and wrinkle the pastry.

In making crescents, as well as the pastry shapes shown on pages 62-67, you may well find yourself with scraps of leftover short-crust or rough puff pastry.

These may be sprinkled with a few bits of butter, gathered into a ball, refrigerated until firm, then rolled again, cut and shaped. Do not try to roll the pastry a third time, however: It will be overworked and tough.

The choice of fillings for the pastry parcels ranges from the fresh pork sausages used on these pages to ground or chopped meat, meat and vegetables, chopped vegetables such as mushrooms or scallions, or even chopped nuts (recipes, pages 134-150). The fillings must be fairly firm and dry—liquids or melting cheese will seep through the pastry. If they require cooking, the fillings must be prepared in advance; they would not cook through in the short time it takes to bake the crescents. In this demonstration, the sausages are poached in water and white wine, then thoroughly drained.

As another precaution against leaks, the cut edges of the crescents should be sealed. To encourage them to stick together, moisten the edges with water, raw egg white or an egg wash—egg yolk mixed with milk or water. Next, brush an egg wash over the pastry parcels, but be careful not to spill any, as it will burn; the egg wash will harden to a crisp, shiny glaze during baking.

Baking sheets to be used for small pastries should be made of heavy metal—such as the carbon steel used in this demonstration—that will not buckle in the oven's heat. To prevent the pastry crescents from sticking while they are baking, you can grease and flour the sheet. A simpler solution is to cover the baking sheet with parchment paper, as shown here, or with aluminum foil.

1 **Preparing the filling.** Transform long pork sausages into small links by twisting them at 1-inch [2½-cm.] intervals. In a partly covered pan, simmer the sausages in a mixture of equal parts of water and white wine for 12 to 15 minutes. Drain the sausages, then cut through the twists to separate the links.

2 **Cutting pastry strips.** Roll pastry— short-crust is used here—into an oblong no more than ¼ inch [6 mm.] thick. Square off the edges with a pastry cutter or a sharp knife to make a rectangle 20 inches [50 cm.] long and 12 inches [30 cm.] wide. Slice the pastry into strips 4 inches [10 cm.] wide. Dust the strips with flour and stack them.

3 **Cutting triangles.** With the pastry cutter, slice diagonally across the stack of strips to form triangles 4 inches [10 cm.] wide at their bases. Peel the triangles apart and lay them out in rows on a lightly floured surface.

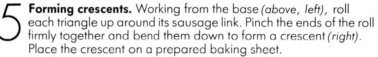

4 **Filling triangles.** Put a dab of Dijon mustard near the base of each triangle and on it lay a sausage link. Using a pastry brush or your finger, dampen the triangle edges with water, egg white or a mixture of yolk and water.

5 **Forming crescents.** Working from the base *(above, left)*, roll each triangle up around its sausage link. Pinch the ends of the roll firmly together and bend them down to form a crescent *(right)*. Place the crescent on a prepared baking sheet.

6 **Baking.** With a pastry brush, coat each crescent lightly with a mixture of egg yolk and water *(below)*. Transfer the baking sheet to a preheated 375° F. [190° C.] oven and bake for about 30 minutes, until the crescents are golden. Let them cool for five minutes, then transfer them individually to a serving tray and serve immediately.

A Catalogue of Parcels

A variety of pastry parcels more substantial than the crescents shown on the previous pages may be formed from circles, squares and rectangles of short-crust or rough puff pastry. As with the crescents, direct handling of the pastry should be minimized to prevent the butter from softening or the pastry from toughening.

Larger packages—demonstrated here and on pages 64-65—readily lend themselves to the use of various types of equipment that help keep warm hands away from the pastry itself. Wax paper, for example, can be used to lift and move larger pieces of pastry without damaging them *(page 64, top, Step 1)*; it also prevents drying if you wish to shape the pastry in advance and store it. Metal tools can replace hands in shaping and decorating: Edges can be sealed with pincer-like pastry crimpers *(Step 4, bottom)*, turnovers such as Cornish pasties can be crimped with a fork, and layered packages can be stamped and sealed together with metal cutters *(page 64, Step 2)*.

The sealed edges and relatively long cooking times of these larger packages allow greater leeway in the choice of filling than is possible with small rolled crescents. Fillings need not always be precooked. For example, the finely diced meat, potato and onion mixture that fills the Cornish pasties here *(recipe, page 136)* will easily cook through while the pastry is baking.

Liquid can be used to enrich fillings without damaging the packages if it is properly handled: The liquid can be funneled in after the pastry has set *(Step 4, top)* or, as with the covered pies in the bottom demonstration *(recipe, page 136)*, the liquid may be combined with such thick, starchy ingredients as potatoes, which will absorb any excess.

Once filled and sealed, most of these larger pastries are brushed with an egg wash and baked *(opposite)*. Notable exceptions are Indian *samosas (page 65; recipe, page 149)*. They are deep fried in hot oil, which would burn an egg wash.

Folding Circles into Turnovers

1 **Cutting circles.** Roll rough puff pastry into a rectangle ⅛ inch [3 mm.] thick. Use the rim of a bowl to stamp out circles 5 inches [12 cm.] in diameter, or use a plate as a pattern and cut around it with a pastry wheel or knife. If you wish to cut smaller pastries, use a biscuit cutter or the rim of a glass.

2 **Filling the pastries.** Prepare a filling; the one used here includes diced round steak, potatoes, chopped onions, thyme, salt and pepper. Place a spoonful of filling slightly off-center on each pastry, and top it with butter. Paint the rim of the pastry with egg wash, fold the pastry over the filling and crimp the edges with the tines of a fork.

Making Miniature Pies

1 **Filling the pies.** Stamp large and small circles from a sheet of rough puff pastry. If you cut out the circles in advance, separate them with wax paper and refrigerate. Press the large circles into the cups of a muffin tin. In each circle, place spoonfuls of grated, parboiled potatoes and grated truffles.

2 **Enriching the pies.** Spoon more potatoes into the pies until each is filled nearly to the top. Into each, spoon heavy cream you have seasoned with salt and pepper, filling the pies to within ¼ inch [6 mm.] of the tops.

3 **Baking.** Paint the pastries with egg wash. Prick the tops with a fork to allow steam to escape. Bake the turnovers for 45 minutes in a preheated 325° F. [160° C.] oven.

4 **Enriching the filling.** Remove the turnovers from the oven. Pierce a hole in the top of each with a funnel, and pour in about 2 tablespoons [30 ml.] of heavy cream. Do not allow the cream to drip onto the pastry: It will burn and blacken.

5 **Completing the baking.** If you like, conceal the holes made by the funnel by placing sprigs of fresh rosemary or thyme in them. Return the turnovers to the oven and bake for 15 minutes more, until they are crisp and golden brown. The herb sprigs will wilt, but they will still be edible.

3 **Covering the pies.** Place a smaller circle of pastry on top of each pie. Do not press the circles down; you may force filling to leak from the edges of the pies.

4 **Crimping edges.** Use pastry crimpers to seal the lid and base of each pie. Paint the pies with egg wash. Do not pierce them; escaping steam may leave the fillings dry. Bake at 325° F. [160° C.] for about 45 minutes, until the pies are golden brown and shrink slightly from the sides of the muffin cups.

5 **Removing the pies.** Lift each pie carefully from its muffin cup and transfer it to a wire rack to cool slightly. Transfer to a platter and serve at once.

Forming Triangular Turnovers

1 **Preparing triangles.** Cut rolled-out pastry into 5-inch [12-cm.] squares. Spoon filling — here, drained, marinated oysters *(recipe, page 138)* and slivers of lemon peel — diagonally along one half of each square. Paint the edges with egg wash and, using wax paper, fold over the uncovered half.

2 **Decorating the triangles.** Press the edges closed, then slash them with the tip of a knife to form a decorative border, and slit the centers to allow steam to escape. Cut small leaf shapes out of pastry scraps and place them on top of each of the turnovers. Brush the decorated turnovers with egg wash.

3 **Baking the triangles.** Put the turnovers on a prepared baking sheet *(page 61)*. Bake them in a preheated 450° F. [230° C.] oven until they are golden, about 15 to 20 minutes. Use a broad spatula to transfer the turnovers to their platter. Serve them immediately.

Bonding Twin Squares

1 **Filling the squares.** Cut rolled-out pastry — in this case, rough puff — into 5-inch [12-cm.] squares. Center a spoonful of filling — here, chopped leeks stewed in butter and thickened with cream — on each. Brush a ¾-inch [2-cm.] egg-wash border around the filling. Cover with another pastry square.

2 **Sealing the squares.** Press the pair of squares lightly but thoroughly together over the egg-washed border around the filling. With a pastry wheel or cookie cutter, trim off the edges, cutting through the center of the egg-wash band. Paint the trimmed, filled squares with more egg wash.

3 **Baking the squares.** With a sharp knife, cut a small cross in the top of each square so that steam can escape. Place the squares on a prepared baking sheet and bake in a preheated 450° F. [230° C.] oven for about 15 to 20 minutes, until they are golden. Transfer the squares to a platter and serve them.

Rolling Up a Filling

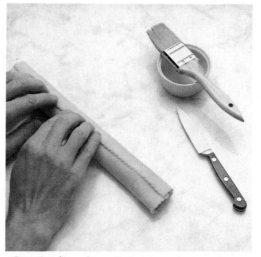

1 **Filling the rectangle.** Cut rolled-out pastry — here, rough puff — into rectangles 12 inches [30 cm.] long and 4 inches [10 cm.] wide. Spoon filling — in this case, ground beef liver, eggs and onion (recipe, page 141) — along the center of each. Smooth the filling into a cylinder shape with a spatula.

2 **Sealing the roll.** Fold one long side of the pastry up over the filling. Brush the second side with egg wash and fold it up to overlap the first; press it lightly to seal the roll. Brush egg wash inside the open ends of the roll and pinch them together. Place the roll, seam side down, on a prepared baking sheet.

3 **Baking.** Make deep diagonal slashes halfway through the roll at 1-inch [2½-cm.] intervals; fold up, seal and slash the other rectangles. Paint the rolls with egg wash. Bake in a preheated 375° F. [190° C.] oven for 45 minutes, until golden. To serve, cut through the slashes to make thick diagonal slices.

Deep Frying Stuffed Cones

1 **Cutting the pastry.** Roll samosa pastry (recipe, page 149) to a thickness of ⅛ inch [3 mm.]. With the rim of a bowl, cut out circles 5 inches [12 cm.] in diameter. Divide each circle in half with a sharp knife or pastry cutter. Paint the edges of each semicircle with water.

2 **Filling the samosa.** Fold each semicircle in half and press the straight edges together to form a cone. Spoon filling into the cone; a traditional mixture of peas and potatoes (recipe, page 149) is used here. Press the curving top edges of the cone together to seal it.

3 **Deep frying.** In a deep pan heat 4 inches [10 cm.] of oil to 375° F. [190° C.] on a deep-frying thermometer. Deep fry a few samosas at a time — to avoid lowering the temperature of the oil — for two to three minutes, turning once. When they are golden, lift them out with a wire skimmer and drain.

Molding Open Tarts

Miniature, open tart shells crisp enough to stand alone and deep enough to hold substantial fillings may be formed either inside tiny individual tartlet pans or over the back of an inverted multiple-tartlet tin or a muffin tin. In either case, short-crust pastry must be used—rising rough puff pastry would overwhelm the small forms—and it must be rolled and shaped carefully, as described on page 9, to ensure that it remains tender.

Individual tartlet pans are available at kitchen-equipment shops in a variety of shapes; the pans at right are oval *barquettes* (French for small boats).

Lining these pans is a simple affair, but because the pastry shells will soften during the initial stage of baking, they require some sort of bracing so that their sides do not collapse. The traditional bracing method is to line the pastry with foil or wax paper, then fill it with dried beans or small aluminum weights whose pressure keeps the sides erect. An easier solution is shown here: The pastry-lined pans are stacked inside one another for baking, so that each pan serves as a brace for the pastry beneath. Only the topmost pastry-lined pan in each stack need be filled with beans or weights.

The main advantage of using individual tartlet pans is their versatility. The pastry shells may be fully baked, cooled and then filled with a precooked mixture or one that can be eaten raw. Or, if you wish to cook a filling in the shells, they may be baked only 10 to 15 minutes to set the pastry and prevent sogginess, then separated from their stacks, filled and returned to the oven to complete the cooking process.

Pastry shaped over the bottom of a multiple-tartlet tin *(below)* cannot, of course, be baked with a filling; on the other hand, shaping can be done quickly—and collapsing pastry is obviously not a problem. Before baking, the shells should be pricked all over to allow the escape of steam, which might otherwise puff and deform the pastry.

Baking in Stacks

1 **Lining barquette pans.** Cut rolled short-crust pastry into ovals. Press the pastry into the pans and slide a knife blade over them to cut off the excess. Stack the pans six deep on a baking sheet. Line each top barquette with wax paper and fill it with beans or with aluminum pieces, as shown here.

An Inside-out Technique

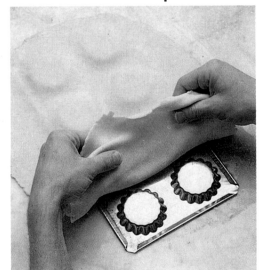

1 **Molding the shells.** Invert a multiple-tartlet tin. Roll short-crust pastry into a rectangle 1/8 inch [3 mm.] thick and one and a half times as large as the tin. Drape the pastry loosely over the tin, allowing it to sink down in the recessed area around the tartlet cups.

2 **Trimming the shells.** Slide a biscuit cutter or a drinking glass that is slightly larger in diameter than the tartlet cups over each cup and press it down to cut a circle in the pastry.

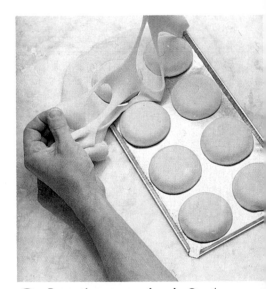

3 **Removing excess dough.** Gently lift the loose pastry away from the tartlet tin. Quickly pat the pastry into a ball and chill it in the refrigerator until you are ready to make the next batch of shells.

2 **Baking and cooling.** Bake the barquettes in a preheated 350° F. [180° C.] oven for 15 minutes, or until the edges are brown, then separate them and bake 15 minutes, until golden. Cool the pans, then invert each one onto your hand and lift it off its pastry. Cool the barquette shells on a cake rack.

3 **Filling the barquettes.** When the barquettes have cooled, add the filling; here, each shell contains halved snails that have been heated in melted snail butter flavored with shallots, chopped parsley and garlic *(recipe, page 93)*. If you wish, reheat the filled barquettes briefly under a broiler.

4 **Baking.** Prick each shell with a fork, refrigerate for 30 minutes, and bake in a preheated 400° F. [200° C.] oven for 10 to 15 minutes, or until golden brown. Cool, then lift each shell off the tin. Cool on a rack before filling; the filling shown in this demonstration is eggs scrambled with cream and butter and garnished by sautéed mushroom slices.

The Special Demands of Phyllo

Filled packages of incomparable lightness and crispness are produced from sheets—or leaves—of phyllo, a translucently thin flour-and-water pastry that is favored by Greek and Middle Eastern cooks. Although it is difficult to make at home, phyllo is widely available, either fresh or frozen, at specialty markets. The pastry is sold in stacks of 25 to 30 sheets, each 16 by 18 inches [40 by 45 cm.], sealed in plastic to keep them moist (because the pastry contains no fat, the sheets quickly become dry and unmanageably brittle when exposed to the air). Fresh phyllo may be kept for up to five days in the refrigerator. Frozen phyllo keeps four to five months; it requires a defrosting period of 24 hours in the refrigerator—still in its package.

Once phyllo is unwrapped, it should be used within a day or two. Remove the number of sheets required, keeping them in a stack, and return the rest in their wrapping to the refrigerator. To divide the sheets quickly into strips or squares for shaping the triangular, square and coiled packages shown here, use scissors to cut through the stack. Then peel off phyllo pieces one by one for folding.

If you are working with phyllo for the first time, you may find it easier to peel off and fold a double layer of pastry; the cooked packages will be less delicate, but the risk of tearing the fragile pastry will be reduced. If your first efforts at folding go rather slowly, cover the phyllo not in use with a dampened towel to keep it moist and flexible. Later, when folding becomes only a matter of seconds, this precaution will not be necessary.

Before filling the phyllo sheets, brush each one generously with melted butter. The butter crisps the pastry during cooking and ensures that each layer remains separate. The filling can consist of almost any combination of ingredients. In the demonstrations at right, baked phyllo triangles and coils are stuffed with a Greek mixture of spinach, feta cheese, beaten egg yolks and seasonings to produce *spanakopitas (recipe, page 139)*. The deep-fried phyllo squares or *briks* demonstrated in the box at far right contain a Tunisian combination: equal amounts of sautéed mushrooms and grated cheese topped with an egg.

Repeated Folds That Yield a Triangle

1 Adding filling. Cut a stack of phyllo lengthwise into three strips. For each triangle, peel off a strip, brush it with melted butter and put filling — a spinach mixture is shown — near the bottom end, slightly left of center. Holding the left corner, fold the right corner over to form a triangle.

2 Folding. Hold the edges of the triangle to keep the filling in place, and fold the triangle up over the strip, aligning the triangle's left edge with the left edge of the phyllo strip. Fold the triangle over again so that this time the right edge of the triangle aligns with the right edge of the phyllo strip *(above)*.

A Cylinder Curled Back on Itself

1 Filling. Cut a stack of phyllo in half across its width. For each coil, peel off a sheet of pastry and brush it with melted butter. Spoon a line of filling — spinach, in this case — across the bottom end of the sheet, leaving margins of pastry 1 inch [2½ cm.] wide on each side and at the bottom.

2 Rolling a tube. Fold both sides of the pastry over the filling to cover the ends; the folds should extend the length of the phyllo. Brush the edges with melted butter. Roll the pastry up from the bottom to enclose the filling in a tube. Press the end flap onto the tube.

A Square with Egg Inside

3 **Finishing the package.** Continue folding over the triangle until you reach the top of the strip. Press the loose end of pastry at the top gently onto the triangular package to seal it.

4 **Baking.** Brush the triangles with melted butter on all sides and put them on a baking sheet. Bake them in a preheated 400° F. [200° C.] oven until they are golden and puffy — about 20 minutes. Using wooden tongs or a spatula to keep from breaking the pastries, transfer them to a platter.

1 **Filling.** Butter a phyllo strip — in this case a double thickness. Spread mushroom filling 4 inches [10 cm.] from one end. Fold in the sides of the strip. Break an egg on the filling and fold up the short end of the strip.

2 **Folding.** Working gently to avoid breaking the egg, fold the filled phyllo end over end the length of the strip. Heat the oil for deep frying to 375° F. [190° C.].

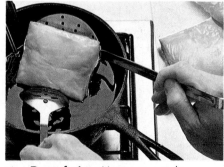

3 **Forming coils.** Twist the tube into a circle and tuck one end under the other, pressing it lightly down so that it will stay in place. Put each coil on a prepared baking sheet; brush with melted butter.

4 **Baking.** Bake the coils in a preheated 400° F. [200° C.] oven until they are crisp and golden — about 20 minutes. Transfer the coils carefully to a platter and serve them immediately.

3 **Deep frying.** Using a spatula, slide the pastry into the hot oil. Deep fry for four to six minutes, or until golden, turning the pastry once with two slotted spatulas or spoons. Drain on paper towels.

Ethereal Confections from Choux

Unlike short crust, rich and sticky *choux* paste *(demonstration, pages 8-9; recipe, page 163)* cannot be rolled or folded. But because this pastry expands dramatically during baking, it makes a delightful vehicle for flavorings and fillings.

The cook may, for instance, incorporate cubes of cheese into the pastry and shape it into a large ring to produce *gougère (right; recipe, page 140)*, a light, savory Burgundian invention customarily accompanied by red wine. An authentic *gougère* is made with Gruyère cheese, but similarly attractive effects can be obtained by substituting cubed Cheddar, or grated Parmesan. An alternative way to treat *choux* paste is to form it into small spheres. As they swell in the oven, the spheres become hollow puffs—ready for almost any filling, from mussels in cream sauce *(recipe, page 138)* to the chicken salad shown in the box below.

To form either puffs or rings, you can spoon mounds of the paste onto a prepared baking sheet or, for a particularly neat effect, pipe the paste through a pastry bag; the cheese for *gougère* should be grated for this procedure.

Both rings and puffs must be baked at a steady high temperature to ensure proper rising. Do not open the oven door until the end of the cooking time: Even a slight drop in temperature could cause a collapse. When the pastries are done, they should be dried to keep them light and crisp. Rings may simply be left in the turned-off oven for five to 10 minutes.

Individual puffs, however, must be dry inside to be successful containers. As soon as they have cooked, pierce each one to provide a vent for steam, then dry the puffs in the turned-off oven. Soft fillings such as *guacamole* can be piped from a pastry bag through the hole in each puff. Heavier fillings will have to be spooned into sliced-open puffs as shown below.

1 **Adding cheese.** Cut Gruyère cheese into small cubes and add about two thirds of the cubes to prepared *choux* pastry. Stir in salt and mustard, and thoroughly blend the ingredients.

Piping Tiny Puffs

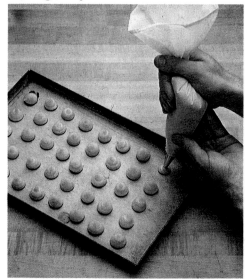

1 **Piping choux puffs.** Fit a pastry bag with a round-tipped tube. Then fill the bag with *choux* paste, twist the bag closed and pipe balls ½ inch [1 cm.] in diameter onto a prepared baking sheet, 3 inches [8 cm.] apart. Brush the tops with egg wash.

2 **Baking and filling.** Bake the puffs in a preheated 375° F. [190° C.] oven for 20 minutes, or until golden. Prick the puffs with a knife and let them dry out in the turned-off oven for 20 minutes. Slice off the tops of the puffs and spoon in filling — chicken and mayonnaise here. Replace the tops.

4 **Smoothing the ring.** Smooth the surface of the pastry circle with a spatula or the flat of a knife. Do not leave any curls of pastry on the top or sides of the circle: They would burn before the *gougère* cooked through.

2 **Making a pattern.** Line a baking sheet with parchment paper, or coat it with butter and flour. Use a saucepan lid as a guide to draw a circular template on the parchment paper or to stamp it into the flour. Beat an egg with cream to form a wash.

3 **Forming a ring.** With a large spoon scoop up the pastry and form mounds in a ring on the baking sheet, using the circle as a guide for the ring's outer edge. Place a second ring of smaller spoonfuls atop the first, centering them between its mounds.

5 **Baking.** Brush the top of the *gougère* with the egg wash, taking care that none drips onto the sheet. Sprinkle the remaining cubed cheese over the *gougère (above)*. Bake in a preheated 375° F. [190° C.] oven for 35 to 40 minutes, until golden brown. Let the ring dry in the turned-off oven for five to 10 minutes. Serve in wedges *(right)*.

A Fried Spiral of Chinese Pastry

A simple flour-and-water mixture similar to the one Greek cooks stretch into gossamer phyllo pastry *(pages 68-69)* is used in China for a variety of sturdy little snacks. Shaped and filled as shown, the pastry can be fried to make crunchy pancakes *(recipe, page 148)* or, with changes in mixing and shaping, it can be steamed *(pages 76-77)* to yield soft dumplings.

Making the basic pastry is not difficult. However, it is important to knead the flour-and-water mixture thoroughly to activate the gluten in the flour, and then let it rest briefly before shaping. These steps will ensure a pastry cohesive and pliable enough to be formed into the thinnest possible pancake, one that will cook through quickly in hot oil.

Assertive fillings lend flavor to the bland pastry. Here, the pastry is filmed with nutty sesame oil, then sprinkled with finely cut scallions. Sausage, ham or shrimp could be used instead of scallions, and melted lard or pungent, dark sesame-seed oil could replace the pale oil. For frying, use bland peanut or vegetable oil that will not detract from the filling.

1 Mixing the pastry. Mound the flour in a bowl, make a well in the center, and gradually stir in water until a sticky dough forms. On a lightly floured surface, knead the pastry *(page 7)* until it is smooth and pliable — about three minutes. Place the pastry in an oiled bowl and cover with a damp cloth.

2 Final kneading. After 15 minutes, transfer the pastry to a lightly floured work surface. Knead the pastry for two minutes, sprinkling it with flour as necessary to keep it from sticking. When the pastry feels soft and smooth, gather it together into a ball.

6 Forming a cylinder. With your fingers, lightly roll the rectangle of coated pastry across its width to form a long cylinder. Pinch the ends closed.

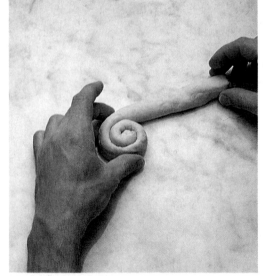

7 Forming a coil. Starting at one end of the cylinder, wind the pastry into a coil. Tuck the loose end of the pastry cylinder underneath the coil.

8 Rolling out the coil. Flatten the coil of pastry slightly with the palm of your hand. Roll it out with a rolling pin, to make a pancake about ¼ inch [6 mm.] thick. Cover the pancake with a cloth to keep it moist and repeat the procedure with the remaining pastry rectangles.

3 **Rolling the pastry.** Cut the ball of pastry into quarters. On a floured surface, lightly roll each quarter into a rectangle about ⅛ inch [3 mm.] thick. Sprinkle each rectangle with salt and roll it once to press the salt into the pastry.

4 **Coating the pastry.** With sharp scissors, cut scallions into fine bits and set them aside. Brush each pastry rectangle with a thin coat of sesame oil.

5 **Adding scallions.** Sprinkle a few of the cut scallions evenly over the entire surface of the rectangle. Pat the scallions lightly to press them in place.

9 **Frying the pancakes.** In a heavy skillet, heat a thin layer of peanut oil until it looks hazy. Add a pancake and fry it over medium heat for about five minutes, turning it once, until both sides are brown and crisp. Transfer the pancake to paper towels to drain *(left)* and fry the remaining pancakes. To serve, cut in quarters with a sharp knife *(above)*.

Pleated Bonnets Cooked in Stages

A flour-and-water pastry that is made in the conventional way *(page 72)* but moistened with boiling rather than cold water *(recipe, page 143)* will be silky and pliable enough to form into the intricate shapes that characterize Chinese dumplings. Most of these dumplings begin with a thin, flat circle of pastry, rolled out from a slice cut from a cylinder. The circle may be gathered into a ball around its filling, crimped into a basket to make an open container *(pages 76-77)*, or pleated into the bonnet shape shown here.

In the shaping process, speed is of the essence: The pastry contains no fat and rapidly becomes dry and brittle when exposed to the air. Work with only a small quantity at a time, covering the rest with a damp towel to help keep it moist.

Because of its lack of fat, this pastry is unsuitable for baking: It would become hard and unpalatable in the dry oven heat. However, the pastry is a perfect candidate for such moist cooking methods as poaching or steaming, as well as for deep frying or pan frying. In this demonstration, two methods are combined: The dumplings are pan fried in a little oil to make their bottoms brown and crisp; then water is added so that the dumplings steam to tenderness.

Like other bland pastries, the wrappers are perfect containers for highly seasoned fillings. Chinese fillings *(recipes, pages 143-145)* are generally based on finely chopped meat or seafood—ground beef is shown in this demonstration— but these ingredients are mixed with a variety of assertive seasonings: scallions, grated fresh ginger root, cabbage, soy sauce and sesame-seed oil.

Additional flavor is usually provided by one or more dipping sauces *(page 76)*. Most of these sauces combine sweet and sour notes: In this demonstration, for example, sweet *hoisin* sauce is thinned and sharpened with vinegar; a second sauce is made of soy sauce, vinegar, sesame-seed oil, chopped chilies and scallions, and freshly grated ginger.

1 **Slicing pastry rounds.** Prepare a filling; lean ground beef, cabbage, scallions and seasonings are used in this demonstration. Divide the pastry into four pieces and shape one of the pieces into a cylinder. Cover the remaining pastry with a dampened kitchen towel. Slice the cylinder into disks that are ½ inch [1 cm.] thick.

2 **Rolling pastry circles.** On a floured surface, flatten each disk of pastry with your hand. Then roll the disk into a circle about 3 inches [8 cm.] in diameter and ⅛ inch [3 cm.] thick. Trim imperfectly shaped circles with a knife or with a cookie cutter.

5 **Frying the dumplings.** Pour a film of vegetable oil into a heavy skillet and heat it until it looks hazy. Add the dumplings, unpleated sides down, and fry for about two minutes over high heat, until the bottoms of the dumplings are brown. Do not crowd the pan: Heat must be able to circulate freely around the dumplings.

6 **Steaming the dumplings.** Holding the lid above the pan to prevent spattering, pour in boiling water. Immediately cover the pan and reduce the heat to medium. Let the dumplings steam for about 10 minutes. If the water has not evaporated by then, lift the lid so that the water will evaporate quickly.

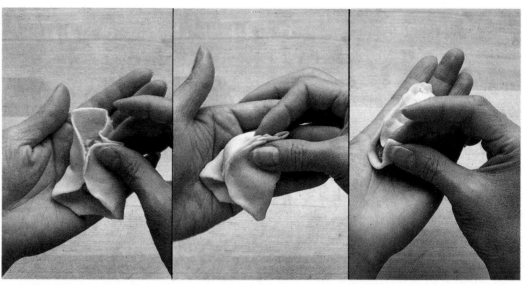

3 **Filling the dumplings.** Cup a pastry circle in one hand and place a spoonful of filling in the center. Leave the border free for pleating.

4 **Pleating the dumplings.** To make pleating easier, pinch the two sides of the pastry circle together at midpoint. Then make a small fold on one edge of the circle *(above, left)* and pinch it against the edge. Press the fold against the opposite edge of the circle, then pinch the pastry together to finish the pleat *(center)*. Continue making folds along the same side of the circle, pressing them to the opposite side *(right)*. Pinch the dumpling ends closed.

7 **Serving the dumplings.** After the water evaporates, let the dumplings fry for a minute to recrisp the bottoms. The tops should look soft and moist at this point. Transfer them to a serving platter at once: Overcooking will make the dumplings disintegrate. Serve the dumplings with dipping sauces; seasoned *hoisin* and soy sauces *(page 76)* are pictured here.

Translucent Baskets Steamed to Succulence

The most delicate of Chinese pastries contain no wheat flour at all. They are formed instead from much less dense wheat starch—a fine powder that is left after the gluten is removed from all-purpose flour—and tapioca flour. The pastry thus created may be shaped, filled and steamed to produce dumplings of petal-like translucency.

The basic pastry is made in the same manner as flour-and-water pastry *(page 143):* Dry ingredients are combined with boiling water, kneaded until they are smooth and cohesive, then allowed to rest, covered with a dampened towel to protect against drying. Because the pastry has minimal gluten, it is vulnerable to tearing while it is being shaped—here, into a basket form. Once torn, the pastry cannot be patched: It must be re-kneaded, then rolled and shaped again.

Wheat-starch pastries should not be baked or fried: They would dry out in the oven and disintegrate in the high heats that frying demands. Instead, the pastries should be gently steamed over boiling water. A Chinese steamer, composed of one or more stackable covered trays set over water in a wok, is used here. But steamers are easy to improvise: You need only a large, tightly covered pan and some sort of rack to hold the pastries above a shallow layer of water so that steam can circulate around them—even a heatproof plate set on a trivet will do.

For a colorful garnish, line the rack with aromatic leaves—spinach, for instance, or Chinese mustard greens, as used here. Be careful not to overcook the pastries: They will steam to doneness in 15 to 20 minutes, and overcooking will cause them to disintegrate.

Fillings should be light, to complement their delicate containers. A shrimp-and-bamboo-shoot combination is shown in this demonstration *(recipe, page 143).* Other possibilities include beef with water chestnuts, and crab with pork.

Rolling rounds. Make a shrimp filling and line a steamer basket with leaves such as these mustard greens. Shape a cylinder from wheat-starch pastry and slice off a few thin rounds *(page 74, Step 1).* Roll each round to a diameter of 3 inches [8 cm.].

Concocting a Dipping Sauce

Mixing a sauce. Combine equal amounts of light soy sauce *(top left)* and Chinese vinegar *(center).* Add soy sauce or vinegar to taste. Add a sprinkling of chopped scallions and a few drops of sesame-seed oil *(right);* nothing more than a chopstick is needed for stirring.

The dipping sauces that add piquant accents to Chinese pastries are made by mixing together two or more of a group of sweet, sour, tart and salty ingredients—all readily available at Oriental markets. The sauces may be prepared in advance or, if you like, the ingredients may be presented in separate dishes at the table, so that each diner can mix them in the proportions he wishes.

Perhaps the most popular dipping-sauce ingredient is soy sauce, a tangy, salty liquid made from fermented soybeans. Of the three kinds available—heavy, dark and light—the last is most often used; it has the thinnest consistency and the most delicate taste.

For a sweet accent, dipping mixtures may include *hoisin* sauce, a purée of ground soybeans, garlic, spices and sugar. *Hoisin* is thick and sweet; to keep it from overwhelming delicate pastries, it usually is thinned with vinegar, which also adds a certain welcome tartness.

Vinegar, in fact, is almost as central to dipping sauces as soy. The best kind to use is mild black Chinese rice vinegar. Slightly more assertive white or yellow Chinese or Japanese rice vinegar or Western cider vinegar may be substituted, but not wine vinegars; they produce sauce too harsh for pastry.

Two other common liquid flavorings are aromatic sesame-seed oil and fiery chili-pepper oil. Both are so potent that they should be added discreetly.

For textural interest, sauces may include solid as well as liquid ingredients. Common additions are shredded fresh ginger root, chopped scallions, grated white radish and chopped chilies.

Sauce components may be used in innumerable combinations. For instance, a tangy sauce especially suitable for seafood-filled pastries is made by steeping grated fresh ginger in vinegar for 30 minutes. A sauce may contain only liquids: Soy sauce and vinegar is a classic combination. But that basic sauce may be enhanced by chopped scallions and sesame-seed oil, as shown at left, or fresh ginger or hot chili oil.

2 **Shaping baskets.** Cup a pastry round in one hand and pinch one edge to fashion a pleat 1 inch [2½ cm.] deep *(above, left)*. Fold the pleat flat against the pastry. Rotate the round slightly and make another pleat, folding it in the same direction as the first pleat *(center)*. Repeat all around the rim to form a basket *(right)*.

3 **Filling the dumplings.** Hold the basket-shaped pastry in one hand and spoon in filling up to the rim. Gently stand the dumpling in the steamer tray and repeat the process with the other pastry rounds. Do not crowd the steamer tray: Steam must circulate freely.

4 **Steaming.** Set the filled steamer tray over boiling water and cover it. Steam the dumplings about 15 minutes, until the pastry is beige-colored and translucent. Serve these dumplings with any of the dipping sauces described in the box on the opposite page.

4
An International Medley

Pizza, pork buns and tortillas are among a number of hearty snacks that retain an ethnic aura and are widely believed to call for special skills: Americans tend to view them as foods to be ordered in restaurants or purchased in ready-made form. In truth, these snacks depend on ingredients as elementary as flour, water, eggs and yeast, and they are prepared with familiar cooking techniques.

Pizza, for example, is nothing more than bread dough flattened and baked with almost any topping, from the ricotta cheese used in Genoa to the tomatoes, mozzarella cheese and herbs of the classic Neapolitan version *(pages 86-87)*. A kindred bread dough, made with milk, not water, can be wrapped around a filling and steamed rather than baked to become soft, opaque Chinese pork buns *(pages 84-85)*. An even simpler dough made with corn flour is flattened to make Mexican tortillas. Depending on how they are fried and garnished, these pale gold disks can be shaped into spicy enchiladas, tacos or *tostadas (pages 88-90)*.

Batters, too, are versatile snack foundations. Pancake batter can be deep fried to form crisp cases for creamy mixtures of meat, fish or vegetables *(pages 80-81)*. And a pancake batter leavened with yeast produces blini—spongy Russian or Scandinavian pancakes *(opposite and pages 82-83)* that may be served with a variety of interesting toppings.

Most of these foods can be prepared with standard equipment found in any kitchen. Part of the pleasure of cooking them, however, lies in learning to use a few special tools—available at kitchen-equipment shops—that give each dish an authentic character and flair. Tortilla dough, for instance, may be flattened with a rolling pin, but a hinged tortilla press makes the procedure so much easier that few Mexican cooks are without one. Pizza attains an ideal crust when it is baked on unglazed tiles rather than in a baking pan, and the large, floppy pie is most easily moved by means of a wooden paddle known as a peel. Blini can be fried in any heavy skillet, but a Scandinavian *plättlagg* with individual compartments will shape the pancakes into uniform small rounds suitable for snacks. And although it may be possible to improvise a mold for deep frying batter cases, the neatest shapes are produced with the aid of Scandinavian rosette irons—small molds attached to long handles—that hold the batter together while it cooks in hot oil.

Wrapped in a napkin that keeps them warm, yeast-leavened blini await their traditional garnishes: melted sweet butter, sour cream, caviar and chopped scallions. The blini are stacked, but in two piles that overlap a bit so that air will circulate to prevent sogginess.

Krustader: Delicate Batter Cups Crisped in Oil

Armed with the long-handled Scandinavian rosette iron shown on these pages and one or more of the interchangeable molds that screw onto its tip, you can turn a simple flour, milk and egg batter into the crisp, wafer-thin cases known as *krustader (recipe, page 150). Krustader* batter—unlike most other mixtures that are molded—is not contained within the mold; rather, it coats the outside surface of the mold and is hardened into a cup by deep frying in hot oil.

To set the batter instantly and prevent it from dispersing in the oil, the mold must be hot; it must also be oiled, so that the fried case is easy to remove. Both requirements can be satisfied by plunging the mold into the hot frying oil, dipping it into the prepared batter, and returning it to the oil to finish the cooking *(Steps 2-4).* The cases emerge from the oil as sturdy containers, suitable for creamy fillings such as the sauced mussels shown here *(recipe, page 138).*

1 Mixing the batter. Sift the flour, then measure it into a deep bowl. In a separate bowl, mix the milk, water, sugar, salt, egg and oil. Gradually pour this mixture into the flour, beating vigorously with a whisk until the batter is smooth. To eliminate any air bubbles, let the batter rest for two hours.

2 Heating the iron. Pour vegetable oil into a deep, heavy pan to a depth of 4 inches [10 cm.] and heat it until it reaches 375° F. [190° C.] on a deep-frying thermometer, or until a cube of bread dropped in the oil browns in 60 seconds. Dip the iron in the hot oil for 15 seconds. Touch the hot iron to a paper towel lightly to remove excess oil.

5 Removing the case. With the help of a fork, gently push down the top edge of the case until it slides off the mold onto a paper towel to drain. Repeat the frying procedure with the remaining batter. The *krustader* should be used at once.

6 Making a sauce. Melt butter in a saucepan set over medium heat and stir in flour to make a roux *(recipe, page 150).* Stir in the liquid used for steaming cleaned fresh mussels *(above);* then stir in white wine and heavy cream, whisking until all lumps disappear.

3 **Coating the iron.** Lower the hot iron slowly into the batter, taking care that the top ¼ inch [6 mm.] of the iron remains exposed. Any batter adhering to the mold's top will cook there, making it hard to slide the fried case off the mold.

4 **Frying the batter.** Plunge the batter-coated iron into the hot oil. After one to one and a half minutes, when the batter begins to turn brown, lift the rosette iron out of the hot oil.

7 **Serving.** Add the shelled mussels and chopped fresh parsley to the hot sauce and reheat for a moment to warm the mussels. Set the containers on a serving platter and fill each with the mussel mixture. Serve immediately; otherwise the *krustader* will become soggy. If you like, set each container on a nest of thinly sliced fresh lettuce.

Blini: Pancake Bases for Savory Toppings

Like all pancakes, blini start with a simple batter of white or buckwheat flour, milk and eggs *(recipes, pages 150-151)*. But the batter is both leavened and lightened to give blini a distinctive character.

The addition of yeast to the batter makes the blini more spongy than other pancakes—and also gives them a faint, pleasant sourness. This yeast-flavored mixture must be allowed to rest for several hours before it is used: As with any batter, the resting period permits the activated gluten in the flour to relax, thus ensuring that the blini will be tender.

To make the pancakes light, beaten egg whites are folded into the rested blini batter. The air in the whites expands during cooking, puffing the blini.

Blini may be cooked by ladling spoonfuls of batter onto any smooth-surfaced griddle or heavy skillet. For perfect shaping of seven blini at a time, use a Swedish cast-iron *plättlagg*, or small-pancake pan, made with circular recesses that mold the blini into uniform rounds.

Any pan used should be brushed with melted butter to give the blini the proper flavor. To prevent burning, the butter must be clarified: Melt it, let it cool and skim off the foam. Let the butter rest for half an hour to settle its milk solids. Finally, pour off the transparent fat, leaving the easily burned solids behind.

Traditionally blini are accompanied by melted butter, caviar and sour cream, but variations abound. Smoked salmon may be substituted for caviar, whipped cream can replace sour cream, and the blini may be garnished with chopped hard-boiled egg, dill or scallions.

1 **Straining the batter.** Dissolve the yeast in warm water *(page 6)*, and whisk it together with flour, egg yolks, salt, sugar, melted butter and milk until the mixture is the consistency of heavy cream. Then strain the batter to eliminate any lumps of flour.

2 **Resting the batter.** Cover the bowl and allow the batter to rest in a warm place—an unlighted oven is ideal—for about two hours. Then fold in stiffly beaten egg whites.

3 **Buttering the pan.** Brush the pan with warm, clarified butter; one coating will last through several batches of blini. Heat the pan slowly until drops of water sprinkled on it hiss and skip.

4 **Forming the blini.** Using a small ladle, fill each depression in the *plättlagg* almost to the top. If you are using a griddle or a skillet, choose a ladle with a capacity of about 3 tablespoons [45 ml.] to produce almost uniformly sized 3-inch [8-cm.] blini.

5 **Cooking the blini.** Cook the blini over medium heat, until the edges begin to brown. Then turn each pancake gently with a narrow spatula, using a fork or knife to support the pancake. Cook them for another minute, until the undersides are browned.

6 **Serving the blini.** To keep them crisp and warm, stack the cooked blini in two piles, overlapping them slightly at the edges, and cover them loosely with a napkin. Then butter the pan if it looks dry and proceed with the next batch. To serve a blini, moisten the top with melted butter, add one spoonful each of caviar and sour cream, and garnish with chopped scallions.

Pork Buns: Dough Cooked in Steam

Savory buns such as those included in most presentations of Chinese *dim sum* snacks are no more than milk-enriched yeast dough *(recipe, page 151)* prepared according to the principles demonstrated on pages 6-7 and wrapped around a filling. If brushed with an egg wash *(pages 60-61)* for color, the buns may be baked to make firm, breadlike snacks. Traditionally, however, the buns are steamed, as shown on these two pages, so that they will emerge distinctively soft and moist.

The fillings for buns cooked using either method are combinations of chopped cooked meats and vegetables, seasoned to yield a tangy surprise within the bland containers *(recipe, page 152)*. For the classic filling demonstrated here, lean pork is marinated in a mixture of soy and *hoisin* sauces that have been highly seasoned with a variety of spices. The pork is then cut into thin strips and suspended in the oven to roast; when cooked in this fashion, large surface areas of the meat

are exposed to the oven heat, which dries it and crisps it.

The means of suspending the strips is a matter of improvisation. In this demonstration, for instance, a long metal skewer is threaded through the centers of the meat strips and balanced between two S hooks—readily available at hardware stores—that are hung from a rod of the uppermost oven rack.

To catch meat drippings and grease, a pan is set below the dangling strips; a layer of water in the pan prevents grease from spattering and smoking.

Cooked until crusty, the meat is then chopped and seasoned again, then enfolded in the prepared yeast dough. The filled packages are steamed by the method described on page 76; however, in the steamer each bun should rest on a separate square of wax paper to prevent the moist dough from sticking to the steamer tray and to facilitate removing the buns when they are done.

1 **Slicing the pork.** With a sharp knife, cut lean pork — here, a Boston shoulder roast — into narrow strips about 1 inch [2½ cm.] thick. Marinate the strips for about three hours at room temperature or for six hours in the refrigerator — in this case in soy and *hoisin* sauces, sugar, grated fresh ginger, chopped garlic and five-spice powder.

5 **Slicing the dough.** On a lightly floured surface, shape the yeast dough into a long cylinder about 2 inches [5 cm.] in diameter. With a sharp knife, slice the cylinder into rounds 1 inch [2½ cm.] thick. Cut six or seven 2-inch [5-cm.] squares of wax paper and set them well apart in the tray of the steamer, ready to hold the buns after they have been filled and shaped.

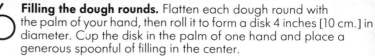

6 **Filling the dough rounds.** Flatten each dough round with the palm of your hand, then roll it to form a disk 4 inches [10 cm.] in diameter. Cup the disk in the palm of one hand and place a generous spoonful of filling in the center.

2 **Roasting the pork.** Attach two S hooks to the back and front of a rod on the highest oven rack; preheat the oven to 350° F. [180° C.]. Place a baking pan containing 1 inch [2½ cm.] of water on the lowest rack. Drain the pork strips and thread a metal skewer through their centers. Slide the skewer into the bottom loops of the S hooks.

3 **Dicing the pork.** Roast the pork for 15 minutes, then increase the oven temperature to 450° F. [230° C.] and roast for an additional 15 minutes, until the strips turn crisp and brown. Remove the skewers from the oven and, when the meat is cool enough to handle, slice it into ½-inch [1-cm.] dice.

4 **Making the filling.** In a large bowl, mix the diced pork with a thick sauce—shown here is a mixture of chopped, sautéed onion and five-spice powder moistened with a little *hoisin* sauce. (If you improvise your own sauce, do not add so much liquid that the sauce becomes runny.) Stir all together well to blend the ingredients.

7 **Steaming.** Gather the edges of the disk around the filling *(above, left)* and twist them together *(above, right).* Place the buns, twisted sides down, on the wax paper in the steamer and let them rise 30 minutes. Steam the buns 20 minutes, until they are shiny *(right).*

Pizza: A Bread Platform for Hearty Sauces

With a few changes in handling to make it elastic and a few tricks in baking to make it crisp and dry, simple bread dough can become the basis for tomato-covered pizza, the quintessential Neapolitan snack *(recipes, pages 154-155)*.

To make the dough supple enough to stretch into the flat disk that forms the base of the pizza, knead it for five minutes longer than you would a dough destined for a loaf. Then, to produce the coarse texture characteristic of pizza, let the dough rise only once before shaping it into a large disk *(Step 3)*.

After the dough is shaped, you will need some means of sliding the unwieldy disk in and out of the oven. A bread board will suffice, or you can use the wooden paddle, known as a peel, that is shown in this demonstration.

Traditionally, pizza is baked directly on bricks or tiles to produce a crisper crust than would be possible if it were baked on a metal pan, which traps oil and fries the dough. For brick-oven results, line the middle shelf of the oven with unglazed quarry tiles. To get the tiles sufficiently hot, heat them in the oven for at least 30 minutes before you slide the pizza onto them.

Pizza dough is baked with a topping, of course, and the choice of toppings is almost limitless. Most have a foundation of fresh, ripe tomatoes, peeled, sliced and strewn uncooked over the dough; alternatively, tomatoes that are not vine-ripened may be peeled, seeded, chopped, then stewed in olive oil to develop their flavor, and puréed into a smooth sauce, as used in this demonstration.

The tomato topping may be covered with nothing more than a sprinkling of shredded cheese—mozzarella or Parmesan, for example—as well as with seasonings such as oregano or basil. More elaborate pizzas may have added layers of mushrooms, green peppers, sausages, meats, sautéed onions or even cooked seafood. Any topping should be added just before you slide the pizza into the oven: If left on the uncooked dough for any length of time, the filling will sink in and make the pizza soggy.

1 **Kneading.** Mix bread dough *(pages 6-7, Steps 1-3)*. With the heel of your hand, knead it on a lightly floured work surface for at least 15 minutes, or until the dough feels silky, elastic and not sticky. Gather the dough into a ball.

2 **Raising the dough.** Coat the inside of a glass or ceramic bowl with olive oil. Place the ball of dough in the bowl and rotate the dough to coat it with the oil. Cover the bowl with a damp towel and put it in a warm, draft-free place for two hours, or until the dough doubles in volume. Punch the dough down *(page 7)*

5 **Assembling the pizza.** Spread tomatoes—a cooked tomato purée is shown here—over the dough without dampening the rim. Sprinkle shredded mozzarella on the tomatoes and add other toppings—in this case, grated Parmesan, chopped basil, whole basil leaves, salt and pepper. Drizzle olive oil over all.

3 **Rolling and shaping.** Divide the dough into four balls and let them rest for a few minutes. On a lightly floured surface, roll one ball of dough at a time into a disk ⅛ inch [3 mm.] thick, rolling just to — but not over — the edge of the dough *(left)*. Then, with your finger tips, gently push some dough outward from the center of the disk *(right)* to build up a rim that will retain the topping.

4 **Transferring the dough to the peel.** Dust a wooden peel lightly with cornmeal. Then grasp the dough disk with your finger tips and — using the same motion you would use to shake out a piece of wet laundry — fling the disk onto the peel. Carefully smooth out the disk with your fingers.

6 **Baking.** Set the edge of the peel on the tile-lined shelf of a preheated 450° F. [230° C.] oven. Use a wooden spatula to push the pizza off onto the tiles *(above)*. Bake for 15 to 20 minutes. Lift the pizza with the spatula to check the bottom *(right)*; when it looks crisp and browned, the pizza is done.

Tortillas: Corn-Dough Wrappers

Among the most versatile of snacks is the tortilla, the thin Mexican pancake classically made from a simple, corn-based dough. These golden disks are eaten folded or flat, sautéed or deep fried, filled or topped with endless combinations of ingredients from chicken to chilies. While tortillas may be bought ready-made, producing them at home is not difficult, and it ensures fresh, tender results.

To make authentic corn tortillas, you will need either *masa* or *masa harina*. *Masa*—dried corn kernels cooked and soaked in a solution of lime and water, then ground with water—is a moist, ready-to-use dough; however, it is not widely available. *Masa harina* is lime-treated dried corn that is ground and sold dry like flour; you can find it at Mexican food stores and many supermarkets.

The first step in making tortillas is to mix *masa harina* with water—and sometimes a little melted shortening, which makes the finished pancakes easy to fold. Small amounts of the dough are then flattened—with a rolling pin or a hinged tortilla press *(box, right)*—and cooked briefly on a griddle *(recipe, page 156)*.

The tortilla can be eaten without further cooking, or—as in this demonstration—it may be sautéed quickly in a little oil to keep it soft, then rolled around a hot filling and topped with sauce to form an enchilada. Two other classic variations are shown on page 90: The tortilla can be fried in oil or lard to produce a flat *tostada,* or it may be folded around a filling and deep fried to become a taco.

In any of its forms, the tortilla marries well with shredded beef, pork or chicken. The meat-covered tortillas are usually topped liberally with other contrasting elements—grated Cheddar or Monterey Jack cheese, chopped tomatoes, peppers and onions, shredded lettuce and thick purées including *guacamole (page 17)* or refried beans *(recipe, page 160)*.

Most tortilla snacks are also garnished with a sauce made from hot chilies, available at specialty markets. The sauce is best when freshly prepared *(Steps 1 and 2; recipe, page 161)*; the chilies' oils, however, can burn the skin and eyes. Wear plastic gloves when trimming chilies, or rinse your hands in cold water afterward to prevent irritation.

Enchiladas: Softened Tortillas Folded over a Filling

1 **Seeding the chilies.** Slit dried chilies — here, mild *ancho* and pungent *mulato* varieties — down one side, then discard the veins and fiery seeds. To heighten their piquancy, briefly toast the chilies in a dry hot pan until they blister. Then soak them in hot water for 15 to 20 minutes to soften them.

2 **Making the sauce.** Purée the chilies, garlic cloves, oregano and cumin in a blender or food mill; strain the purée. Heat a little oil in a saucepan and in it simmer the purée over medium heat for about 10 minutes. Add meat stock and milk and stir the sauce for about five minutes. Set it aside.

The Basics of Pressing and Cooking

Forming tortillas. Shape tortilla dough *(recipe, page 156)* into small balls. To prevent sticking, lay a plastic sandwich bag on the bottom half of an open tortilla press; place a ball of dough on the bag. Cover the dough with another plastic bag *(above, left)*, then close the press quickly and firmly. Open it and peel both bags from the dough. Immediately place the tortilla on a preheated griddle *(center)* and cook it for two minutes, turning it twice; it should be slightly puffed and its edges dry. Wrap cooked tortillas in a napkin *(right)* to keep them warm and flexible.

3 **Making filling.** Poach a 2½- to 3-pound [1¼- to 1½-kg.] chicken. Let it cool, and strip the meat from the bones. With two forks, tear the meat into fine shreds. Mix the chicken shreds with the chili sauce and set aside until you are ready to assemble the enchiladas.

4 **Softening tortillas.** Warm 1 inch [2½ cm.] of vegetable oil in a skillet over medium heat until bubbles form around a shred of tortilla when it is dropped into the pan. Overlap several tortillas, holding them like a fan, and slide them into the pan *(left)*; the oil will prevent sticking. Within 30 seconds the tortillas will wilt and color on the edges. Immediately lift them vertically from the oil, using a skimmer and fork. Lean the tortillas against the sides of a colander so that they drain completely.

5 **Folding enchiladas.** Prepare garnishes — in this instance, grated Monterey Jack cheese and chopped onion. Reheat the sauce if necessary. Dip two tortillas into the sauce, one at a time, then overlap them on a plate and spoon the chicken mixture in a thin line across them. With a fork and spoon, lift the overlapped tortillas along one long side and fold them over the filling.

6 **Serving the enchiladas.** Spoon additional chicken and chili sauce over the enchiladas, garnish them with the onions and cheese, and serve them immediately. Once filled and sauced, enchiladas will quickly become soggy.

Tostadas: Crisp Tortillas Heaped with Garnishes

1 **Frying tortillas.** Let tortillas *(page 88)* dry for at least two hours. Heat oil in a skillet until a drop of water tossed in hisses. Fry the tortillas — do not crowd them — for a minute on each side; they should be golden, with crisp edges. Drain the *tostadas* on paper towels.

2 **Garnishing the tostadas.** Prepare refried beans *(recipe, page 160)*. Support a *tostada* in one hand and spread on it a layer of the beans. Then pile the *tostada* high with garnishes — in this case, grated Cheddar cheese, *guacamole*, shredded lettuce and a sauce of sour cream *(beef tacos recipe, page 158)* that resembles the slightly sour heavy cream available in Mexico.

Tacos: Tortillas Deep Fried with a Filling Inside

1 **Filling and folding.** To make them soft and flexible, steam tortillas for a few moments on a wire rack set over boiling water. Place a little poached shredded chicken *(recipe, page 157)* in the center of each tortilla. Fold the tortilla in half over the filling and join the halves with wooden picks.

2 **Frying the tacos.** Put the tortillas in a deep-frying basket, and lower it slowly into a deep pan containing 4 inches [10 cm.] of oil heated to 350° F. [180° C.] on a deep-frying thermometer. Fry the tacos for four or five minutes, until crisp and golden brown. Remove them with tongs and drain them on paper towels.

3 **Adding the garnishes.** Remove the picks and gently pry open the taco shells. Add shredded lettuce and grated cheese, then moisten the filling by adding a spoonful of *salsa*, a spicy tomato-and-chili sauce *(recipe, page 160)*. Sprinkle chopped fresh coriander leaves over the tacos.

Anthology of Recipes

Drawing upon the cooking traditions and literature of more than 20 countries, the editors and consultants for this volume have selected 205 published recipes for the Anthology that follows. The selections range from the simple to the unusual—from homely cheeseburgers and club sandwiches to pork-stuffed Chinese dumplings and an exotic Moroccan turnover made of phyllo pastry and stuffed with brains and a raw egg.

Many of the recipes were written by world-renowned exponents of the culinary art, but the Anthology also includes selections from rare and out-of-print books and from works that have never before been published in English. Whatever the sources, the emphasis in these recipes is always on fresh, natural ingredients that blend harmoniously.

Since many early recipe writers did not specify amounts of ingredients, the missing information has been judiciously added. In some cases, instructions have been expanded. Where appropriate, clarifying introductory notes have also been supplied; they are printed in italics. Modern terms have been substituted for archaic language, but to preserve the character of the original recipes and to create a true anthology, the authors' texts have been changed as little as possible.

The recipes are organized according to the kind of snack they produce. Recipes for fillings and sauces are grouped by the uses appropriate for them: Chinese pastry fillings, for example, accompany recipes for suitable pastry wrappers. Recipes for standard preparations—short-crust and rough puff pastry, sandwich bread and a range of sauces among them—are positioned at the end of the Anthology. Unfamiliar cooking terms are explained in the combined General Index and Glossary that appears at the end of the book.

Apart from the primary components, all recipe ingredients are listed in order of use, with the customary U.S. measurements and the new metric measurements provided in separate columns. The metric quantities given here reflect the American practice of measuring such solid ingredients as flour or sugar by volume rather than by weighing them, as European cooks do.

In order to make the quantities simpler to measure, many of the figures have been rounded off to correspond to the graduations that are now standard on metric spoons and cups. One cup, for example, equals 237 milliliters; wherever practicable in these recipes, however, a cup appears as a more readily measurable 250 milliliters.)

Similarly, weight, temperature and linear metric equivalents have been rounded off slightly. For these reasons, the American and metric figures are not equivalent, but using one set or the other will produce equally good results.

Spreads and Dips

*Recipes for basic butters, spreads and sauces appear
in Standard Preparations, pages 161-167.*

Farmer's Wife Butter

Beurre Fermière

To make 1 ⅓ cups [325 ml.] butter

5	hard-boiled egg yolks	5
½ lb.	unsalted butter, softened	¼ kg.
	salt and ground pepper	
	cayenne pepper	
3 tbsp.	dry white wine	45 ml.
	strained fresh lemon juice	
1 tsp.	Dijon mustard (optional)	5 ml.

Put the egg yolks through a sieve into a bowl and blend in
the butter. Add salt and black pepper to taste, a dash of the
cayenne, the wine, lemon juice to taste, and mustard if desired. Mix well.

HENRI PAUL PELLAPRAT
THE GREAT BOOK OF FRENCH CUISINE

Green Butter

The butter you use must be the best possible, firm and cold.
Novelty rests with yourself: You can ring the changes upon
pounded anchovies, sardines, soft herring roe, lobster, crab
and shrimp; you can use capers, parsley, chervil, watercress,
garden cress, sour gherkins and olives. By the judicious selection of your ingredients, all of which are agreeable in
fancy butter, you will avoid sameness and secure success.

To make about ½ cup [125 ml.] butter

8 tbsp.	unsalted butter	120 ml.
about ½ lb.	fresh spinach	about ¼ kg.
8	oil-packed flat anchovy fillets	8
about ¼ cup	fresh parsley sprigs	about 50 ml.
1 tsp.	finely chopped capers	5 ml.

Boil the spinach, drain it thoroughly, squeeze the leaves
through a piece of muslin, and save all the green coloring so
obtained in a bowl or saucer. Pass the anchovies through a

hair sieve and save the pulp. Blanch the parsley, drain, and
mince as fine as possible enough parsley to fill a tablespoon
[15 ml.]. Pound the capers to a paste.

Having these ingredients ready, first color the butter by
working into it, as lightly as you can, enough of the spinach
coloring to secure the tint you require. Always order a little
more spinach than you think you may want, to be on the safe
side. Let the color be pale green rather than dark green.

Lastly, add the other things by degrees, and when they
are thoroughly incorporated, trim the butter into a neat
shape, or sundry pretty patlets, and set it in the icebox or
over a dish containing crumbled ice.

A. KENNEY HERBERT
COMMONSENSE COOKERY FOR ENGLISH HOUSEHOLDS

Flower Butter

To make 1 cup [¼ liter] butter

½ lb.	unsalted butter	¼ kg.
1 cup	violet, rose or nasturtium petals, or clover blossoms, washed, drained well and dried	¼ liter

Whip the butter to a cream. Pack a layer of violet, rose or
nasturtium petals or clover blossoms in the bottom of a 12-
ounce [375-ml.] jar and cover them with a piece of perforated
wax paper. Mold the butter into a square or ball smaller than
the jar. Place the molded butter on the paper. Place another
piece of perforated wax paper on top of the butter and sprinkle the remaining petals on top of the paper. Cover the jar
tightly and refrigerate it for several hours. Use this flower-
flavored butter as a spread on fanciful cuts of bread.

ARNOLD SHIRCLIFFE
EDGEWATER SANDWICH AND HORS D'OEUVRES BOOK

Dill Butter

Dillsmör

*The technique of preparing compound butter is demonstrated
on pages 10-11.*

To make about ½ cup [125 ml.] butter

2 tsp.	finely cut fresh dill	10 ml.
7 tbsp.	unsalted butter	105 ml.
2	eggs, hard-boiled and coarsely chopped	2
	thin slices white bread, or rye crackers	
	cooked crab claws	

Whip the butter until creamy, then mix it with the eggs and
dill. Spread the dill butter on white bread or rye crackers,
and decorate with crab claws.

GRETE WILLINSKY
KULINARISCHE WELTREISE

Snail Butter

Beurre d'Escargots

This butter mixture takes its name from its classic use as a flavoring for snails, but it can be used whenever a pungent spread is appropriate. The amount of parsley may be increased as desired to give the mixture a richer, greener color.

You may store the snail butter in an earthenware jar in the refrigerator.

	To make about 5 cups [1 ¼ liters] butter	
2 lb.	unsalted butter, slightly softened	1 kg.
3 tbsp.	crushed garlic	45 ml.
2 tbsp.	chopped shallots	30 ml.
3 tbsp.	chopped blanched almonds	45 ml.
1½ tbsp.	coarse salt	22 ml.
¼ tsp.	freshly ground pepper	1 ml.
	grated nutmeg	
½ cup	finely chopped fresh parsley	125 ml.

Mix in a mortar the garlic, shallots, almonds, salt, pepper and a dash of nutmeg. With the pestle, pound these ingredients into a smooth paste. Then add the parsley and the butter. Again with the pestle, grind all the ingredients until they are homogenized.

PAUL BOCUSE
PAUL BOCUSE'S FRENCH COOKING

Lobster Butter

Beurre de Homard (à Froid)

	To make about ¾ cup [175 ml.] butter	
8 tbsp.	unsalted butter	120 ml.
	meat from the claws of a cooked lobster, finely chopped, and a little of the soft shell	
¼ cup	heavy cream	50 ml.
	salt	
	cayenne pepper	

Beat the butter in an electric mixer until it is creamy. Add the finely chopped lobster. Crush the lobster shell in a blender, and add it to the butter mixture. Add the cream and blend until quite smooth. Season with salt to taste and a few grains of cayenne pepper. Rub through a fine strainer.

DIONE LUCAS AND MARION GORMAN
THE DIONE LUCAS BOOK OF FRENCH COOKING

Soused Camembert

The techniques of shaping and molding a cheese disk are shown on pages 32-33.

	To make one 5-inch [13-cm.] disk	
2	ripe Camembert cheeses (about 10 oz. [350 g.] each)	2
⅔ cup	dry white wine	150 ml.
8 tbsp.	butter, softened	120 ml.
	salt	
	cayenne pepper (optional)	
	brandy	
3 cups	fine, fresh white bread crumbs, spread on a baking tray and toasted in a 325° F. [160° C.] oven for 7 minutes	¾ liter
6 tbsp.	finely chopped fresh parsley	90 ml.

Scrape the crusts from the cheeses; cut the cheeses into quarters and soak them overnight in the white wine.

Remove the cheeses from the wine; dry them gently and cream them thoroughly with the softened butter and, if desired, a little of the marinating liquid. Add a little salt and cayenne, if necessary, and flavor with a little brandy. Press the cheese mixture into a plain round 5-inch [13-cm.] flan ring set on a foil-lined baking sheet. Chill until the cheese is firm, about four hours.

Turn the cheese upside down onto the toasted bread crumbs and remove the flan ring and foil. Coat the bottom of the cheese with the toasted bread crumbs and the sides with the parsley. Serve with bread or crackers.

ROBERT CARRIER
ROBERT CARRIER'S ENTERTAINING

Creamed Camembert Cheese

Crème de Camembert

To make one 2½-cup [625-ml.] cheese

1	ripe Camembert cheese (10 oz. [⅓ kg.]), whole or in sections	1
about ¾ cup	dry white wine	about 175 ml.
5 tbsp.	unsalted butter, softened	75 ml.
about ½ cup	fine fresh bread crumbs, toasted in a 350° F. [180° C.] oven for about 2 minutes	about 125 ml.

Scrape off the Camembert skin carefully and thoroughly and let the cheese stand in a bowl, covered with dry white wine, for 12 hours. Drain it, wipe the cheese dry and cream it thoroughly with the butter. Shape the Camembert cream into the form of the original cheese, coat it on all sides with toasted crumbs and chill it well before serving.

NARCISSA G. CHAMBERLAIN AND NARCISSE CHAMBERLAIN
THE FLAVOR OF FRANCE IN RECIPES AND PICTURES, VOLUME II

Filled Edam Cheese

The authors note that instead of spicing the cheese pieces removed from the shell, you can mash these pieces with enough heavy cream to produce an easily spread mixture that will preserve the characteristic flavor of the Edam or Gouda.

To make 1 stuffed cheese

1	small Edam or Gouda cheese	1
2 tsp.	Worcestershire sauce or dry red wine	10 ml.
1 tbsp.	prepared mustard	15 ml.
	cayenne pepper	
1 or 2 tbsp.	mixed fresh herbs, finely chopped, or mixed dried herbs, crumbled	15 or 30 ml.

Hollow out a small Edam or Gouda cheese and crumble into fine bits the pieces you have removed. Combine these with the Worcestershire sauce or wine, the mustard, cayenne and herbs, and beat them to a smooth paste. Refill the cheese shell with this paste. Serve the stuffed cheese surrounded by toasted crackers.

IRMA S. ROMBAUER AND MARION ROMBAUER BECKER
JOY OF COOKING

Herbed Cream Cheese

I like to mold this in a ring, then shortly before serving unmold it onto a platter and garnish it with herbs and fresh vegetables. To unmold, dip the mold in warm water for 10 seconds and invert it onto your platter. Refrigerate immediately to stop the surface from melting.

To make 1½ cups [375 ml.] cheese

½ lb.	cream cheese, softened	¼ kg.
3 or 4	scallions including the green tops, chopped	3 or 4
2	small garlic cloves, finely chopped or crushed to a paste	2
½ tsp.	dry mustard	2 ml.
½ tsp.	Worcestershire sauce	2 ml.
¼ cup	chopped fresh parsley	50 ml.
¼ cup	chopped fresh dill (omit if fresh dill is unavailable)	50 ml.
2 to 4 tbsp.	chopped fresh basil (optional)	30 to 60 ml.
¼ cup	chopped ripe olives	50 ml.
1 to 2 tbsp.	fresh lemon juice	15 to 30 ml.
	salt, preferably sea salt	
	freshly ground pepper	

In a large mixing bowl, whip the softened cheese and add the other ingredients. Mix well, then add salt and pepper to taste. Mold in a bowl or ring, or in a mound on a platter. Cover and refrigerate, or serve immediately. (If the cream cheese is runny or soft, 15 minutes in the refrigerator will stiffen it up.)

MARTHA ROSE SHULMAN
THE VEGETARIAN FEAST

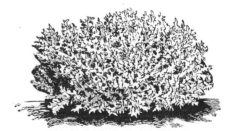

Cream Cheese with Thyme

Fromage au Thym

The peasants of Savoie make a very good cheese called Banon, which is prepared with either sheep's milk or goat's milk and treated with thyme and rosemary. It is, of course, difficult to find except locally. But there is no reason why it should not be prepared at home quite successfully. Those who live in the country probably make cream cheeses occasionally; in any case, they can be got from a farm. Indeed, the cream cheeses sold in shops would also do.

To make 1 pound [½ kg.] flavored cheese		
1 lb.	cream cheese, preferably homemade, softened	½ kg.
	salt	
2 to 3 tsp.	crumbled dried thyme leaves	10 to 15 ml.
2 to 3 tsp.	crumbled dried rosemary leaves	10 to 15 ml.

Work the cheese a little and add salt to taste, then model the cheese into a ball. Rub a few leaves of dried thyme and rosemary all over the cheese, wrap it, and refrigerate it for about a week so that it is well flavored.

X. MARCEL BOULESTIN
BOULESTIN'S ROUND-THE-YEAR COOKBOOK

Liptauer Cheese

The classic accompaniment is icicle radishes, but red radishes, cucumber sticks, celery and fennel can all be used. The best bread to serve with this dish is thin caraway rye.

To serve 8 to 10		
1 lb.	cream cheese	½ kg.
½ cup	unsalted butter	125 ml.
½ cup	creamed cottage cheese	125 ml.
2 tbsp.	heavy cream	30 ml.
1 tbsp.	anisette	15 ml.
2 tsp.	caraway seeds	10 ml.
1 tbsp.	paprika	15 ml.
1 cup	finely chopped onions	¼ liter
10	oil-packed flat anchovy fillets, chopped	10
⅔ cup	capers, rinsed and drained well	150 ml.
2	bunches white radishes	2

With an electric mixer, beat the cream cheese and butter until very light and creamy. Add the cottage cheese and whip until fluffy. Thin with the heavy cream and flavor with the anisette. Add the caraway seeds and mix well.

Mound the cheese decoratively on a serving plate. Use a spatula to smooth the surface and to make decorative indentations around the sides. Dust the top with paprika, preferably medium-sweet Hungarian paprika.

This recipe may be made up early in the morning and refrigerated until evening; just be sure to cover it. Take it out of the refrigerator about one half hour before serving.

When serving, set out small dishes containing chopped onion, chopped anchovies and drained capers as condiments for the Liptauer cheese. Also set out icy-cold white radishes.

JULIE DANNENBAUM
JULIE DANNENBAUM'S CREATIVE COOKING SCHOOL

Cheese Brick

Mimolette cheese is a deep orange, Cheddar-like French cheese. The author suggests that the cheese brick might alternatively be coated with chopped or ground walnuts, cashews or pistachios, paprika, or very finely chopped fresh herbs such as fennel, dill, basil or chervil.

To make one 10-inch [25-cm.] cheese log		
½ lb.	Mimolette or Cheddar cheese, shredded	¼ kg.
3 oz.	cream cheese, softened	100 g.
¼ tsp.	crushed garlic	1 ml.
¼ cup	chopped pecans	50 ml.
1½ tbsp.	chili powder	22 ml.
½ tbsp.	ground cumin	7 ml.

Blend the cheeses well and add the garlic and pecans. Form this mixture into a brick about 10 inches [25 cm.] long, and chill long enough for it to hold its shape. Mix the chili powder and cumin, and spread it on wax paper. Press the cheese brick in the mixture and coat it evenly. Chill, and cut into slices when ready to serve.

DAVID KOLATCH (EDITOR)
COMPLETELY CHEESE

Cheese of the Seven Herbs

To make about 1 cup [¼ liter] cheese		
1 cup	shredded Cheddar cheese	¼ liter
2 tbsp.	heavy cream	30 ml.
3 tbsp.	sherry or hard cider	45 ml.
2 tbsp.	finely chopped mixed herbs: parsley, sage, thyme, tarragon, chives, chervil and winter savory	30 ml.
	salt and pepper	

Put the cheese, cream, sherry or cider, and herbs into the top part of a double boiler set over simmering water. Season, and stir over very gentle heat until the mixture is creamy and pale green in color. While the mixture is still warm, pour it into small pots. Cool before serving.

BEE NILSON (EDITOR)
THE WI DIAMOND JUBILEE COOKBOOK

Good Health Cheese

Le Fromage de Santé

The vieux marc called for in this recipe is a pungent brandy distilled from the grape skins and seeds after wine is made. The author suggests using crottin de Chavignol as the cheese. If unavailable, substitute chèvre blanche.

Good health cheese should be eaten from the little earthenware pot in which it matures. It once had the reputation of combating all ills.

To make about 2 cups [½ liter] cheese

½ lb.	dry goat cheese, grated	¼ kg.
about ⅔ cup	goat's milk, or ⅓ cup [75 ml.] cow's milk mixed with ⅓ cup heavy cream	about 150 ml.
1 tbsp.	Roquefort cheese, scraped from the slice with a knife	15 ml.
about ⅓ cup	*vieux marc*	about 75 ml.

Soak the goat's cheese in the goat's milk or in the milk-cream mixture for 30 minutes. Knead the cheese mixture to a smooth paste. It should be soft, but not runny. When well mixed, add the Roquefort, which should be creamy and very blue; knead again and place the mixture in a bowl in a cool place, covered with a cloth, for 24 to 48 hours.

After this, take a tall glazed earthenware pot and moisten the inside well with marc or brandy. Stir 4 tablespoons [60 ml.] of marc or brandy into the cheese and pack it into the pot, pressing well down to avoid air bubbles. If the paste has become too thick, which is unusual, thin it with a little more of the milk. Cover the top with wax paper soaked in marc or brandy, then put on the lid.

Store the cheese in a cool place for 15 days before using. It is ideal spread on country bread or rye bread for picnics, on its own or with freshly ground pepper added.

ALBIN MARTY
FOURMIGUETTO: SOUVENIRS, CONTES ET RECETTES DE LANGUEDOC

Liptó Cheese Spread

Körözött Júhtúró

Liptó is a soft, white, mild and milky-tasting sheep's-milk cheese made in Hungary and obtainable from some imported-cheese stores. If not available, substitute Bryndza —a creamy, soft Roquefort-type cheese, made in the United States as well as in Central Europe.

The cheese that is the base of the spread originally came from a northern Hungarian area called Liptó. The Austrians, who made a similar mixture, called the spread itself *Liptauer*, or more correctly, *Liptauer garniert*. Since in Hungary Liptó is the name only of the cheese itself, this causes undue mix-ups in non-Hungarian recipes. If you are unable to buy the real sheep's-milk cheese, a very similar product called Bryndza, which comes from Rumania, can generally be purchased in the better cheese stores.

The same cheese spread was made in Trieste with Gorgonzola cheese substituting for the sheep's-milk cheese and *mascarpone*, a fresh cream cheese, replacing the butter.

To make 3 cups [¾ liter] spread

½ lb.	Liptó cheese, or substitute Bryndza cheese	¼ kg.
8 tbsp.	butter, softened	120 ml.
1 tsp.	paprika	5 ml.
½ tsp.	prepared mustard	2 ml.
½ tsp.	crushed caraway seeds	2 ml.
1	small onion, grated	1
½ tsp.	anchovy paste	2 ml.

Sieve the cheese and mix it with the softened butter and all of the other ingredients until the spread is light red in color and evenly mixed. Refrigerate. Serve with wedges of good crusty bread or toast, accompanied by young radishes, green peppers or scallions.

GEORGE LANG
THE CUISINE OF HUNGARY

Cream Cheese Mousse

Petit Suisse

To make one 4-cup [1-liter] cheese

½ lb.	small-curd creamed cottage cheese (1 cup [¼ liter])	¼ kg.
½ cup	plain yogurt	125 ml.
½ cup	sour cream	125 ml.
1½ cups	heavy cream	375 ml.

Put the cottage cheese and yogurt in a blender jar and blend until smooth. Mix the sour cream and heavy cream, and beat until stiff enough to fall from the beater in large blocks. Mix one third of the cream into the cottage-cheese-yogurt blend, then fold in the remainder.

Line a 6-cup [1½-liter] wicker basket or *coeur à la crème* mold with one layer of cheesecloth rinsed under cold water. Turn the cheese mixture into the basket. Fold the cheese-cloth over the cheese mixture. Place the basket or mold over a mixing bowl and refrigerate at least 24 hours. The mixture should lose at least ⅔ to ¾ cup [150 to 175 ml.] whey.

MADELEINE M. KAMMAN
WHEN FRENCH WOMEN COOK

Yogurt-Cheese Cubes

The first time you try the recipe, do it a couple of days ahead of time so you can see how it works for you. If the cheese does not become firm enough to cube, pack it into an attractive small dish and serve it with a spreader.

To make about 4 cups [1 liter] cheese cubes

1 quart	plain yogurt	1 liter
3 tbsp.	ground anise	45 ml.
	salt	
3 cups	chopped walnuts (about ¾ lb. [⅓ kg.])	¾ liter

Line a colander or sieve with three thicknesses of clean cheesecloth. Blend the yogurt with anise and salt to taste, and pour the mixture into the cheesecloth. Pull the ends of the cheesecloth together and tie them. Do this around noon and allow the cheese to drain at room temperature overnight. In the morning, the cheese should be firm enough to cut into cubes. Heap the cheese cubes on a serving plate and sprinkle them generously with the walnuts.

GERI HARRINGTON
THE SALAD BOOK

Persian Yogurt Cheese with Cucumbers

To make about 2 cups [½ liter] cheese

4 cups	plain yogurt	1 liter
2	medium-sized cucumbers, peeled, seeded (if seeds are large) and finely chopped	2
¼ cup	red onion, very finely chopped	50 ml.
4	radishes, grated	4
½ cup	finely chopped walnuts	125 ml.
¼ cup	dried currants	50 ml.
1 tbsp.	finely cut fresh dill	15 ml.
1 tbsp.	finely chopped fresh mint	15 ml.
	salt	
	lettuce leaves	

Line a strainer or colander with a clean muslin cloth wrung out in cold water or with a few layers of dampened cheesecloth. Stir the yogurt and pour it into the cloth. Tie the oppo-

site corners of the cloth together securely to form a bag. Suspend the bag from a hook for eight hours or overnight, placing a bowl underneath to catch the drippings. The whey will drain away, leaving a soft, creamy white cheese. When the yogurt has become firm enough to spread, remove it from the bag and place it in a dish.

To flavor the yogurt cheese, combine all the ingredients except the lettuce and mix thoroughly. With an ice-cream scoop, shape the mixture into balls and arrange them on a serving platter lined with the lettuce leaves. Serve chilled.

SONIA UVEZIAN
THE BOOK OF YOGURT

Green Chili with Cheese

Chile con Queso

To make about 4 cups [1 liter] dip

4 oz.	canned peeled green chilies, seeded and chopped	125 g.
½ lb.	Monterey Jack cheese, cubed	¼ kg.
1	small onion, finely chopped	1
2 tbsp.	butter	30 ml.
1 cup	chopped, seeded, peeled tomatoes	¼ liter
1 cup	heavy cream	¼ liter
	salt and pepper	

Wilt the onion in the butter—about five minutes. Add the tomatoes, chilies, and salt and pepper to taste; simmer for 15 minutes, then add the cubed cheese. When the cheese begins to melt, add the cream. Serve as a dip with toasted tortillas.

ELENA ZELAYETA
ELENA'S SECRETS OF MEXICAN COOKING

Mock Crab Sandwiches

To make about ½ cup [125 ml.] spread

¼ cup	grated sharp cheese	50 ml.
¼ tsp.	salt	1 ml.
¼ tsp.	paprika	1 ml.
¼ tsp.	dry mustard	1 ml.
2 tbsp.	butter	30 ml.
1 tsp.	anchovy paste	5 ml.
1 tbsp.	finely chopped ripe olives	15 ml.
1 tsp.	fresh lemon juice	5 ml.

Mix all of the ingredients to a paste, and spread between lightly buttered slices of white bread.

WOMAN'S WORLD BOOK OF SALADS AND SANDWICHES

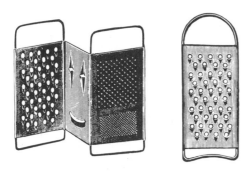

Egg and Avocado Appetizer

Picante de Huevos

To make about 4 cups [1 liter] spread

6	eggs, hard-boiled and chopped	6
2	avocados, halved, pitted, peeled and finely chopped	2
1	fresh hot chili, finely chopped, or ¼ tsp. [1 ml.] cayenne pepper	1
1	onion, finely chopped	1
3 tbsp.	chopped fresh parsley	45 ml.
2 tbsp.	vinegar	30 ml.
1½ tsp.	salt	7 ml.

Combine the eggs, avocados, chili or cayenne, onion, parsley, vinegar and salt. Mix well and chop until very smooth and well blended. Chill. Serve on toast or on lettuce leaves.

MYRA WALDO
THE COMPLETE ROUND-THE-WORLD COOKBOOK

Avocado Dip

Guacamole

The word *guacamole* comes from the Nahuatl words for "avocado" *(ahuacatl)* and "mixture" or "concoction" *(molli)* — and what a beautiful "concoction" *guacamole* is, pale green sparked with the coriander's darker green and the red of the tomato. *Guacamole* is usually eaten in Mexico at the beginning of a meal with a pile of hot, freshly made tortillas and other *botanas* (snacks) like crisp pork skins *(chicharrónes)* or little pieces of crispy pork *(carnitas)*. It will also often accompany a plate of tacos. It is so delicate that it is best eaten the moment it is prepared. There are many suggestions for keeping it — covering it airtight, leaving the pit in, and so forth — but they will help only for a brief time; almost immediately the delicate green will darken and the fresh, wonderful flavor will be lost.

To make 1 ¾ to 2 cups dip

2	avocados	2
¼	small onion, finely chopped	¼
2	serrano chilies or any other fresh hot green chilies, finely chopped	2
4	large sprigs fresh coriander, leaves only	4
¼ tsp.	salt	1 ml.
1	large tomato, about ½ lb. [¼ kg.], peeled and chopped	1
Onion-coriander garnish		
¼	small onion, finely chopped	¼
6	sprigs coriander, leaves only, roughly chopped	6

In a *molcajete,* or using a regular pestle and mortar, grind the onion, chilies, coriander and salt together until they are almost smooth.

Cut the avocados in half. Remove the pits, scoop out the flesh with a wooden spoon and mash it roughly into the ingredients in the *molcajete.* Mix well together to make sure that the ingredients are thoroughly incorporated, then stir in the chopped tomato. Adjust the salt, if necessary. Sprinkle with the onion-and-coriander garnish, and serve at once.

DIANA KENNEDY
RECIPES FROM THE REGIONAL COOKS OF MEXICO

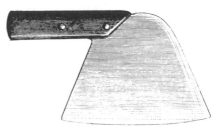

Celery, Apple and Watercress Sandwich Filling

To make about 2 cups [½ liter] filling

½ cup	chopped celery	125 ml.
½ cup	diced unpeeled apple	125 ml.
½ bunch	watercress (about 1 cup [¼ liter])	½ bunch
⅓ cup	mayonnaise (recipe, page 166)	75 ml.
¼ tsp.	salt	1 ml.

Wash the watercress and look it over for any bad leaves. Drain and chop it fine. Mix it with the other ingredients.

FLORENCE BROBECK
THE LUNCH BOX AND EVERY KIND OF SANDWICH

Eggplant Filling

Berinjela

This mixture may be used as a sandwich filling or canapé topping, or even as a dip.

To make about 1 cup [¼ liter] filling

1 cup	chopped cooked eggplant	¼ liter
3	green olives, pitted	3
¼	garlic clove	¼
½ tsp.	vinegar	2 ml.
	salt and pepper	
2 to 3 tbsp.	mayonnaise (recipe, page 166)	30 to 45 ml.

Blend the eggplant with the olives and garlic in a blender or chop the mixture very fine. Add vinegar and season to taste. Mix well with enough mayonnaise to bind the mixture.

MARGARETTE DE ANDRADE
BRAZILIAN COOKERY

Garlic-flavored Eggplant Purée

Salad of Aubergines

This purée is also called baba ghanoush, its Lebanese name. As the author notes, the eggplants—in England called by their French name aubergines—will have a slightly smoky flavor if broiled or, preferably, grilled over charcoal. To broil or grill them, pierce their skins in two or three places and set them 3 inches [8 cm.] from the heat source. Cook, turning them frequently, for about 20 minutes, or bake them on a sheet in a preheated 350° F. [180° C.] oven for one hour.

A good dish from Greece and the Near East, where it is often served as a *meze.* You dip slices of bread into the salad and eat it while drinking your apéritif.

To make about 6 cups [1 ½ liters] purée

2	garlic cloves, mashed to a paste	2
3 or 4	large eggplants	3 or 4
	salt and pepper	
	olive oil	
½	lemon	½
	chopped fresh parsley	

Broil the eggplants in their skins. When they are soft, peel them and pound the flesh in a mortar with the garlic, salt and pepper. Add, drop by drop, a little olive oil, as for a mayonnaise. When it is a thick purée, add the juice of half a lemon and a handful of chopped parsley.

ELIZABETH DAVID
A BOOK OF MEDITERRANEAN FOOD

Cucumber Yogurt Dip

Tzatzíki Soúpa

To make about 2 cups [½ liter] dip

1	large cucumber, peeled and finely grated	1
2 cups	plain yogurt	½ liter
1 tbsp.	olive oil	15 ml.
¾ tbsp.	wine vinegar	12 ml.
about ¼ tsp.	salt	about 1 ml.
½ tsp.	finely chopped fresh mint	2 ml.
1	small garlic clove, crushed	1
	chopped fresh parsley	

Blend together the yogurt, olive oil, vinegar, salt to taste, fresh mint and garlic. Add the grated cucumber, stir well, and chill for at least one hour. Before serving, sprinkle chopped parsley over the top.

ANNE THEOHAROUS
COOKING AND BAKING THE GREEK WAY

Bean Dip

Frijoles para Sopear

The jalapeña sauce called for is a bottled relish containing green jalapeño peppers and both green and red tomatoes. It is available where Mexican foods are sold.

To make about 2 cups [½ liter] dip

½ cup	dried pink or red beans	125 ml.
¼ tsp.	salt	1 ml.
4 to 6 tbsp.	freshly melted lard or bacon drippings	60 to 90 ml.
1 cup	sour cream	¼ liter
	jalapeña sauce	

Soak the beans in 1 quart [1 liter] of water overnight for faster cooking. Discard any beans that float to the surface. Then add more water to cover, salt, and bring the beans to a boil. Boil for 10 minutes, then reduce the heat and cook the beans slowly until they are very tender—about two hours. Drain. Mash the beans with a potato masher. Transfer them to a heavy skillet, add 2 tablespoons [30 ml.] of the hot lard or bacon drippings (drippings improve the flavor), and cook until all of the fat is absorbed by the beans. Be sure to stir often to prevent sticking. Transfer the beans to a bowl.

Heat additional fat in the heavy skillet. The more fat the better, most people think. Add the mashed and fried beans and cook, stirring, until the beans are completely dry.

Thoroughly cool the beans. Mash them and combine them with the sour cream. Mix well and add as much jalapeña sauce as desired.

ELENA ZELAYETA
ELENA'S SECRETS OF MEXICAN COOKING

Peanut Butter

You can substitute almonds, cashews or filberts for the peanuts; a combination of almonds and filberts is especially good. Don't overbrown any of the nuts; filberts should be roasted just until their skins crack. After roasting filberts, rub off as much of the husks as possible.

To make about 1 ¾ cups [425 ml.] spread

3 cups	shelled raw peanuts (about 1 lb. [½ kg.])	¾ liter
½ to 1 tsp.	salt	2 to 5 ml.
½ to 1 tsp.	sugar	2 to 5 ml.
2 tbsp.	peanut oil	30 ml.

Preheat the oven to 300° F. [150° C.]. Spread the nuts in a jelly-roll or roasting pan and roast them for 20 minutes,

shaking the pan now and then; they should be light gold. Cool the peanuts.

For creamy peanut butter, first put half of the cooled nuts in the container of a food processor (or the jar of a blender) with half of the salt, sugar and oil. Process the mixture to a creamy consistency (stopping the action and scraping down the sides of the container often with a spatula), then empty the peanut butter into a bowl and process the remaining nuts, salt, sugar and oil.

For chunky peanut butter, use the processor to chop about one third of the nuts coarse; set them aside, then process the remaining nuts to a creamy consistency with the salt, sugar and oil. Stir the mixture together with the chopped nuts. Or use a blender by processing half of the nuts at a time and scraping down the sides of the container and under the blades several times. Process the mixture into as crunchy a texture as you wish. It is not necessary to chop part of the nuts first for blender-made chunky peanut butter.

Store the peanut butter in a covered jar in the refrigerator; it will keep for about two weeks.

HELEN WITTY AND ELIZABETH SCHNEIDER COLCHIE
BETTER THAN STORE-BOUGHT

Hummus with Tahini

Tahini is a paste made from ground sesame seeds. It is obtainable in cans or jars in Oriental or Middle Eastern groceries. The technique of making hummus is shown on page 14.

To make about 3 cups [¾ liter] dip

2 cups	dried chick-peas, soaked in water overnight and drained	½ liter
3 tbsp.	*tahini*	45 ml.
3 to 4 tbsp.	fresh lemon juice, strained	45 to 60 ml.
4	garlic cloves, crushed to a paste	4
	salt	
1 tbsp.	chopped fresh parsley	15 ml.
4 tbsp.	olive oil	60 ml.

Blanch the chick-peas, in enough water to cover them, for about 30 minutes; then drain and cool them. Rub off the skins from as many of the chick-peas as possible.

Simmer the chick-peas in fresh water for two to three hours, or until they are tender. Then purée them in a food processor or blender. Separately beat together the *tahini*, 3 tablespoons [45 ml.] of lemon juice, the garlic and salt, and combine this mixture with the chick-peas until you have a smooth paste. Taste, and add more lemon juice if desired. To serve, mound the paste on a dish, garnish with parsley and sprinkle the top with oil.

EL MUNDO GASTRONOMICO

Garlic Sauce with Pine Nuts

Skordalia

Pine nuts, often marketed under their Italian name pignolia, are the small, cream-colored, slightly oil-flavored kernels from the cones of the stone pine. They are available where Mediterranean foods are sold.

To make about 4 cups [1 liter] sauce

6	garlic cloves	6
½ cup	pine nuts	125 ml.
1 tsp.	salt	5 ml.
4 cups	mashed potatoes, made from 3 medium-sized potatoes, boiled, peeled, pounded to a paste and cooled	1 liter
½ cup	vinegar or fresh lemon juice	125 ml.
2½ cups	olive oil	625 ml.
1	egg	1
½ cup	warm water (optional)	125 ml.

In a mortar mash the garlic with the salt. Add the pine nuts and pound until they are well blended. Add the mashed potatoes. Transfer the mixture to a bowl. Clean the mortar with the vinegar or lemon juice and add this liquid to the mixture. Gradually add the olive oil, beating with an electric beater. When all of the oil is absorbed, add the egg and continue beating until the sauce is smooth. For a thinner sauce, beat in the warm water.

THE WOMEN OF ST. PAUL'S GREEK ORTHODOX CHURCH
THE ART OF GREEK COOKERY

Pimiento Spread

To make 1 cup [¼ liter] spread

3 oz.	chopped pimiento, juice reserved (about ½ cup [125 ml.])	100 g.
1 tbsp.	heavy cream	15 ml.
½ tsp.	Worcestershire sauce	2 ml.
	Tabasco sauce	
	salt and pepper	
¼ lb.	cream cheese, cut into chunks	125 g.

Put into a blender the chopped pimiento with its juice and the cream. Blend to purée the pimiento. Add the Worcester-

shire sauce, a dash of Tabasco, and salt and pepper to taste. Blend the ingredients again.

Keep the blender running while you are adding the cream cheese. Scrape the spread from the blender into a container, cover tightly, and refrigerate until needed. Serve on Melba rounds or plain crackers.

CAROL CUTLER
THE SIX-MINUTE SOUFFLÉ AND OTHER CULINARY DELIGHTS

Sunflower Seed Dressing

Created as a dressing for slaws and green salads, this mixture of sunflower seeds and yogurt also makes a tangy dip for raw vegetables.

To make about 1 ½ cups [375 ml.] dip

⅓ cup	sunflower seeds	75 ml.
1	garlic clove	1
	salt, preferably sea salt, and freshly ground pepper	
1 tbsp.	chopped fresh herbs (parsley, tarragon, thyme, dill)	15 ml.
2 tbsp.	fresh lemon juice	30 ml.
1 cup	plain yogurt	¼ liter

In a blender or food processor, grind the sunflower seeds fine, almost to a butter. Add the garlic, salt and pepper and herbs, then blend in the lemon juice and the yogurt and mix until you have a smooth sauce. Adjust the seasoning.

MARTHA ROSE SHULMAN
THE VEGETARIAN FEAST

Black Radish Canapé

To make about ½ cup [125 ml.] spread

2	black radishes, peeled and finely chopped	2
1	small onion, finely chopped	1
2 tbsp.	sour cream or plain yogurt	30 ml.
1 tbsp.	fresh lemon juice	15 ml.
⅛ tsp.	salt	½ ml.

Combine the black radishes with the onion, sour cream or yogurt, lemon juice and salt. Serve spread on thin slices of pumpernickel bread.

IRMA S. ROMBAUER AND MARION ROMBAUER BECKER
JOY OF COOKING

Green-Olive Relish with Coriander, Cyprus-Style

To make about 2 cups [½ liter] spread

1 ½ cups	green Spanish-type olives	375 ml.
2 tsp.	coriander seeds, crushed or ground to a paste	10 ml.
¼ cup	olive oil	50 ml.
¼ cup	red wine vinegar	50 ml.
2	large garlic cloves, crushed to a paste	2

Drain the olives. Remove and discard the pits, then chop the flesh of the olives and combine it in a small bowl with the oil, vinegar, garlic and coriander. Cover the mixture and refrigerate it overnight, stirring it a few times. Serve the relish on toast.

VILMA LIACOURAS CHANTILES
THE FOOD OF GREECE

Fresh Herb Dip

To make about 1 cup [¼ liter] dip

1 tbsp.	finely cut fresh chives	15 ml.
1 tbsp.	finely chopped fresh parsley	15 ml.
1 tbsp.	finely cut fresh dill	15 ml.
1	garlic clove, crushed to a paste or finely chopped	1
¾ cup	sour cream	175 ml.
¼ cup	plain yogurt	50 ml.
	fresh lemon juice	
	salt and pepper	

Thoroughly mix all of the ingredients. Taste and adjust the seasonings. Refrigerate. Serve as a dip with raw vegetables.

WOLF TRAP ASSOCIATES
WOLF TRAP PICNIC COOKBOOK

Chopped Chicken Liver

To make about 2 ½ cups [625 ml.] spread

½ lb.	chicken livers, cleaned and quartered	¼ kg.
4 tbsp.	rendered chicken fat (or substitute butter)	60 ml.
1	medium-sized onion, diced	1
2	eggs, hard-boiled and chopped	2
½ tsp.	salt	2 ml.
¼ tsp.	pepper	1 ml.
	thyme	
	lettuce leaves, or bread or crackers	

Melt the fat or butter in a skillet; sauté the livers and onion for about eight minutes, or until the livers are cooked and the onion is golden. Drain the livers and onion, reserving the fat. Cool. Chop the livers, and mix them with the onion and the fat. Combine the liver mixture with the eggs; stir in the salt, pepper and a pinch of thyme. Chill. Serve the mixture in lettuce cups or as a spread for bread or crackers.

IDA BAILEY ALLEN
BEST LOVED RECIPES OF THE AMERICAN PEOPLE

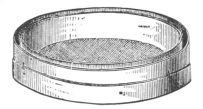

Deviled or Potted Chicken Spread

To make about 2 ½ cups [625 ml.] spread

2 cups	chopped cooked chicken	½ liter
¼ cup	chopped boiled or baked ham	50 ml.
⅛ tsp.	grated nutmeg	½ ml.
	white pepper	
½ tsp.	salt	2 ml.
3 tbsp.	butter	45 ml.
1 tbsp.	fresh lemon juice, or ½ tsp. [2 ml.] freshly grated lemon peel	15 ml.

Using the fine disk of a food grinder, grind together three times the chicken, ham, nutmeg, a pinch of white pepper, the salt, butter, and lemon juice or peel. You may further press this mixture through a fine wire sieve or knead it gently before storing it, covered and refrigerated. The spread will keep longer if the top is coated with clarified butter.

IRMA S. ROMBAUER AND MARION ROMBAUER BECKER
JOY OF COOKING

Chicken Chestnut Spread

To make 1 cup [¼ liter] spread

1 cup	chopped cooked chicken	¼ liter
4 or 5	peeled cooked chestnuts	4 or 5
2 tbsp.	finely chopped celery	30 ml.
	salt and pepper	
	mayonnaise (recipe, page 166)	

Purée the chestnuts. Mix these with the chopped chicken meat, the finely chopped celery, salt and pepper to taste and enough mayonnaise to bind.

JAMES BEARD
HORS D'OEUVRE AND CANAPÉS

Chicken and Almond Sandwich Filling

To make about 2 cups [½ liter] filling

1 cup	finely chopped cooked chicken	¼ liter
1 cup	finely chopped blanched almonds	¼ liter
½ cup	heavy cream	125 ml.
¾ tsp.	salt	4 ml.
¼ tsp.	paprika	1 ml.
	pepper	

Mix the chicken and blanched almonds together. Blend them with the cream and season with the salt, paprika and a dash of pepper. Use with either white or whole-wheat bread.

FLORENCE A. COWLES
1001 SANDWICHES

Fish Roe Dip

Taramosalata

Tarama is the Greek name for the coral-pink roe of the female gray mullet. It is obtainable, usually salt-preserved in jars, where Greek foods are sold.

To make 1 ½ to 2 cups [375 ml. to ½ liter] dip

½ cup	tarama	125 ml.
1	small onion, finely grated	1
1 to 2 cups	olive oil	¼ to ½ liter
4	slices firm homemade-style white bread, the crusts removed	4
8 to 12 tbsp.	fresh lemon juice	120 to 180 ml.

Mash the *tarama* and add the grated onion. Add a little of the olive oil and beat the *tarama* mixture to a smooth paste.

Moisten the bread by soaking it briefly in water, then squeeze out the excess water. Continue beating the *tarama* mixture, adding small bits of moistened bread alternately with more of the olive oil and the lemon juice. When it is ready to serve, *taramosalata* should be cream-colored and should have the consistency of a thick mayonnaise.

THE WOMEN OF ST. PAUL'S GREEK ORTHODOX CHURCH
THE ART OF GREEK COOKERY

Estonian Fish Paté

Skoombria

To make about 5 cups [1 ¼ liters] spread

1 lb.	fresh cod or other firm white fish, cut into large chunks	½ kg.
¼ cup	flour	50 ml.
	salt and pepper	
½ cup	vegetable oil	125 ml.
3	onions, finely chopped	3
4	carrots, grated	4
4	allspice berries	4
1 tsp.	paprika	5 ml.
1¼ cups	tomato sauce (recipe, page 167)	300 ml.
⅓ cup	ketchup (recipe, page 167)	75 ml.
1	bay leaf	1
1 to 2 tbsp.	fresh lemon juice	15 to 30 ml.
	lemon wedges	
	parsley sprigs	

Dredge the cod in the flour that has been seasoned with salt and pepper. Heat ¼ cup [50 ml.] of the oil in a large pot or heavy casserole. Add the cod and cook it over medium heat for 10 to 12 minutes, until it is barely done. Remove the cod with a slotted spoon and set it aside.

Add to the oil the onions, carrots, allspice berries and paprika. Cook them over low heat for five minutes. Return the cod to the pot. Add the tomato sauce, ketchup, bay leaf, and salt and pepper to taste. Stir and mash thoroughly. Cover and simmer the mixture for 45 minutes, stirring frequently. While the mixture is simmering, add the remaining oil sparingly, as needed, to keep it moist. Remove the bay leaf and allspice berries.

Cover the *skoombria* and refrigerate it for 24 hours. Before serving, add the lemon juice and stir to blend it in thoroughly. Mound the *skoombria* on a serving platter and garnish it with parsley and lemon wedges. Serve with thinly sliced black bread and butter.

MELANIE MARCUS
COOKING WITH A HARVARD ACCENT

Salt Cod with Garlic

Brandade de Morue

To make about 3 cups [¾ liter] spread

1 lb.	salt cod, soaked in several changes of cold water for 12 hours, and drained	½ kg.
1	garlic clove, mashed to a paste	1
½ cup	olive oil	125 ml.
½ cup	heavy cream	125 ml.

Place the salt cod in a saucepan, cover it with cold water and simmer for 15 minutes, or until the fish is tender. Drain again, remove all of the skin and bones and, in a sturdy bowl, pound the flesh to a pulp with a potato masher.

Put the pulp in a deep saucepan, add the mashed garlic, put the pan over low heat and, with a wooden spoon, beat in the olive oil and cream by alternate spoonfuls. The finished mixture should be white, creamy and as smooth as possible. Serve it warm with crusty bread.

ROBERT FARRAR CAPON
PARTY SPIRIT

Shad Roe Sandwich Spread

To make about 3 cups [¾ liter] spread

1	medium-sized shad roe, poached in lightly salted water for 8 minutes, trimmed, and membranes removed	1
3	hard-boiled egg yolks	3
about 12 tbsp.	butter, softened, and beaten until creamy	about 180 ml.
½ tsp.	paprika	2 ml.
	Tabasco sauce	
1 tsp.	anchovy paste	5 ml.
	salt	

Mash the roe together with the egg yolks. Add an equal amount of creamed butter, the paprika, a few drops of Tabasco sauce, the anchovy paste and salt to taste. Spread between thin, buttered slices of bread. Slices of lemon, peeled and salted, may be put between rounds of buttered bread and passed with the shad roe sandwiches.

RUTH BEROLZHEIMER, EDITOR
THE AMERICAN WOMAN'S COOK BOOK

Crab Meat à la Mornay

To make about 4 cups [1 liter] dip

1 lb.	cooked crab meat, flaked	½ kg.
8 tbsp.	butter	120 ml.
1	small bunch scallions, white parts only, finely chopped	1
½ cup	finely chopped fresh parsley	125 ml.
2 tbsp.	flour	30 ml.
2 cups	light cream	½ liter
2 cups	grated Swiss cheese	½ liter
1 tbsp.	dry sherry	15 ml.
	cayenne pepper	
	salt	

Melt the butter in a heavy pot and sauté the scallions until soft but not browned, about five minutes. Blend in the flour, cream and cheese and stir until the cheese is melted. Add the sherry and the cayenne pepper and salt to taste, and gently fold in the crab meat. Serve in a chafing dish with Melba-toast rounds as a dip, or serve in patty shells.

ST. STEPHEN'S EPISCOPAL CHURCH
BAYOU CUISINE

Hot Anchovy Dip

Bagna Cauda

The technique of making bagna cauda is demonstrated on page 20. The truffle, although traditional —and desirable— is not essential to the success of this dip.

To make about 1 ½ cups [375 ml.] dip

½ cup	oil-packed flat anchovy fillets, finely chopped	125 ml.
8 tbsp.	butter	120 ml.
¼ cup	olive oil	50 ml.
6	garlic cloves, finely chopped	6
1	truffle, sliced thin	1

Combine the butter, olive oil and garlic in the top of a double boiler. Place over hot water and cook over low heat, stirring constantly until the butter melts. Remove from the heat, but do not remove the top of the double boiler from the hot water. Add the anchovies and truffle, stirring well. Set the mixture aside for 10 minutes before using the *bagna cauda* as a dip for crisp raw vegetables.

ROMEO SALTA
THE PLEASURES OF ITALIAN COOKING

Potted Shrimp Spread for Sandwiches

Brown bread, spread with a very thin layer of mayonnaise rather than butter, is good for this spread.

To make about 2 cups [½ liter] spread

1 lb.	cooked shrimp, shelled, deveined and chopped	½ kg.
6 tbsp.	fresh lemon juice	90 ml.
2 tsp.	grated lemon peel	10 ml.
⅛ tsp.	grated nutmeg	½ ml.
1 cup	melted butter	¼ liter
	salt and freshly ground pepper	

Push the shrimp twice through the finest disk of a meat grinder, then beat in the lemon juice, lemon peel, nutmeg, ¾ cup [175 ml.] of melted butter, and salt and pepper to taste. Or, in a blender, blend the shrimp, lemon juice, lemon peel, nutmeg and ¾ cup of melted butter. Taste for seasoning and season with salt and pepper.

Spoon into jars or custard cups, and pour melted butter over the surface to seal.

NIKA HAZELTON
THE PICNIC BOOK

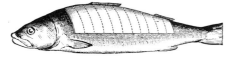

Salmon Spread

To make about 1 ½ cups [375 ml.] spread

1 cup	flaked cooked salmon	¼ liter
¼ tsp.	salt	1 ml.
¼ tsp.	pepper	1 ml.
⅓ cup	finely chopped green pepper	75 ml.
¼ cup	finely chopped scallions	50 ml.
1 tbsp.	fresh lemon juice	15 ml.
2 to 3 tbsp.	mayonnaise *(recipe, page 166)*	30 to 45 ml.
	watercress	
	cucumber slices	

Combine the flaked cooked salmon, salt, pepper, green pepper, scallions and lemon juice with just enough mayonnaise to bind them. Garnish the bowl with watercress and cucumber slices. The spread is delicious on dark or rye bread.

DIANE MACMILLAN
THE PORTABLE FEAST

Salmon Cream

Laxkräm

To make about ¾ cup [175 ml.] spread

2 oz.	smoked salmon	75 g.
2	eggs, hard-boiled	2
4 tbsp.	butter or mayonnaise *(recipe, page 166)*	60 ml.
3 to 4 tbsp.	finely cut fresh dill	45 to 60 ml.
	salt and pepper (optional)	

Chop the salmon and eggs fine. Mix them with the butter or mayonnaise and the dill. Cream the mixture until it is smooth. Taste for seasoning. Add salt and pepper, if desired.

J. AUDREY ELLISON
THE GREAT SCANDINAVIAN COOKBOOK

Tuna Sunflower-Seed Spread

To make about 3 cups [¾ liter] spread

13 oz.	canned tuna, drained	⅓ kg.
½ cup	shelled sunflower seeds	125 ml.
1	small red onion, finely chopped	1
½ tsp.	dried basil	2 ml.
about ½ cup	mayonnaise *(recipe, page 166)* or plain yogurt	about 125 ml.
	salt and pepper	

Mix all of the ingredients well and serve on crackers, bread, or cucumber or zucchini rounds.

SHARON CADWALLADER
SHARON CADWALLADER'S COMPLETE COOKBOOK

Tuna as a Cocktail Spread

To make about 2 cups [½ liter] spread

7 oz.	canned tuna, drained and mashed	200 g.
½ cup	capers, rinsed and drained	125 ml.
2 tbsp.	mayonnaise *(recipe, page 166)*	30 ml.
1 tsp.	paprika	5 ml.
2 tbsp.	fresh onion juice	30 ml.
3	egg whites, stiffly beaten	3
	toast fingers	

Blend all of the ingredients except the toast. Spread the mixture on fingers of toast and place them under the broiler until lightly browned and puffy, about five minutes.

JAMES BEARD
JAMES BEARD'S NEW FISH COOKERY

Deviled Ham

To make 1 ½ cups [375 ml.] spread

1½ cups	cubed cooked ham, trimmed of all membrane (about ¾ lb. [⅓ kg.])	375 ml.
¼ cup	cubed firm ham fat	50 ml.
1½ tsp.	horseradish mustard or other hot prepared mustard	7 ml.
2 tsp.	white wine vinegar	10 ml.
	pepper sherry or bottled hot pepper sauce	
¼ tsp.	anchovy paste	1 ml.
⅛ tsp.	finely chopped garlic	½ ml.
	grated nutmeg	
	ground cloves	
	ground pepper	
	ground ginger	
	ground thyme or finely crumbled dried thyme leaf	

Grind the ham and fat fairly fine in a food processor. Add the mustard, vinegar, pepper sherry, anchovy paste, garlic and a pinch each of nutmeg, cloves, pepper, ginger and thyme. Process until the mixture is rather like a coarse paté.

If you are using a blender, process half of the ham and fat and scrape the mixture into a bowl. Then add the seasonings to the blender jar, process the rest of the ham and fat and combine it with the mixture in the bowl. If the mixture is too coarse, process it again in two batches.

Taste the deviled ham for seasoning, then pack it into a jar, cover, and refrigerate it overnight or longer to let the flavors mingle. The spread will keep for up to two weeks.

HELEN WITTY AND ELIZABETH SCHNEIDER COLCHIE
BETTER THAN STORE-BOUGHT

Beef and Watercress Spread

To make about ½ cup [125 ml.] spread

2 oz.	lean beef round, in one piece	75 g.
2 or 3	sprigs fresh watercress	2 or 3
2 tbsp.	butter	30 ml.
	salt and pepper	
½ tsp.	dry mustard	2 ml.

Shred the beef by scraping it with the back of a knife. In a mortar, pound the beef to a paste with the butter and salt and pepper to taste. Mix in the mustard. Finally, pound in the watercress.

MOIRA MEIGHN
SIMPLIFIED COOKING AND INVALID DIET

Tongue Spread

To make about 2 cups [½ liter] spread

½ lb.	cooked smoked tongue	¼ kg.
1 tbsp.	finely chopped sour gherkin	15 ml.
1 tbsp.	finely cut fresh chives or finely chopped shallot	15 ml.
1	egg, hard-boiled	1
1 tsp.	Dijon mustard	5 ml.
	mayonnaise (recipe, page 166)	

Chop the tongue very fine. Add the gherkin, the chives or shallot, the hard-boiled egg and the mustard. Bind this with sufficient mayonnaise to make a stiff paste.

JAMES BEARD
HORS D'OEUVRE AND CANAPÉS

Steak Tartare

To make 2 cups [½ liter] spread

1 lb.	lean beef sirloin or round, cut into chunks	½ kg.
1	egg yolk	1
4 tbsp.	finely chopped onion	60 ml.
2	garlic cloves, finely chopped	2
	salt and freshly ground black pepper	
1 tbsp.	Worcestershire sauce	15 ml.
	finely chopped fresh parsley	
¼ cup	Cognac	50 ml.
	thinly sliced rye, pumpernickel or white bread	
	chopped, hard-boiled egg	
	capers, rinsed and drained (optional)	
	caviar (optional)	

Grind the beef twice and, in a mixing bowl, combine it with the egg yolk, most of the finely chopped onion, the garlic, salt and pepper to taste, the Worcestershire sauce, 2 tablespoons [30 ml.] of parsley and the Cognac. Mix thoroughly, cover the bowl tightly and refrigerate until ready to serve. Spread the tartar steak on rounds of rye bread or fingers of pumpernickel or toasted white bread. Top with chopped onion, or hard-boiled egg and parsley and, if desired, capers or caviar.

ROBERT CARRIER
ROBERT CARRIER'S ENTERTAINING

Canapés and Sandwiches

Recipes for Basic Bread and Sandwich Bread appear in Standard Preparations, pages 164 and 165.

Cornets of Smoked Salmon

A cornet, in food terminology, is any food rolled into the shape of a horn. These are most delicious examples.

To make about 40 cornets

1 lb.	smoked salmon, ½ lb. [¼ kg.] ground, and ½ lb. thinly sliced	½ kg.
	white pepper	
1 tbsp.	Cognac	15 ml.
8 tbsp.	butter	120 ml.
	fresh parsley or watercress sprigs	

Add a dash of the pepper, Cognac and butter to the ground salmon and mix well. Cut the sliced salmon into 1½-inch [4-cm.] squares. Form the squares into cornets and, with a pastry tube, fill each with the ground mixture. Arrange the cornets attractively, spaced well apart, on plates or platters, using a few sprigs of parsley or watercress for garnish.

CHARLOTTE ADAMS
THE FOUR SEASONS COOKBOOK

Salami Layers

To make 6 wedges

8	very thin slices of salami	8
2 tbsp.	Neufchâtel cheese, softened	30 ml.
2 tsp.	finely cut fresh chives	10 ml.
2 tsp.	finely chopped dill pickle	10 ml.

Spread seven salami slices with the cheese, using about 1 teaspoon [5 ml.] for each slice. Sprinkle the cheese with the chives and pickle. Stack the cheese-coated slices one on top of another, and cover the stack with the remaining salami slice. Cut the stack into six equal wedges.

CLARENCE HERISKO
DRINKS AND SNACKS FOR ALL OCCASIONS

Curried Chicken Balls

To make about 60 balls

2 cups	chopped cooked chicken (about ½ lb. [¼ kg.])	½ liter
2 tsp.	curry powder	10 ml.
½ lb.	cream cheese, softened	¼ kg.
1½ cups	chopped blanched almonds (about 6 oz. [175 g.])	375 ml.
4 tbsp.	mayonnaise *(recipe, page 166)*	60 ml.
3 tbsp.	chopped chutney	45 ml.
1 tsp.	salt	5 ml.
1 cup	grated fresh coconut	¼ liter

Thoroughly cream the cream cheese and then add the chicken, almonds, mayonnaise, chutney, salt and curry powder. Shape the mixture into walnut-sized balls. Roll each ball in the coconut. Chill the balls until ready to serve.

MARIAN FOX BURROS AND LOIS LEVINE
THE ELEGANT BUT EASY COOKBOOK

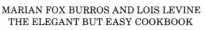

Parmesan Onion Rounds

To make 48 open-faced sandwiches

¾ cup	freshly grated Parmesan cheese	175 ml.
1 cup	very thin slices white onion	¼ liter
1 cup	mayonnaise *(recipe, page 166)*	¼ liter
48	bread rounds, made from thinly sliced, firm-textured white bread, cut into disks 2 inches [5 cm.] in diameter	48

Preheat the oven to 375° F. [190° C.].

Toast the bread rounds on one side. Blend the mayonnaise and the cheese. Put a thin slice of onion on the untoasted side of each round, and top the onion with a generous spoonful of the mayonnaise-cheese mixture. Bake for 10 to 12 minutes, until the tops are puffed and golden. Watch carefully, for they burn easily. Serve warm.

JUNIOR LEAGUE OF THE CITY OF NEW YORK
NEW YORK ENTERTAINS

Roquefort Cheese Sandwich

To make eight 1-inch [2 ½-cm.] finger sandwiches

½ cup	Roquefort cheese, mashed to a paste (2 oz. [75 g.])	125 ml.
2 tbsp.	butter	30 ml.
	salt and pepper	
4	thin slices sandwich bread, crusts removed	4
	finely chopped fresh parsley (optional)	
	finely cut fresh chives (optional)	

Work the cheese into a paste with the butter, using a knife. Then season to taste with salt and pepper. When it is quite smooth, spread the paste on two slices of the bread, cover the paste with another bread slice, press the two halves carefully together and cut the sandwiches into fingers. If desired, parsley or chives, or both, may be mixed with the cheese. The paste may also be spread on crackers in place of bread.

OSCAR TSCHIRKY
THE COOKBOOK BY "OSCAR" OF THE WALDORF

Onion Canapés

The preparation of Melba toast is shown on pages 36-37.

To make 36 canapés

1 cup	finely chopped onion	¼ liter
36	toasted Melba rounds	36
	butter, softened	
3 tbsp.	mayonnaise *(recipe, page 166)*	45 ml.
1 tbsp.	Worcestershire sauce	15 ml.
	paprika	

Butter the toasted rounds. Mix together the onions, mayonnaise, Worcestershire sauce and a dash of paprika in a small bowl. Place about a teaspoonful [15 ml.] of the mixture on top of each round and place the rounds on a baking sheet. Put them under the broiler until the tops are golden brown—about two minutes. Serve hot.

BONITA WAGNER
NIBBLERS AND MUNCHERS

Fresh Tomato and Chive Appetizers

Croûtons aux Tomates et à la Ciboulette

The crème fraîche called for in this recipe may be available at French food markets. If not, make it from the heavy —but not ultrapasteurized —cream usually sold in health-food stores. Add about 1 ½ teaspoons [7 ml.] of buttermilk to 1 cup [¼ liter] of cream. Stirring, heat to 85° F. [30° C.]. Pour the mixture into a crock, cover, and set in a warm place for six to eight hours, or until it thickens. Refrigerate until ready to use.

To make 8 canapés

8	slices bread, ¼ inch [6 mm.] thick, cut from a small French loaf; or 8 circles, 2 ½ inches [6 cm.] in diameter, cut from slices of sandwich bread	8
2 tbsp.	butter, softened	30 ml.
Tomato-chive topping		
2	ripe tomatoes, peeled, seeded and coarsely chopped	2
	salt and pepper	
2 tbsp.	*crème fraîche* or heavy cream	30 ml.
1 tbsp.	finely chopped shallots	15 ml.
1 tbsp.	finely cut fresh chives	15 ml.
1 tsp.	fresh lemon juice	5 ml.
about ½ tsp.	Tabasco sauce	about 2 ml.

Butter the pieces of bread on both sides and toast them on both sides under the broiler, or fry them in the butter as you would croutons.

Season the tomatoes and mix them with all of the other ingredients (except the toast) in a bowl, then place the bowl in the refrigerator for at least one hour to chill thoroughly. Spread the tomato-chive mixture evenly over the eight pieces of toast. Serve cold.

MICHEL GUÉRARD
MICHEL GUÉRARD'S CUISINE GOURMANDE

Savory Brazil-Nut Spread

The technique of cutting and toasting Melba rounds is explained on pages 36-37.

To toast Brazil nuts, spread the shelled nuts on a baking sheet and bake in a 350° F. [180° C.] oven for 15 to 18 minutes, turning occasionally to brown evenly. Cool.

To make 20 canapés

	toasted Brazil nuts, ½ cup [125 ml.] finely chopped and ⅓ cup [75 ml.] crushed	
½ lb.	liverwurst	¼ kg.
2 tbsp.	mayonnaise *(recipe, page 166)*	30 ml.
1 tsp.	prepared mustard	5 ml.
20	Melba-toast rounds	20

Mash the liverwurst and blend it with the mayonnaise and mustard. Mix in the chopped Brazil nuts. Spread the mixture on the toast rounds and garnish the edges with the crushed nuts. Place the canapés under a broiler until they are heated through, about three minutes, and serve hot.

IDA BAILEY ALLEN
BEST LOVED RECIPES OF THE AMERICAN PEOPLE

Chicken Drums

To toast almonds, place them in a shallow pan in a 350° F. [180° C.] oven for 10 minutes, turning them frequently to brown them evenly.

To make 12 canapés

1 cup	finely chopped cooked chicken	¼ liter
¼ cup	finely chopped celery or fennel	50 ml.
1 tbsp.	grated onion	15 ml.
1 tbsp.	finely chopped green pepper	15 ml.
1 tbsp.	chopped fresh parsley	15 ml.
about 10 tbsp.	mayonnaise *(recipe, page 166)*	about 150 ml.
	salt and freshly ground pepper	
6	thin slices white bread or challah, sliced lengthwise from the loaf	6
½ cup	chopped toasted almonds	125 ml.

Combine the chicken, celery or fennel, onion, green pepper and parsley in a bowl. Stir in enough mayonnaise to moisten the mixture, about 5 or 6 tablespoons [75 or 90 ml.]. Season to taste with salt and black pepper.

Spread half of the bread or challah slices with the chicken mixture. Cover with the remaining slices and, using a 1½-inch [4-cm.] biscuit cutter, cut four rounds from each sandwich. Brush the cut edge with, or roll it in, the remaining 4 tablespoons [60 ml.] of mayonnaise and then in the nuts. Refrigerate until serving time.

JEAN HEWITT
THE NEW YORK TIMES WEEKEND COOKBOOK

Bacon and Tomato Canapés

To make 12 canapés

24	bread rounds, cut from thinly sliced sandwich bread	24
2 to 4 tbsp.	butter	30 to 60 ml.
4 tbsp.	horseradish butter *(recipe, page 163)*	60 ml.
12	thin tomato slices	12
6	slices bacon, broiled or fried until crisp, drained and crumbled	6

Remove a small circle from the center of 12 of the bread rounds. Sauté the bread in butter and spread the uncut rounds with horseradish butter; lay on these a thin slice of tomato of the same circumference as the bread. Place the cutout slices on top and fill the spaces with bacon.

LUCY G. ALLEN
A BOOK OF HORS D'OEUVRE

Cream and Anchovy Canapés

Canapés à la Crème

To make 12 canapés

⅓ cup	heavy cream, whipped	75 ml.
3	thin slices firm-textured white bread, cut into 12 rounds, each about 1½ inches [4 cm.] across	3
3 tbsp.	butter	45 ml.
12	oil-packed flat anchovy fillets, drained	12

Fry the bread in the butter until the rounds are a pale color on both sides. Roll the anchovies into cylinders and place them on the bread. Cover the anchovies with the whipped cream and serve at once.

MRS. DE SALIS
SAVOURIES À LA MODE

Oysters on Toast

Huitres Tartinettes

To make 12 canapés

12	live oysters, shucked, their liquor strained and reserved	12
3	egg yolks	3
4 tbsp.	butter, softened	60 ml.
	fresh lemon juice	
12	thin bread rounds, cut from a sandwich loaf and toasted	12

Place the oysters on an ovenproof plate and sprinkle them with their liquor. Place the plate in a preheated 350° F. [180° C.] oven. As soon as the liquid begins to bubble a little, remove the plate from the oven. Immediately spread each round of toast with a mixture of the egg yolks and the butter. Place a poached oyster on each toast round. Sprinkle the oysters with drops of lemon juice and serve.

LA CUISINE LYONNAISE

Liver Paté Loaf

Leverpostei

Slices of liver paté are a traditional topping for smorrebrod sandwiches. Sprats are small fish caught in the fjords of Norway and are obtainable canned —as sprats or Brisling anchovies —where Scandinavian foods are sold. If necessary, 10 oil-packed flat anchovy fillets may be substituted for the five sprats called for in this recipe.

To make about 4 cups [1 liter] paté

1¼ lb.	calf or pork liver, soaked for 1 hour in cold water and a little vinegar, drained, and the skin and membranes removed	⅔ kg.
¼ lb.	lean fresh or salt pork	125 g.
5	canned oil-packed sprats, skinned, boned and mashed to a paste	5
2 tbsp.	milk	30 ml.
1 tbsp.	finely chopped onion	15 ml.
1 to 2 tsp.	salt	5 to 10 ml.
½ tsp.	pepper	2 ml.
½ tsp.	ground cloves	2 ml.
¾ cup	cracker meal	175 ml.
3	eggs, beaten	3
½ lb.	thinly sliced sheets of fresh pork fat	¼ kg.

Grind the liver twice, using the fine disk of a food grinder. Grind the pork three times and mix it with the liver. Add the

mashed sprats, milk, onion, spices, cracker meal and the eggs. Line a greased loaf-pan bottom and sides with slices of the pork fat, pour in the liver mixture and place the remaining pork-fat slices on top. Bake in a hot water bath in a preheated 350° F. [180° C.] oven for one and one half hours. Turn out on a platter and serve cold, sliced medium thick.

ALICE B. JOHNSON
THE COMPLETE SCANDINAVIAN COOKBOOK

Red Cabbage with Apples

Rödkal med Äpplen

This braised cabbage is traditionally used as a topping for smorrebrod sandwiches.

To make about 6 cups [1 ½ liters] braised cabbage

1	large head red cabbage, halved, cored and cut into thin shreds	1
4	cooking apples, peeled, cored and sliced	4
1	small onion, finely chopped	1
3 tbsp.	wine vinegar	45 ml.
3 tbsp.	water	45 ml.
1 tsp.	salt	5 ml.
½ tsp.	pepper	2 ml.
1 tbsp.	sugar	15 ml.
4 tbsp.	butter	60 ml.
3 or 4 tbsp.	red wine	45 or 60 ml.

Put the cabbage in a heavy enameled, stainless-steel or tin-lined pot with the onion, vinegar, water, salt and pepper. Cover the pot tightly and cook over low heat for two and one half to three hours.

At the end of the first hour of cooking, add the apples and the sugar. Cover the pot again and continue the slow cooking. No more water or vinegar should be required if the cabbage is a fresh, moist head; it will cook in its own juices. A few minutes before serving, add the butter and wine.

FLORENCE BROBECK AND MONIKA B. KJELLBERG
SMÖRGÅSBORD AND SCANDINAVIAN COOKERY

Swedish Marinated Salmon

Thin slices of marinated salmon are a traditional topping for smorrebrod sandwiches.

	To make 2 pounds [1 kg.] marinated salmon	
2 lb.	fresh salmon, filleted, but the skin left on	1 kg.
24	white peppercorns	24
3 tbsp.	sugar	45 ml.
4 tbsp.	salt	60 ml.
3 to 4 cups	fresh dill leaves (2 or 3 bunches)	¾ to 1 liter

Crush the peppercorns and mix them with the sugar and salt. Rub the fish with this mixture, and layer the fillets in a bowl with the dill. Refrigerate for 24 hours under a plate with a weight on top. Turn the fish occasionally and scrape off the seasoning before serving.

E. DONALD ASSELIN, M.D.
SCANDINAVIAN COOKBOOK

Herring Salad
Sillsalad

When this salad is served as a topping for smorrebrod, one of the herring fillets may be sliced and set on top of the other ingredients, as shown on page 48.

	To make 6 portions	
2	salt herring fillets, soaked overnight in cold water and drained	2
4 or 5	potatoes, boiled and peeled	4 or 5
2 or 3	pickled beets	2 or 3
1	dill pickle	1
1 or 2	apples	1 or 2
1 or 2 tbsp.	chopped onion	15 or 30 ml.
	salt and white pepper	
	beet juice (optional)	
7 tbsp.	heavy cream, whipped (optional)	105 ml.

Cut the herring, potatoes, beets, pickle and apple into small, uniform cubes and mix them carefully. Add the onion and seasoning to taste, including juice from the beets, if desired. For a richer salad, add the whipped cream. Put the salad into a bowl or pack it into a mold. Chill the salad for at least three hours before serving.

J. AUDREY ELLISON
THE GREAT SCANDINAVIAN COOK BOOK

Roquefort with Walnuts on Hot Toast
Tartines de Roquefort aux Noix

	To make about 6 open-faced sandwiches	
7 oz.	Roquefort cheese	200 g.
5 tbsp.	butter, softened	75 ml.
3½ oz.	freshly shelled walnuts (about 1 cup [½ liter])	100 g.
2 tbsp.	Armagnac or Cognac	30 ml.
	freshly ground pepper, preferably white pepper	
1	round loaf country-style bread, 3 or 4 days old, cut into thick slices	1

Place the butter in a 2-quart [2-liter] mixing bowl and, using a wooden spoon, work it into a paste. Then mix in the chopped walnuts. Put the Roquefort on a soup plate and mash it well with a fork. Then blend in the Armagnac or Cognac and add four or five good turns of the pepper mill. Combine the cheese with the butter and nuts, mixing until all of the ingredients are thoroughly incorporated.

Either in your oven or under the broiler, toast the bread slices. While the toast is still hot, spread it with the cheese mixture and serve at once. You can accompany these cheese toasts with celery hearts and radishes. They also marry well with grapes, and with pear quarters wiped with lemon juice.

ROGER VERGÉ
ROGER VERGÉ'S CUISINE OF THE SOUTH OF FRANCE

Almond Soufflé Sandwiches

	To make 4 open-faced sandwiches	
½ cup	chopped almonds (about 2 oz. [75 g.])	125 ml.
2	eggs, the yolks separated from the whites	2
½ tsp.	Worcestershire sauce	5 ml.
½ cup	shredded Cheddar cheese	125 ml.
1 tbsp.	mayonnaise (recipe, page 166)	15 ml.
1 tbsp.	chopped fresh parsley	15 ml.
½ tsp.	salt	2 ml.
4	slices toast	4

Beat the egg yolks until they are thick. Add the almonds, Worcestershire sauce, cheese, mayonnaise and parsley. Beat the egg whites with the salt until they are stiff and fold them into the yolk mixture. Pile the mixture lightly on the toast. Heat the sandwiches under the broiler until they are puffy and lightly browned, about five minutes.

WOMAN'S DAY COLLECTOR'S COOK BOOK

Reblochon Toast

Croûtes au Reblochon

Reblochon—a soft, French cheese—can be found in the United States from July to February or March. If the Reblochon is hard, wait until it creams (ripens).

To make 6 open-faced sandwiches

1	creamy Reblochon cheese, cut into slices ¼ inch [6 mm.] thick	1
6	slices cracked-wheat or whole-wheat bread	6
6	small slices unsalted butter, cut about ⅙ inch [about ½ cm.] thick	6
6	slices prosciutto from the center cut	6
6 tbsp.	fresh bread crumbs	90 ml.
3 tbsp.	chopped fresh parsley	45 ml.
6 tbsp.	heavy cream	90 ml.
	salt and freshly ground pepper	

Remove the crust from the bread; toast the bread very lightly. Spread one small slice of butter on each slice of bread. Set the bread slices in a jelly-roll pan. Top each buttered side with one slice of prosciutto and enough slices of Reblochon to completely cover the ham.

Mix the bread crumbs, parsley, heavy cream, a pinch of salt and the pepper together. Spread a thin layer of the mixture over the Reblochon. Bake in a preheated 375° F. [190° C.] oven until heated through. Serve before the Reblochon starts "running away" from you.

MADELEINE M. KAMMAN
WHEN FRENCH WOMEN COOK

Cheese and Green-Pepper-Ring Sandwiches

To make 12 sandwiches

½ lb.	cream cheese, softened	¼ kg.
2	medium-sized green peppers	2
	mayonnaise *(recipe, page 166)*	
	butter	
	sour cream (optional)	
2 tbsp.	finely cut fresh chives	30 ml.
	salt and black pepper	
24	thin slices firm-textured white bread	24

Wash the peppers and cut off the tops, removing the seeds and the ribs. Season the cream cheese with the chives, salt and black pepper. Add sour cream to thin the cheese, if it is needed. Mash the mixture to a smooth consistency. Fill the peppers with the seasoned cream cheese. Chill the peppers thoroughly until the filling is firm—about two hours.

When ready to serve, cut the peppers crosswise into thin slices. Cut 12 slices of the bread into rounds slightly larger in diameter than the pepper slices. Spread the rounds with mayonnaise. Lay a pepper slice on each round. Cover the pepper slice with a round of buttered bread cut ½ inch [1 cm.] smaller than the bottom round, so the pepper rings show.

FLORENCE BROBECK
THE LUNCH BOX AND EVERY KIND OF SANDWICH

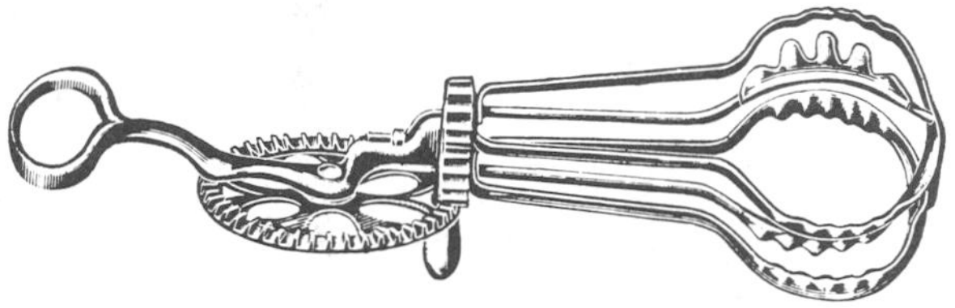

Sassy Carnival Rolls

Panini Rustici

The mortadella called for here is an Italian bologna, studded with pieces of fat, obtainable where Italian foods are sold.

To make 12 rolls

1 lb.	ricotta cheese	½ kg.
2	eggs	2
½ tsp.	salt	2 ml.
½ lb.	mozzarella cheese, diced	¼ kg.
¼ lb.	salami, chopped	125 g.
¼ lb.	prosciutto, chopped	125 g.
¼ lb.	mortadella, chopped	125 g.
6	hard sesame-seed rolls, cut in half	6
½ cup	freshly grated Parmesan cheese	125 ml.
	freshly ground black pepper	
4 tbsp.	butter, cut into small bits	60 ml.

Preheat the oven to 350° F. [180° C.]. Combine the ricotta, eggs, salt, mozzarella, salami, prosciutto and mortadella. Using a palette knife, spread the ricotta mixture over the halved rolls. Sprinkle the tops with the grated Parmesan, pepper and butter.

Place the rolls on a baking sheet and bake for 10 to 15 minutes. Remove the rolls from the oven and put them under a hot broiler long enough to toast the grated cheese—two to three minutes. Serve them hot. If you wish to use *Panini Rustici* as canapés, cut them into quarters.

ANNA MUFFOLETTO
THE ART OF SICILIAN COOKING

Cheese and Sausage Sandwiches

Crostini di Ricotta e Salsiccie

To make 24 open-faced sandwiches

½ lb.	ricotta cheese	¼ kg.
3	sweet Italian poaching sausages	3
3 tbsp.	cold water	45 ml.
½ tsp.	salt	2 ml.
⅓ cup	freshly grated Parmesan cheese	75 ml.
6 tbsp.	olive oil	90 ml.
4 tbsp.	unsalted butter	60 ml.
12	slices firm-textured white bread, crusts removed and slices halved	12
3½ oz.	Fontina or Gruyère cheese, thinly sliced and cut into rectangles the size of the halved bread slices	125 g.

In a bowl, mix the ricotta cheese and cold water. Add the salt and Parmesan cheese and mix until smooth and creamy.

Prick the sausages with a fork and cook in ¼ cup [50 ml.] of water in a skillet, over low heat, until the water evaporates. Continue cooking until the sausages become lightly browned on all sides and thoroughly cooked. Drain the sausages on paper towels, peel them, then chop them fine and stir the sausage meat into the cheese mixture.

Preheat the oven to 325° F. [160° C.]. Heat the oil and butter in a large, heavy skillet. Add the bread slices and fry them on one side only. Drain the slices on paper towels. Spread the fried sides of the bread with the cheese-sausage mixture. Place the slices on a well-greased baking sheet and bake them for five minutes.

Remove the sandwiches from the oven and top each with Fontina or Gruyère cheese. Return them to the oven for about a minute, until the cheese melts.

FRANCESCO GHEDINI
NORTHERN ITALIAN COOKING

Hot Mushroom Sandwich

To make 1 open-faced sandwich

6 to 8	small fresh mushrooms	6 to 8
6 tsp.	butter	30 ml.
¼ tsp.	fresh lemon juice	1 ml.
	pepper	
½ tsp.	chopped fresh parsley	2 ml.
1	slice whole-wheat bread, toasted	1

Stem the mushrooms; chop the stems and sauté them in 2 teaspoons [10 ml.] of the butter. Combine 2 teaspoons of the remaining butter with the lemon juice, a pinch of pepper and the parsley. Spread the slice of toast with the butter mixture. Sprinkle the sautéed mushroom stems on the toast; top with the raw mushroom caps, gill sides down.

Melt the remaining butter, brush it over the mushroom caps and set the toast slice in a covered dish. Bake in a preheated 350° F. [180° C.] oven for 12 to 15 minutes, until the mushroom caps are tender.

JANICE MURRAY GILL
NOVA SCOTIA DOWN-HOME COOKING

Toasted Bread and Garlic

El Pan de Costra al Ajo (Málaga)

The bitter Seville-orange juice in this recipe may be replaced by 1 tablespoon [15 ml.] of lemon juice mixed with 2 tablespoons [30 ml.] of sweet orange juice.

To make 1 open-faced sandwich

2 or 3	garlic cloves	2 or 3
1	dried red chili	1
3 tbsp.	Seville-orange juice	45 ml.
	salt and pepper	
1 tbsp.	oil	15 ml.
1	slice firm-textured white bread	1

Pound the garlic in a mortar with the chili, and salt and pepper to taste. Stir in the orange juice and then the oil. Spread the mixture on the bread, and bake in a preheated 350° F. [180° C.] oven for five to 10 minutes before serving.

ELIZABETH CASS
SPANISH COOKING

Fried Banana Sandwich

To make 1 open-faced sandwich

1	small banana, sliced	1
2 tbsp.	butter	30 ml.
	ground cinnamon	
1	slice hot corn bread, buttered	1

Fry the banana slices in butter and sprinkle heavily with cinnamon. Serve on corn bread dripping with butter.

CORA, ROSE AND BOB BROWN
10,000 SNACKS

Salmon Tartare with Caviar

If you prefer a less dramatic presentation, mix the salmon *tartare* in the kitchen and serve it on bread.

To make 8 open-faced sandwiches

1⅓ lb.	fresh salmon fillets	700 g.
2 tbsp.	black caviar	30 ml.
	butter, softened	
2	large slices pumpernickel bread	2
2	egg yolks	2
1 tbsp.	olive oil	15 ml.
1	lemon	1
¾ tbsp.	Worcestershire sauce	12 ml.
1½ tbsp.	capers, rinsed and drained	22 ml.
1 tbsp.	finely chopped onion	15 ml.
1½ tsp.	Dijon mustard	7 ml.
	salt (optional)	
	ground pepper	
	lettuce leaves	

Chop the salmon very fine. Butter the pumpernickel slices smoothly to the edges. Then top each slice with salmon. Press a hollow in the salmon on each slice, and put an egg yolk into each hollow. Sprinkle caviar lavishly on the egg yolks and salmon. Bring the plate of caviar-topped salmon to the table, along with a well-chilled bowl, the rest of the ingredients and a wire whisk.

At the table, spoon the egg yolks gently from the salmon into the chilled bowl, then whip vigorously with the whisk. Add the olive oil, drop by drop, beating hard until it forms a thin, mayonnaise-like sauce. Gently whisk in the juice of the lemon, a scant tablespoon of Worcestershire sauce, the capers, onion, mustard and a dash of salt and pepper. Now toss the salmon and caviar gently in the sauce with two forks until just mixed. Taste for seasoning. Cut each pumpernickel slice into four pieces. Place the salmon *tartare* evenly on each piece. Make a casual crisscross pattern on top with the tines of a fork. Garnish with a bit of lettuce.

MARY LOUISE LAU
THE DELICIOUS WORLD OF RAW FOODS

Toast with Ham and Cheese

Croustillons Remois

To make 6 open-faced sandwiches

¼ lb.	diced cooked ham (about ¾ cup [175 ml.])	125 g.
1½ cups	grated Gruyère cheese (about ¼ lb. [125 g.])	375 ml.
¾ cup	blanched almonds (about ¼ lb. [125 g.])	175 ml.
1 tbsp.	butter	15 ml.
1 tbsp.	flour	15 ml.
	salt	
	cayenne pepper	
½ cup	milk	125 ml.
6	slices of toast	6

Pulverize the almonds in a blender. Mix them with the ham and the cheese. Melt the butter in a saucepan. Remove the pan from the heat and stir in the flour. Season to taste with salt and cayenne. Blend in the milk carefully and return the sauce to the heat. Stir constantly until the sauce boils. Remove from the heat. Mix the sauce with the ham mixture and stir well until the cheese melts slightly and becomes sticky. Then spread the toast slices with the mixture. Place the slices on a baking sheet and broil them until the mixture bubbles and browns, about five minutes. Serve at once.

PAUL MAYER
PARIS . . . AND THEN SOME

Marrow Crusts

To make 8 open-faced sandwiches

2	beef marrow bones, each about 4 inches [10 cm.] long	2
	water	
8	slices firm-textured white bread, toasted and buttered	8
	finely chopped fresh parsley	
	salt	
	black pepper	

Remove the marrow carefully from the bones and soak it in lukewarm water for one hour. Shortly before serving time, cut the marrow into 1-inch [2½-cm.] slices; place the slices in cold water, bring the water to a boil and pour it off immediately. Spread the marrow on very hot toast, sprinkle the tops with a little parsley, lots of salt and a little black pepper. Pass under the broiler. Serve immediately.

SIGRID SCHULTZ
OVERSEAS PRESS CLUB COOKBOOK

Toast with Mussels and Bacon

To make 4 open-faced sandwiches

4	large slices firm-textured white bread, toasted	4
about 30	live mussels, scrubbed and bearded, steamed for 2 minutes and shucked	about 30
3 to 4 tbsp.	butter	45 to 60 ml.
4 to 6	slices bacon	4 to 6
1 tbsp.	chopped fresh parsley	15 ml.

Fry the mussels in the butter for two or three minutes, or until slightly firm. Remove the pan from the heat and cover it to keep the mussels hot. Cut the bacon slices crosswise into strips and fry them until crisp. Drain the bacon. Put the mussels on the toast and top with the bacon. Sprinkle with parsley, and serve.

BENGT PETERSEN
DELICIOUS FISH DISHES

Brandied Lobster Sandwich

To make 4 open-faced sandwiches

1 cup	coarsely chopped cooked lobster meat (about ¼ lb. [125 g.])	¼ liter
2 tbsp.	brandy	30 ml.
1 tbsp.	butter	15 ml.
1½ tbsp.	flour	22 ml.
¾ cup	milk	175 ml.
1 tbsp.	tomato paste	15 ml.
2 tbsp.	finely chopped fresh parsley	30 ml.
½ tsp.	salt	2 ml.
	grated nutmeg	
	finely chopped fresh tarragon	
	pepper	
	butter, softened	
about ¼ cup	shredded Gruyère, Swiss or Jarlsberg cheese	about 50 ml.
4	slices firm-textured white bread	4

Melt the butter in a saucepan and stir in the flour with a whisk. Add the milk all at once and stir with the whisk. Heat until thickened and bubbly, stirring constantly. Remove from the heat. Add the tomato paste and mix well. Add the brandy, parsley, salt, a pinch of nutmeg, a pinch of tarragon, and pepper to taste, and mix again. Add the lobster meat,

return the pan to the heat and simmer gently for about three minutes, stirring occasionally.

Preheat the broiler. Arrange the bread slices on a baking sheet and toast one side under the broiler. Turn the slices and butter the untoasted sides. Spoon the lobster mixture over the toast. Sprinkle each slice with 1 tablespoon [15 ml.] or more of the cheese. Broil the sandwiches until the cheese melts and the lobster mixture is bubbly and lightly browned. Serve immediately.

ANITA BORGHESE
THE GREAT SANDWICH BOOK

Pan Basquaise

To make 4 to 6 open-faced sandwiches

4 tbsp.	olive oil	60 ml.
4	large red peppers, roasted, peeled and finely sliced	4
⅔ cup	flaked oil-packed tuna, preferably tuna packed in olive oil	150 ml.
	salt and freshly ground black pepper	
2 tbsp.	wine vinegar	30 ml.
4 tbsp.	finely chopped fresh parsley	60 ml.
3	garlic cloves, finely chopped	3
2	loaves French bread	2
4	eggs, hard-boiled and sliced	4
8	ripe Greek olives	8

Heat 3 tablespoons [45 ml.] of the oil in a heavy 10-inch [25-cm.] skillet. Add the peppers and cook them over high heat for two or three minutes; then add the tuna, salt and pepper, continuing to cook until the tuna is heated through. Add the vinegar, 2 tablespoons [30 ml.] of the parsley, and the garlic, and cook the mixture until the vinegar has evaporated, or for about two more minutes. Remove the pan from the heat, taste the mixture for seasoning and set aside.

Cut the loaves of bread in half lengthwise and then crosswise into 4-inch [10-cm.] pieces. Place on a baking sheet and toast in the oven until warm and crisp, but not brown.

Place the bread on a serving platter and top it with the pepper-and-tuna mixture. Garnish with sliced eggs and top each slice with an olive, pitted and cut in half lengthwise. Dribble a little oil over each piece of bread and sprinkle the top with the remaining parsley. Serve the sandwiches warm or at room temperature.

PERLA MEYERS
THE PEASANT KITCHEN

The Reuben Sandwich

To make 4 open-faced sandwiches

4	large slices rye bread	4
	butter, softened	
	Russian dressing *(recipe, page 166)*	
¾ lb.	cooked corned beef, thinly sliced	⅓ kg.
½ lb.	thoroughly drained sauerkraut	¼ kg.
4	large slices Swiss or Gruyère cheese	4

Preheat the oven to 400° F. [200° C.]. Toast the bread lightly and butter it. Cover the buttered sides with Russian dressing. Arrange the corned beef over the dressing. Top the corned beef with sauerkraut and cheese. Place the sandwiches on a baking sheet. Cook in the oven for five to seven minutes, until the sandwiches are heated through and the cheese begins to melt. Run them under the broiler for a minute or so to brown the cheese. Cut in half and serve at once.

ANITA BORGHESE
THE GREAT SANDWICH BOOK

Italian Fried Cheese Sandwiches

Mozzarella in Carrozza

The technique of frying egg-coated cheese sandwiches is shown on pages 54-55. A traditional accompaniment to Mozzarella in Carrozza is an anchovy sauce made by combining 16 drained and finely chopped oil-packed flat anchovy fillets with ½ cup [125 ml.] olive oil, 2 tablespoons [30 ml.] of fresh lemon juice and two mashed garlic cloves. Stir over low heat until the anchovies melt.

To make 16 or 32 small sandwiches

16	slices firm homemade-style white bread, each cut ¼ inch [6 mm.] thick	16
16	slices whole-milk mozzarella cheese, each cut ¼ inch [6 mm.] thick	16
2	eggs	2
¼ tsp.	salt	1 ml.
1 tsp.	water	5 ml.
about 1 cup	fine white bread crumbs	about ¼ liter
	oil for deep frying	

Trim the crusts from the bread slices and cut each slice into halves or quarters. Cut the slices of mozzarella slightly smaller than the slices of bread and assemble the sandwiches, pressing the edges of the bread together. Beat together the eggs, salt and water. Dip the sandwiches into the beaten egg mixture, coating both sides and all the edges

well. Let the sandwiches stand to become well impregnated, then dip the edges in fine bread crumbs to seal them.

In a small skillet, fry the sandwiches, a few at a time, to a fine golden color in hot oil almost 1 inch [2½ cm.] deep, turning them to brown both sides. Drain the sandwiches on absorbent paper and serve immediately on a hot plate.

NARCISSA G. CHAMBERLAIN & NARCISSE CHAMBERLAIN
THE FLAVOR OF ITALY

Cheese and English-Walnut Sandwiches

The English author of this recipe probably assumed her readers would use a Cheddar cheese. Any firm, flavorful cheese — Edam, Gruyère, Emmenthal, or Monterey Jack —is suitable.

To make 4 to 6 sandwiches

¼ lb.	cheese, grated (about 1 cup [¼ liter])	125 g.
¼ lb.	walnuts, thinly sliced (about 1 cup [¼ liter])	125 g.
8 tbsp.	butter	125 g.
	salt	
	paprika	
8 to 12	slices whole-wheat bread	8 to 12

Work the butter to a cream, and add the seasonings and the grated cheese gradually; then mix in the nuts, which should be sliced very thin. Spread the mixture upon slices of bread and press them together in pairs.

JANET McKENZIE HILL
SALADS, SANDWICHES AND CHAFING-DISH DAINTIES

Danish Prince

To make 2 sandwiches

2	eggs, hard-boiled	2
1 tbsp.	chopped scallion	15 ml.
3	radishes, sliced	3
	salt and pepper	
1 tbsp.	grated sharp cheese	15 ml.
3 tbsp.	mayonnaise *(recipe, page 166)*	45 ml.
2	crusty rolls	2

Chop the eggs. Add the scallion and radishes, and salt and pepper to taste. Fold the grated cheese into the mayonnaise and mix them lightly with the egg mixture. Spread the filling on the rolls.

RUTH CHIER ROSEN
JUST BETWEEN US

Mushroom Sandwiches

To prepare the scrambled eggs for this recipe, first beat the eggs lightly with 1 teaspoon [5 ml.] of water. Melt 1 tablespoon [15 ml.] of butter in a small skillet over medium heat, pour in the eggs and stir them until they begin to form soft curds. Remove the skillet from the heat and stir until the eggs are smooth and thick.

This makes a delicious sandwich that tastes like chicken.

	To make 2 sandwiches	
¼ lb.	fresh mushrooms	125 g.
½ tsp.	fresh lemon juice	2 ml.
2 tbsp.	butter	30 ml.
	salt and pepper	
	cayenne pepper	
2	eggs, lightly scrambled	2
3 tbsp.	freshly grated Parmesan cheese	45 ml.
4	thin slices firm-textured white bread	4

Cook the mushrooms mixed with the lemon juice in the butter for eight minutes; remove them from the heat and chop them. Then pound the mushrooms to a paste in a mortar. Season with salt, pepper and a pinch of cayenne. Add the egg and the cheese and mix well. Pile the mixture onto two bread slices, cover with the other two slices and serve.

ALICE B. TOKLAS
THE ALICE B. TOKLAS COOK BOOK

Onion Rings

	To make 12 sandwiches	
12	paper-thin onion slices, each about 1½ inches [4 cm.] in diameter	12
6	thin slices firm white homemade-style bread, or use 12 slices challah	6
about ½ cup	mayonnaise (recipe, page 166)	about 125 ml.
about ¾ cup	very finely chopped fresh parsley	about 175 ml.

With a 1½-inch [4-cm.] cookie cutter, cut four rounds from each slice of bread or two rounds from each challah slice. Arrange the rounds in 12 pairs. Spread each round with mayonnaise. Put an onion slice on a bread round, salt the onion lightly, then top it with a second bread round.

When all 12 sandwiches are assembled, spread some mayonnaise on a piece of wax paper and have the chopped parsley ready in a bowl. Take a sandwich between your thumb and forefinger and roll the edges first in the thinly spread mayonnaise, then in the chopped parsley. Make sure there are no bare spots; if there are, dab a bit of mayonnaise on each spot and dip the sandwich again in parsley. Place the sandwiches on wax paper on a flat tray or baking sheet and cover them with wax paper. Chill well.

IRMA RHODE
COOL ENTERTAINING

Cucumber and Nasturtium Sandwich

	To make 3 or 4 sandwiches	
2	medium-sized cucumbers, peeled, halved, seeded and finely chopped	2
3 or 4	nasturtium leaves	3 or 4
	onion juice	
	cayenne pepper	
	mayonnaise (recipe, page 166)	
6 or 8	thin slices brown bread, buttered	6 or 8

To the chopped cucumber, add a little onion juice, a dash of cayenne pepper and enough mayonnaise to spread. For each sandwich, spread one slice of brown bread with the mixture, lay a nasturtium leaf (not flower) over it and put the other slice of bread on top. Serve at once.

FLORENCE A. COWLES
1001 SANDWICHES

Club Sandwich

	To make 1 sandwich	
2	slices egg bread	2
	butter, softened	
2 or 3	slices cooked chicken	2 or 3
	salt	
	paprika	
1	tomato, sliced	1
1 tbsp.	mayonnaise (recipe, page 166)	15 ml.
1 or 2	slices bacon, fried until crisp and drained	1 or 2
	lettuce leaves	

Toast and butter the bread. Lay the slices of chicken on one piece of the toasted bread and season lightly with salt and paprika. On top, put the tomato slices, spread the mayonnaise on them, and crumble the bacon over that. Garnish with the lettuce and cover with a second piece of toast.

ALDEN ROBERTSON
THE NO BALONEY SANDWICH BOOK

Corn Dog

To make 6 corn dogs

½ cup	yellow cornmeal	125 ml.
6	frankfurters	6
½ cup	flour	125 ml.
1 tbsp.	sugar	15 ml.
1 tsp.	dry mustard	5 ml.
1 tsp.	baking powder	5 ml.
½ tsp.	salt	2 ml.
½ cup	milk	125 ml.
1	egg, lightly beaten	1
1 tbsp.	melted shortening	15 ml.
6	skewers or sticks	6

Combine the cornmeal, flour, sugar, mustard, baking powder and salt, mixing well. Add the milk, egg and shortening, mixing until very smooth. Pour the mixture into a tall glass.

Put the frankfurters on sticks. Dip them into the cornmeal batter to coat them evenly. Deep fry in oil heated to 375° F. [190° C.] until golden brown, about two minutes. Drain on paper towels.

LYDIA SAIGER
THE JUNK FOOD COOKBOOK

Stuffed Frankfurters

To make 4 sandwiches

4	frankfurters	4
2	medium-sized onions, thinly sliced	2
1 tbsp.	butter	15 ml.
2	slices Cheddar cheese, cut into long strips	2
4	thin slices bacon	4
4	frankfurter rolls, toasted	4
	prepared mustard	

Sauté the onions in the butter until they are golden brown — about 10 minutes.

Cut a lengthwise slit in each frankfurter. Fill the frankfurters with the sautéed onions and place two cheese strips in each frankfurter. Wind one bacon slice in a spiral around each frankfurter and secure the bacon with wooden picks.

Broil the frankfurters on a rack 5 inches [13 cm.] from the heat, turning them often, until the cheese melts and the bacon and frankfurters are brown. Remove the wooden picks and serve in lightly toasted frankfurter rolls with mustard.

MARY AND VINCENT PRICE
A TREASURY OF GREAT RECIPES

Texas Jailhouse Chili

Chili molido is a pure chili powder made without the addition of the herbs and spices found in most commercial powders. It is available where Mexican foods are sold.

The author notes that if a less hot chili is desired, 1 tablespoon [15 ml.] of additional paprika may be substituted for 1 tablespoon of the chili molido. If you are preparing the chili to make chili dogs, the quantities called for may be reduced to the fractional proportion desired.

To make about 6 cups [1 ½ liters] chili

½ lb.	beef suet, finely chopped	¼ kg.
2½ lb.	coarsely ground beef chuck	1¼ kg.
3	garlic cloves, finely chopped	3
1½ tbsp.	paprika	22 ml.
1 tbsp.	ground cumin	15 ml.
1 tbsp.	salt	15 ml.
1 tbsp.	white pepper	15 ml.
1½ tbsp.	diced green pepper	22 ml.
1 tsp.	dried coriander	5 ml.
3 cups	water	¾ liter
3 tbsp.	*chili molido*	45 ml.

Melt the suet in a Dutch oven. Add the meat and brown it. Add all of the other ingredients and cook, covered, for four hours. Add more water while cooking, if necessary.

THE JUNIOR LEAGUE OF HOUSTON
HOUSTON JUNIOR LEAGUE COOK BOOK

Breaded Liver Sandwiches

Liver Hrinky

To make 2 large sandwiches

½ lb.	thinly sliced calf's liver, sautéed in butter for 5 minutes, drained, and ground in a food processor or grinder	¼ kg.
2 tsp.	grated onion	10 ml.
3 to 4 tbsp.	butter	45 to 60 ml.
	salt and pepper	
	milk, cream sauce or stock (optional)	
4	slices bread	4
1	egg, lightly beaten	1
⅓ cup	milk	75 ml.
	dry bread crumbs	

Cook the onion in 1 tablespoon [15 ml.] of the butter over low heat until lightly browned, about five minutes. Combine it with the liver and season with salt and pepper to taste. The mixture may be moistened slightly with milk, cream sauce or stock. Make two large sandwiches, using the liver mixture as a filling. Cut the sandwiches into triangles or rectangles. Dip each piece in the beaten egg diluted with the milk, then coat with the bread crumbs. Sauté the pieces in the remaining butter until browned on both sides. Serve at once.

SAVELLA STECHISHIN
TRADITIONAL UKRAINIAN COOKERY

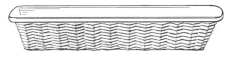

Greek Meatball Sandwich

Keftedes Sandwich

To make 10 sandwiches

½ lb.	ground beef	¼ kg.
½ lb.	ground lamb, veal or pork	¼ kg.
1	egg	1
1 cup	dry white bread crumbs	¼ liter
1	large onion, grated	1
1 tbsp.	tomato paste	15 ml.
¼ cup	dry white wine	50 ml.
1	garlic clove, finely chopped	1
½ tsp.	oregano	2 ml.
1 tsp.	chopped fresh mint	5 ml.
	flour	
about 1 tbsp.	olive oil	about 15 ml.
about 1 tbsp.	butter	about 15 ml.
10	hard oblong rolls	10

Beat the egg lightly. Add the bread crumbs and mix well. Add the beef and the lamb, veal or pork and mix well. Add the onion, tomato paste, wine, garlic, oregano and mint, and work the mixture together until it is well combined. Cover and refrigerate it for about one hour.

Cut the rolls open lengthwise without cutting all the way through. Pull out some of the soft centers and reserve them for another use. Form the meat mixture into 1-inch [5-cm.] balls, flatten them slightly and dredge them in flour. Fry the meatballs, a small batch at a time, in the oil and the butter until they are nicely browned all over, adding more oil and butter if necessary. Put four meatballs into each roll along with some of the pan drippings. Serve immediately.

ANITA BORGHESE
THE GREAT SANDWICH BOOK

Fried Ham and Cheese Sandwich

Croque-Monsieur

The slices of cheese and ham should be cut to the same shape as the bread slices, but a fraction of an inch smaller.

	To make 6 sandwiches	
6	slices boiled ham	6
12	slices Gruyère cheese	12
12	slices firm-textured white bread, crusts removed	12
	butter, softened	
	grated nutmeg	
	pepper	
3	eggs, beaten with 3 tbsp. [45 ml.] water	3
3 to 6 tbsp.	butter	45 to 90 ml.
3 to 6 tbsp.	vegetable oil	45 to 90 ml.

Spread each slice of bread generously with the butter. On the buttered side of six of the bread slices, arrange a slice of cheese, a slice of ham and another slice of cheese. Sprinkle the top slice of cheese with nutmeg and a little pepper. Add the remaining six slices of bread, buttered sides down.

Pour the egg mixture into a shallow dish and into it dip both sides of each of the six sandwiches.

In a skillet, heat 3 tablespoons [45 ml.] each of the butter and oil and brown the *croques* on each side for five minutes, or until golden. Add more butter and oil, if necessary. Keep the prepared *croques* warm until all are ready to be served.

ROBERT ACKART
THE CHEESE COOKBOOK

Cheeseburger

The technique of making a cheeseburger is shown on page 51.

	To make 4 cheeseburgers	
1 lb.	ground beef	½ kg.
	salt and pepper	
4	slices cheese	4
4	hamburger buns	4

Form your hamburgers into eight very thin, 2-ounce [75-g.] cakes. Salt and pepper them and place a slice of cheese just smaller than the hamburger cake on half of the hamburgers. Top with the other halves and broil or pan broil for about two minutes on each side. Serve in buttered, toasted buns.

JAMES BEARD
THE JAMES BEARD COOKBOOK

Wild West Burger

To make 4 sandwiches

1 lb.	ground beef	½ kg.
½ cup	grated Cheddar cheese	125 ml.
4	slices bacon, cut in half and partially cooked	4
4	hamburger buns	4
	ketchup (recipe, page 167)	

Mix the ground beef with the cheese and form it into four patties. Broil the patties for about six minutes on one side. Turn, top with bacon, and broil for a few minutes more, or until the bacon is crisp. Serve on buns, with ketchup.

LYDIA SAIGER
THE JUNK FOOD COOKBOOK

Italian Hero

Pepperoncini are small, whole pickled peppers; they are sometimes marketed as Tuscan peppers.

To make 4 to 6 portions

1	long loaf Italian white or whole-wheat bread	1
	mayonnaise (recipe, page 166), (optional)	
1	large tomato, very thinly sliced	1
	olive oil	
	crushed or finely chopped fresh basil	
1	medium-sized cucumber or zucchini, very thinly sliced	1
	salt	
	freshly ground pepper	
1	sweet red onion, very thinly sliced	1
¼ lb.	provolone cheese, thinly sliced	125 g.
¼ lb.	Genoa salami, thinly sliced	125 g.
1	green pepper, sliced into paper-thin rings, seeds removed	1
	finely chopped pepperoncini	

Slice the loaf in half lengthwise and spread it lightly with mayonnaise, if desired. Layer with thin slices of tomato and sprinkle lightly with olive oil and sweet basil. Next layer with the cucumber or zucchini and sprinkle with salt and pepper. Then layer with the onion, cheese, salami and green pepper, and sprinkle with *pepperoncini*. Repeat the layers and place the top of the bread over the layered filling.

DIANE MACMILLAN
THE PORTABLE FEAST

The Hero

The technique of broiling and peeling peppers is explained on page 50. Pepperoncini, or Tuscan peppers, are pickled, mild-flavored peppers.

To make 4 portions

1	large loaf Italian bread	1
	olive oil	
1	garlic clove, cut	1
¼ lb.	Gorgonzola cheese, softened	125 g.
1 lb.	Italian sandwich meats (about ¼ lb. [125 g.] each of 4 or more of the following meats: Genoa salami, prosciutto, mortadella, *cappicola*, salami and pepperoni)	½ kg.
¼ to ½ lb.	provolone or Taleggio cheese	125 to 250 g.
6	*pepperoncini* (optional)	6
2 or 3	broiled, peeled green peppers (optional)	2 or 3
	oil-packed flat anchovy fillets	
	small hot peppers (optional)	
	vinegar	

Cut the bread open lengthwise. Brush the cut sides with oil. Rub the garlic clove over the oil. Spread the bottom half of bread with the Gorgonzola. Arrange layers of meat over it. Cover the meat with a layer of provolone or Taleggio cheese. Cover the cheese with *pepperoncini* and/or roasted sweet peppers, a few anchovies and a few hot peppers, if desired. Sprinkle lightly with vinegar. Cover the filling with the top of the bread and wrap the loaf tightly in aluminum foil. At the picnic site, cut the bread into four portions.

ANITA BORGHESE
THE GREAT SANDWICH BOOK

Linguiça Rolls

The linguiça called for in this recipe is Portuguese, garlic-flavored, smoked pork sausage. Spanish chorizo or other garlicky smoked sausage may be substituted.

It is very easy to make an at-home version of the popular *linguiça* rolls served at wayside stands throughout coastal

New England. Try to obtain the New England type of frank-furter rolls if you can: the ones split down the center top.

	To make 6 rolls	
1 lb.	*linguiça*, cut into small chunks	½ kg.
1	onion, finely chopped	1
6	frankfurter rolls	6

Fry the *linguiça* with the onion until well browned. Divide the *linguiça* mixture evenly among the rolls.

MARGARET H. KOEHLER
RECIPES FROM THE PORTUGUESE OF PROVINCETOWN

Toast à l'Anglaise

	To make 4 sandwiches	
4	slices rare roast beef	4
4 tbsp.	butter	60 ml.
2 tsp.	Dijon mustard	10 ml.
	Worcestershire sauce	
	salt and freshly ground pepper	
1 tbsp.	vegetable oil	15 ml.
3	medium-sized onions, thinly sliced	3
8	slices firm-textured white bread with the crusts removed	8
½ cup	clarified butter	125 ml.
4	dill gherkins, thinly sliced lengthwise	4
4	sprigs parsley	4

Combine 2 tablespoons [30 ml.] of the butter and the mustard in a small bowl. Add a few drops of Worcestershire sauce and a pinch each of salt and pepper. Mash the mixture with a fork until smooth, then set this mustard butter aside.

Heat the remaining butter and the oil in a heavy skillet. Add the onions, cover, and cook over low heat for 30 minutes, or until they are very soft and lightly browned. Drain the onions and set them aside.

Spread the bread slices with the mustard butter. Place a slice of roast beef on half of the bread slices, top the meat with a little of the onion mixture, and cover with the remaining slices of bread.

Heat the clarified butter in a large skillet, add the sandwiches, and sauté them on both sides until they are nicely browned. Transfer the sandwiches to a serving platter and top each one with a dill gherkin and a sprig of parsley. Serve the sandwiches immediately.

PERLA MEYERS
THE PEASANT KITCHEN

Beef-Tongue Sandwich

To cook the tongue, soak it in cold water for one hour. Put it in a pan with an onion, carrot, celery rib, bouquet garni, a few peppercorns and 1 teaspoon [5 ml.] of salt. Add water to bare-ly cover, then bring to a boil, skim, and simmer until the tongue is tender, about 45 minutes a pound [½ kg.]. When it is cool enough to handle, skin and trim the tongue and return it to the cooking liquid to cool completely.

	To make 4 to 6 sandwiches	
½ lb.	boiled beef tongue	¼ kg.
2	hard-boiled egg yolks	2
1 tbsp.	prepared mustard	15 ml.
	salt	
	cayenne pepper	
2 to 3 tbsp.	cream	30 to 45 ml.
	butter	
8 to 12	slices bread	8 to 12

Chop the tongue, put it into a mortar with the egg yolks, mustard, salt and cayenne to taste, and pound it all to a paste. Dilute the paste with the cream. Butter the bread, spread the slices with the tongue mixture, and press them together in pairs. Cut the sandwiches into halves, put them on a paper doily or a napkin placed on a dish, and serve.

OSCAR TSCHIRKY
THE COOK BOOK BY "OSCAR" OF THE WALDORF

Frogs' Legs Sandwich

	To make 1 sandwich	
6	small frogs' legs or 2 large frogs' legs	6
1 or 2 tbsp.	butter	15 or 30 ml.
	tartar sauce (recipe, page 166)	
2	thin slices toast	2
	lettuce leaves	

Sauté the frogs' legs in butter for five to 10 minutes—depending on size—or until tender, and then detach the flesh from the bones. Chop the flesh fine and mix with enough tartar sauce to bind it. Spread it on thin slices of toast, press on the upper bread slice, and cut the sandwich into finger shapes. Serve the fingers warm on leaves of lettuce.

ARNOLD SHIRCLIFFE
THE EDGEWATER SANDWICH AND HORS D'OEUVRES BOOK

Oyster-Loaf Sandwich

Corn flour is the milled product of yellow or white corn. It tastes like cornmeal and has the texture of wheat flour. Creole mustard is a pungent prepared mustard made from brown mustard seeds. As a substitute, you may use any strong-flavored prepared brown mustard.

In the 19th Century, according to tradition, a New Orleans husband who had spent the night in the French Quarter saloons brought this oyster-loaf sandwich home to his wife as a *médiatrice*, or peacemaker. Called a "poor boy" in New Orleans, this kind of sandwich is known in other parts of the United States as a hero, a grinder or a submarine.

To make 1 long sandwich

1 pint	live medium-sized oysters, shucked (about 12)	½ liter
¼ tsp.	cayenne pepper	1 ml.
¼ tsp.	freshly ground black pepper	1 ml.
2	eggs	2
½ cup	light cream	125 ml.
⅛ tsp.	salt	½ ml.
1 cup	unsifted corn flour or all-purpose flour	¼ liter
1½ cups	soft fresh bread crumbs	375 ml.
1	loaf French or Italian bread (about 15 inches [38 cm.] long and 3 inches [8 cm.] wide)	1
4 tbsp.	butter, melted	60 ml.
	vegetable oil for deep frying	
1½ cups	finely shredded lettuce	375 ml.
1	large tomato, sliced ¼ inch [6 mm.] thick	1

Creole tartar sauce

1	egg yolk	1
½ cup	olive oil	125 ml.
1 tsp.	Creole mustard	5 ml.
about ⅛ tsp.	cayenne pepper	about ½ ml.
2 tbsp.	finely chopped scallion, including 2 inches [5 cm.] of the green top	30 ml.
2 tbsp.	finely chopped fresh parsley, preferably flat-leafed parsley	30 ml.
2 tbsp.	finely chopped dill pickle	30 ml.

To make the tartar sauce, first whisk the egg yolk vigorously in a deep bowl until it thickens. Beat in the oil, ½ teaspoon [2 ml.] at a time, making sure each addition is absorbed before adding more. The sauce should have the consistency of thick cream. Add the Creole mustard, cayenne and salt, and beat until the sauce is smooth. Then stir in the chopped scallions, parsley and pickles, and taste for seasoning.

Pat the oysters dry with paper towels and season them on all sides with the cayenne and black pepper. In a shallow bowl, beat the egg to a froth with a wire whisk or fork, add the cream and salt, and mix well. Spread the corn flour or all-purpose flour on one piece of wax paper and the bread crumbs on another piece.

Roll one oyster at a time in the flour and, when it is evenly covered, immerse it in the egg mixture. Then turn the oyster about in the crumbs to coat it on all sides. Arrange the oysters in one layer on a plate and refrigerate them while you prepare the bread.

Preheat the oven to 350° F. [180° C.]. With a sharp knife, slice the loaf of bread horizontally in half. Pull out all of the white crumbs from both the top and bottom to create two boatlike shells of the crusts. With a pastry brush, spread the melted butter evenly inside both halves of the loaf. Place the shells on a baking sheet and bake in the middle of the oven for 15 minutes, or until they are crisp and lightly brown.

Meanwhile, pour vegetable oil into a deep fryer or large, heavy saucepan to a depth of about 3 inches [8 cm.] and heat the oil until it reaches a temperature of 375° F. [190° C.]. Deep fry the oysters six at a time, turning them with a slotted spoon for two to three minutes, or until the coating is crisp and golden brown. As they brown, transfer them to paper towels to drain.

To assemble the oyster loaf, spread the tartar sauce inside both the bottom and top parts of the loaf. Scatter the shredded lettuce on the bottom half of the loaf and arrange the tomato slices and finally the oysters over it. Set the top part of the loaf in place, slice the loaf crosswise into four portions and serve at once.

FOODS OF THE WORLD
AMERICAN COOKING: CREOLE AND ACADIAN

Sweet Chocolate Sandwich

German chocolate is a sweet cooking chocolate, named for its inventor, Samuel German. It is available at most food stores. The author suggests that orange marmalade may be added to the chocolate mixture.

To make 1 sandwich

½ oz.	German chocolate	25 g.
1 tbsp.	hot water	15 ml.
	salt	
2	thin slices firm-textured white bread, buttered	2

Melt the chocolate in the upper part of a double boiler set over simmering water. Add the tablespoon [15 ml.] of hot water and stir until smooth. Add a bit of salt, and spread the chocolate mixture between generously buttered slices of white bread.

FLORENCE A. COWLES
1001 SANDWICHES

Fig Sandwiches

The rose water called for in this recipe is a flavoring produced in the Middle East and India by distilling the oil of rose petals. It is available at pharmacies and specialty food shops.

To make about 1 cup [¼ liter] spread

¼ lb.	dried figs	125 g.
¼ cup	water	50 ml.
⅓ cup	blanched almonds	75 ml.
	rose water	
1 to 2 tbsp.	fresh lemon juice	15 to 30 ml.
	ladyfingers, or white or yellow cupcakes, halved crosswise	

Chop the figs very fine, add the water, and cook to a smooth paste; add, also, the almonds, chopped very fine and pounded to a paste with a few drops of rose water and the lemon juice. When cold, spread the mixture upon ladyfingers or halved cupcakes, white or yellow, press another ladyfinger or cupcake half above the mixture, and serve upon a handsome doily-covered plate.

JANET MCKENZIE HILL
SALADS, SANDWICHES AND CHAFING-DISH DAINTIES

Canton Ginger Sandwich

Canton ginger is boiled, syrup-preserved ginger root.

To make 2 or 3 sandwiches

2 tbsp.	finely chopped Canton ginger	30 ml.
3 oz.	cream cheese, softened	100 g.
1 to 2 tbsp.	heavy cream	15 to 30 ml.
½ cup	finely chopped blanched almonds	125 ml.
1 tsp.	fresh lemon juice	5 ml.
¼ tsp.	salt	1 ml.
¼ tsp.	paprika	1 ml.
4 to 6	thin slices plain or toasted white bread	4 to 6
	lettuce leaves	
	watercress sprigs	

Thin the cream cheese with the cream and mix in the ginger, almonds, lemon juice, salt and paprika. If the mixture is too thin, place it in the refrigerator and thoroughly chill it, or add additional cream cheese. Spread the mixture on two or three slices of freshly made toast or plain bread, and press a second slice on top of each one. Trim the crusts, cut the sandwiches into the desired shapes and serve the pieces on leaves of lettuce. Garnish with watercress.

ARNOLD SHIRCLIFFE
THE EDGEWATER SANDWICH AND HORS D'OEUVRES BOOK

Stuffed Vegetables

Filled Beets

To make 24 filled beets

24	tiny beets, boiled for 30 to 40 minutes, drained, peeled and trimmed	24
1 cup	mustard-flavored vinaigrette (recipe, page 165)	¼ liter
3 oz.	cream cheese, softened	100 g.
¼ cup	chopped walnuts	50 ml.

Remove the centers from the beets. Toss these beet cups with the vinaigrette, cover, and marinate for 24 hours. Drain the beet cups and pat them dry. Reserve 2 teaspoons [10 ml.] of the marinade and mix it with the cream cheese and walnuts. Fill the cups with the cream-cheese mixture.

ALICE SCHRYVER AND FRANCILLE WALLACE
THE COMPLETE HORS D'OEUVRES COOKBOOK

Egg and Endive

To make 12 to 16 stuffed endives

3	eggs, hard-boiled and chopped	3
2 or 3	heads Belgian endive	2 or 3
2 tbsp.	crumbled Roquefort or blue cheese	30 ml.
about 2 tbsp.	mayonnaise (recipe, page 166)	about 30 ml.
	salt and black pepper	
¼ tsp.	Tabasco sauce	1 ml.
6 to 8	oil-packed flat anchovy fillets, halved lengthwise	6 to 8
	chopped fresh parsley	

Place the eggs in a mixing bowl and add the cheese and mayonnaise. Stir and, if necessary, add more mayonnaise to bind the mixture. Season to taste with salt, pepper and Tabasco. Pull apart the endive leaves. Spread the egg mixture inside the endive leaves and lay half of an anchovy lengthwise over each filled leaf. Garnish with the chopped parsley. Chill and serve.

JEAN HEWITT
THE NEW YORK TIMES LARGE TYPE COOKBOOK

Stuffed Brussels Sprouts

To make 12 stuffed Brussels sprouts

12	Brussels sprouts	12
½ cup	chopped cooked corned beef	125 ml.
¼ cup	mayonnaise *(recipe, page 166)*	50 ml.
¼ tsp.	dry mustard	1 ml.

Remove the centers from the 12 raw Brussels sprouts. Soak the Brussels-sprouts cups in ice water for half an hour. Drain them. Fill the Brussels sprouts with a mixture of the remaining ingredients.

ALICE SCHRYVER AND FRANCILLE WALLACE
THE COMPLETE HORS D'OEUVRES COOKBOOK

Stuffed Celery

To make about 48 pieces

1	celery heart, ribs separated and trimmed	1
6 oz.	cream cheese	175 g.
1 tsp.	white vinegar	5 ml.
1 tbsp.	light cream	15 ml.
1 tsp.	curry powder	5 ml.
5 tbsp.	finely chopped chutney	75 ml.

Soften the cream cheese to room temperature. Blend together the white vinegar, light cream and curry powder. Add the cream cheese and work the mixture into a smooth paste. Stir in the chutney and refrigerate for several hours, overnight if possible. About one hour before serving, stuff the mixture into the celery ribs and cut them into 1-inch [2½-cm.] pieces.

ANN ROE ROBBINS
TREADWAY INNS COOKBOOK

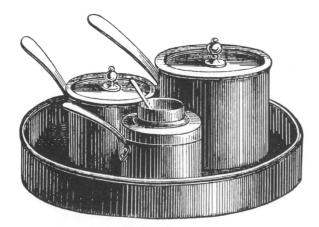

Celery Stuffed with Caviar

To make about 48 pieces

2	celery hearts, ribs separated and trimmed	2
½ lb.	cream cheese	¼ kg.
1 tbsp.	grated onion	15 ml.
⅓ cup	chopped fresh parsley	75 ml.
⅓ cup	red caviar	75 ml.
	salt and pepper	

Mix the cream cheese with the onion and parsley until soft, then gently fold in the caviar. Season with salt and pepper. Stuff the celery ribs with the caviar mixture, cut the ribs into 2-inch [5-cm.] pieces and refrigerate until serving time.

RENÉ VERDON
THE WHITE HOUSE CHEF COOKBOOK

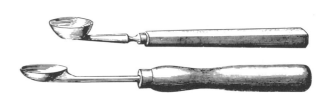

Filled Cucumber Cups

To make about 16 cucumber cups

2	cucumbers, peeled in stripes with a serrated knife	2
1 cup	vinaigrette *(recipe, page 165)*	¼ liter
2 tbsp.	finely chopped fresh parsley	30 ml.
4	slices smoked salmon, finely chopped	4
about ¾ cup	tartar sauce *(recipe, page 166)*	about 175 ml.
	freshly grated horseradish	

Cut the fluted cucumbers—the green skin is corrugated with long white lines—across into 1-inch [2½-cm.] slices. Take out the center of each slice with a large melon baller, leaving enough cucumber at the sides and bottom to make a thin cup. Marinate the cups in vinaigrette for at least one hour, turning them often. Spread the parsley out on wax paper, drain the cucumber cups and dip the top edge of each one into the parsley to make a green border. Bind the chopped salmon with a little tartar sauce and fill the cucumber cups with this mixture. Sprinkle each cup with a few raspings of horseradish and serve the cups very cold with additional tartar sauce.

LILLIAN LANGSETH-CHRISTENSEN
COLD FOODS FOR SUMMER AND WINTER

Stuffed Mushrooms

Champignons Farcis

To make 40 to 50 stuffed mushrooms

1 lb.	very small fresh mushrooms	½ kg.
2 tbsp.	butter	30 ml.
½	garlic clove, mashed to a paste	½
	salt and pepper	
1 tsp.	finely chopped fresh parsley	5 ml.
about 2 tbsp.	dried bread crumbs, seasoned with oregano and parsley	about 30 ml.
	oil	

Remove the mushroom stems from the caps, trim off the root ends and chop the stems. Sauté these briefly in the butter. After two or three minutes, add the garlic, salt and pepper, and the parsley. Cook together for another two minutes, remove from the heat, and mix in enough seasoned bread crumbs to make a light stuffing. Fill the mushroom caps with this, and put them in a well-oiled shallow baking dish. Pour a few drops of oil over each mushroom, and bake them in a preheated 350° F. [180° C.] oven for 10 to 15 minutes until they are barely soft and the stuffing is lightly browned; they must not be overcooked.

NARCISSE CHAMBERLAIN
FRENCH MENUS FOR PARTIES

Viennese Stuffed Mushrooms

If shallots are unavailable, substitute one small onion.

To make 12 to 16 stuffed mushrooms

12 to 16	large fresh mushrooms, 2 to 3 inches [5 to 8 cm.] in diameter, plus ½ lb. [¼ kg.] small fresh mushrooms	12 to 16
6 oz.	cream cheese, softened	175 g.
3 tbsp.	butter	45 ml.
2	large shallots, finely chopped	2
	salt and freshly ground white pepper	
2 tbsp.	finely cut fresh dill	30 ml.
2 tbsp.	freshly grated Parmesan cheese	30 ml.
	parsley sprigs	

Carefully remove the stems from the large mushrooms, chop them fine and set aside. Wipe the mushroom caps carefully with damp paper towels. Set aside. Chop the remaining ½ pound [¼ kg.] of mushrooms fine.

Heat 2 tablespoons [30 ml.] of the butter in a small, heavy skillet. Add the finely chopped mushrooms, the re-served mushroom stems and the shallots, and cook the mixture over high heat until it is lightly browned and all of the liquid has evaporated. Season with salt and pepper.

In a mixing bowl combine the cream cheese, dill and the mushroom mixture. Add the Parmesan, then mash the mixture with a fork until it is well blended. Taste and correct the seasoning; chill for 30 minutes.

Preheat the broiler. Butter a baking dish with the remaining butter. Fill the reserved mushroom caps with the mushroom-and-cream-cheese mixture, then place them under the broiler and cook for three to five minutes, or until lightly browned. Do not overcook. Carefully transfer the mushrooms to a serving platter, garnish with sprigs of parsley and serve immediately.

PERLA MEYERS
THE PEASANT KITCHEN

Cheese-stuffed Mushrooms

This is one of my most successful cocktail goodies. The trick is to use a well-flavored cream cheese, like the herb-and-garlic French Boursin. If necessary, cream cheese can be doctored up with Tabasco, onion juice, a little mashed garlic and whatever herbs one likes. I repeat, the cheese must have plenty of flavor.

To make about 50 stuffed mushrooms

1 lb.	small mushrooms, all of the same size	½ kg.
about ½ cup	fresh lemon juice	about 125 ml.
1	small round Boursin cheese, at room temperature	1

Remove the stems from the mushrooms and dip the mushrooms immediately in the lemon juice, on all sides to prevent darkening. Put the prepared mushrooms on kitchen paper to dry. Save the stems for soup. Fill the cavity of each mushroom with a little of the cheese.

Put the mushrooms in a serving dish, cover with plastic wrap and refrigerate until chilled.

NIKA HAZELTON
THE PICNIC BOOK

Stuffed Cherry Tomatoes

To make 48 stuffed tomatoes

48	cherry tomatoes	48
½ lb.	shrimp, poached in lightly salted water for 4 minutes, drained, shelled and cut into small pieces	¼ kg.
1 tbsp.	finely chopped fresh tarragon	15 ml.
6 tbsp.	finely chopped sour pickles	90 ml.
1 tbsp.	finely chopped shallots	15 ml.
1 tbsp.	finely chopped fresh parsley	15 ml.
1 tbsp.	Dijon mustard	15 ml.
1	garlic clove, finely chopped (optional)	1
1	egg, hard-boiled and finely chopped (optional)	1
2 cups	mayonnaise *(recipe, page 166)*	½ liter
	salt and freshly ground pepper	

Combine the tarragon, pickles, shallots, parsley and mustard with the mayonnaise; add the garlic and hard-boiled egg, if desired. Season to taste with salt and pepper.

Cut the top from each cherry tomato and scoop out the insides with a demitasse spoon, leaving a shell. Fill the tomato shells with the mayonnaise mixture. Garnish each tomato with a piece of shrimp. A very thin slice can be cut off the bottom of any tomato that will not stand up easily.

JUNIOR LEAGUE OF THE CITY OF NEW YORK
NEW YORK ENTERTAINS

Stuffed Radishes

To make 12 stuffed radishes

12	radishes	12
about 4 tbsp.	cream cheese, softened	about 60 ml.
	finely cut fresh chives	
	salt and white pepper	

Select good-sized radishes of a round shape rather than long, and scrub them well but leave a green leaf at the base of each one. Cut a slice from the top and, using a small knife, remove the center. Fill the space with cream cheese highly seasoned with chives, salt and white pepper.

LUCY G. ALLEN
A BOOK OF HORS D'OEUVRE

Eggs

Stuffed Eggs Delmonico

To make 12 stuffed egg halves

6	eggs, hard-boiled	6
½ cup	very finely chopped almonds	125 ml.
2 tsp.	vinegar	10 ml.
⅛ tsp.	dry mustard	½ ml.
½ tsp.	salt	2 ml.
½ tsp.	Worcestershire sauce	2 ml.
⅛ tsp.	Tabasco sauce	½ ml.
2 tbsp.	mayonnaise *(recipe, page 166)*	30 ml.

Cut the eggs in half lengthwise, remove the yolks and put them through a sieve or mash them with a fork. Combine the yolks with the remaining ingredients and blend. Fill the egg-white cavities lightly.

JULIE BENELL
KITCHEN MAGIC

Italian Deviled Eggs

Uova Ripiene

To make 16 stuffed egg halves

8	eggs, hard-boiled	8
3½ oz.	canned tuna, drained and flaked	100 g.
½ cup	chopped pitted ripe olives	125 ml.
¼ cup	capers, rinsed and drained	50 ml.
8	oil-packed flat anchovy fillets, rinsed, patted dry and sliced	8
3 tbsp.	fresh lemon juice	45 ml.
	wine vinegar	
2 to 4 tbsp.	olive oil	30 to 60 ml.
	sliced pimientos	

Slice the eggs in half lengthwise. Scoop out the yolks and place them in a bowl. Reserve the whites. Add to the egg yolks the tuna, olives, parsley, capers and anchovies. Mash and blend thoroughly. Add the lemon juice, a dash of vinegar and enough of the olive oil to make a moist mixture. Combine thoroughly and then stuff the mixture into the egg whites. Garnish each egg with pimiento. Spread the excess stuffing on celery and crackers.

MELANIE MARCUS
COOKING WITH A HARVARD ACCENT

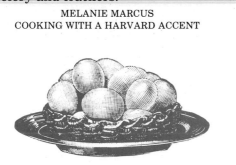

Stuffed Eggs with Curry Flavor

The most important thing is to rice the yolks. Two crushed or mashed egg yolks would fill only about 2 tablespoons [30 ml.], whereas two riced yolks fill more than ⅓ cup [75 ml.]. And even after they have been beaten with butter and mayonnaise, riced yolks still retain a much greater volume than if they had been crushed. Do not salt and pepper the basic yolk mixture until after the other ingredients have been added. When the yolk mixture contains butter, chill the eggs for at least two hours before serving.

To make 16 stuffed egg halves

8	eggs, hard-boiled	8
2 tsp.	curry powder	10 ml.
1 to 2 tbsp.	butter, softened	15 to 30 ml.
4 tbsp.	mayonnaise *(recipe, page 166)*	60 ml.
1½ tsp.	heavy cream, or 2 tbsp. [30 ml.] whipped cream (optional)	7 ml.
	salt and pepper	
1 tsp.	finely chopped onion	5 ml.
16	small cooked shrimp (about ¼ lb. [125 ml.])	16
	fresh dill leaves	

Cut the eggs in half lengthwise, take out the yolks and rice them through a coarse sieve. Stir the curry powder into the soft butter until it is smooth, then whip the butter into the yolks with the mayonnaise, using a fork.

Add the cream, if desired, to make the yolk mixture lighter and smoother. Season the mixture with salt and pepper and add the onion. Pipe the mixture into each egg white through a wide fluted tube, forming a large rosette. Press one shrimp down deep into each rosette and garnish each egg with a little dill pressed down next to one side of the shrimp.

LILLIAN LANGSETH-CHRISTENSEN
COLD FOODS FOR SUMMER AND WINTER

Eggs and Tuna

Uova al Tonno

To make 10 stuffed egg halves

5	eggs, hard-boiled and halved lengthwise	5
3 oz.	canned tuna	100 g.
2 tsp.	capers, rinsed, drained and finely chopped	10 ml.
1 tbsp.	chopped fresh parsley	15 ml.
3 tbsp.	mayonnaise *(recipe, page 166)*	45 ml.
¼ tsp.	salt	1 ml.
	freshly ground pepper	
	fresh parsley leaves or 10 whole capers (optional)	

Remove the yolks from the eggs and put the yolks through a sieve. Put the tuna through the sieve. Put the egg yolks, tuna, capers, parsley, mayonnaise, salt and a little freshly ground pepper into a bowl; mix well.

Fill the egg-white halves to overflowing with this mixture. Decorate each half with a leaf of parsley or one whole caper, if desired.

WILMA PEZZINI
THE TUSCAN COOKBOOK

Deviled Eggs without Mayonnaise

To make 12 stuffed egg halves

6	eggs, hard-boiled	6
¾ cup	chicken stock *(recipe, page 161)*	175 ml.
2 tsp.	unflavored powdered gelatin, softened in 3 tbsp. [45 ml.] cold water	10 ml.
1 tsp.	prepared mustard	5 ml.
1 tsp.	chopped fresh parsley	5 ml.
½ tsp.	salt	2 ml.
½ tsp.	Worcestershire sauce	2 ml.

Cut the eggs in half crosswise, remove the yolks, and cut off the tips from the narrower ends of the egg whites to make straight-standing cups. The broader ends of the eggs usually do not require leveling. Press the yolks through a sieve.

Heat the chicken stock to the boiling point; add the softened gelatin and stir to dissolve it. Reheat the stock a bit if necessary. Add the mustard, parsley, salt and Worcestershire sauce. Chill the mixture until it begins to jell. Beat the mixture lightly, then add the egg yolks. The mixture should now be just right for pressing through a pastry tube. If not, refrigerate it until it is a bit firmer.

Using the pastry tube, fill the egg cups with the mixture.

IRMA RHODE
COOL ENTERTAINING

Stuffed Eggs à la Russe

To make 12 stuffed egg halves

6	eggs, hard-boiled	6
4 to 6 tbsp.	caviar	60 to 90 ml.
2 to 3 tbsp.	mayonnaise *(recipe, page 166)*	30 to 45 ml.
12	tomato slices	12
¼ cup	vinaigrette *(recipe, page 165)*, mixed with 1 tbsp. [15 ml.] chopped fresh parsley	50 ml.
	parsley sprigs	

Cut the hard-boiled eggs into halves and cut a slice off the bottom of each half to make it stand up. Cut out the yolks, fill the egg-white halves with caviar, and cover the tops of the whites with a little mayonnaise, with which the sieved egg yolks have been mixed. Season the tomato slices with the vinaigrette. Serve the eggs on the tomato slices. Dish up and garnish with parsley.

IRENE HIRST (EDITOR)
HORS D'OEUVRES AND SALADS

Totally Stuffed Eggs, Indian-Style

To make 6 stuffed eggs

6	large eggs, hard-boiled	6
1 tbsp.	butter, softened	15 ml.
	salt and pepper	
1 tsp.	finely chopped onion	5 ml.
2 tsp.	finely chopped capers	10 ml.
1 tbsp.	finely chopped pimiento	15 ml.
	lettuce leaves (optional)	
3	large tomatoes, halved and hollowed	3
½ cup	mayonnaise *(recipe, page 166)*, flavored with ½ tsp. [2 ml.] curry powder	125 ml.

While they are still hot, cut the eggs in half lengthwise; keep each pair of halves together. Take out the yolks and mash them with the butter, salt and pepper to taste, onion, capers and pimiento. Shape the paste into yolk-sized rounds and press them into half of the egg whites. Close each egg white with the second half and wrap each reassembled egg tightly in wax paper. Chill them for at least one hour. Remove the wax paper and arrange the eggs on lettuce leaves or in tomato halves and serve them with curry mayonnaise.

LILLIAN LANGSETH-CHRISTENSEN
COLD FOODS FOR SUMMER AND WINTER

Pickled Eggs

Oeufs Vieux-Garçons

Pickled in this fashion, the eggs must be refrigerated after the jar in which they are packed is closed. Their flavor will be spicy after five to six days—and will sharpen over the 30-day maximum suggested by the author.

Here is a curious recipe given by E. Richardin in his book, *L'Art du Bien Manger*. The eggs will be best appreciated by lovers of pickles.

To make 12 pickled eggs

12	eggs	12
1 quart	vinegar	1 liter
1 tbsp.	ground allspice	15 ml.
1 tbsp.	ground ginger	15 ml.
1 tbsp.	black pepper	15 ml.

Boil the eggs for 12 minutes; cool them in cold water and shell them. Bring the vinegar—seasoned with the allspice, ginger and pepper—to a boil, reduce the heat to low and let it cook for 10 minutes. Place the eggs in a jar; pour the boiling vinegar over them. When the vinegar is quite cold, close the jar. These pickled eggs can be kept for a month.

J. BERJANE
FRENCH DISHES FOR ENGLISH TABLES

Tea Eggs

Star anise is a licorice-flavored dried spice that looks like an eight-pointed star about an inch [2½ cm.] across. Five-spice powder is a combination of five ground spices: anise and fennel seeds, cinnamon, cloves, and the hot but lemony Szechwan pepper. Both star anise and five-spice powder are available at Oriental food stores.

To make 12 eggs

12	large eggs, hard-boiled	12
2	whole star anise, or 2 tsp. [10 ml.] five-spice powder	2
2 tbsp.	black tea leaves	30 ml.
1¼ quarts	water	1¼ liters
2 tbsp.	salt	30 ml.

Lightly crack the eggshells with the back of a spoon while the eggs are still warm. (Be sure not to separate the shells from the eggs.) Put the eggs, star anise or five-spice powder, and tea leaves into a 4-quart [4-liter] saucepan. Add the water and salt. Bring the water to a boil, reduce the heat, cover, and simmer for 1½ hours. Remove the eggs from the cooking liquid and refrigerate before serving them.

EVA LEE JEN
CHINESE COOKING IN THE AMERICAN KITCHEN

Red Caviar Roll

Rolling an egg sponge is demonstrated on pages 28-29.

To make a roll about 10 inches [25 cm.] long

4 tbsp.	red caviar	60 ml.
4	eggs, the yolks separated from the whites	4
	olive oil	
9 tbsp.	flour	135 ml.
4 tbsp.	butter	60 ml.
1¼ cups	milk, heated to lukewarm	300 ml.
	salt	
2 tsp.	superfine sugar	10 ml.
	grated nutmeg	
4 to 6 tbsp.	finely cut fresh chives	60 to 90 ml.
	sour cream	

Caviar and cream cheese filling

3 or 4 tbsp.	red caviar	45 or 60 ml.
6 oz.	cream cheese, softened	175 g.
1 or 2 tbsp.	fresh lemon juice	15 or 30 ml.
	freshly ground pepper	
¾ cup	heavy cream	175 ml.

Preheat the oven to 400° F. [200° C.]. Line a 15½-by-10½-inch [39-by-26-cm.] jelly-roll pan with foil; brush the foil with olive oil and dust it with 1 tablespoon [15 ml.] of the flour, shaking out the excess.

To make the roll, first melt the butter in a small saucepan. Add 4 tablespoons [60 ml.] of the flour and cook, stirring over low heat to blend thoroughly. Gradually stir in the hot milk and cook, stirring constantly until the sauce thickens—about two minutes. Bring to a boil and simmer, stirring, for three to four minutes. Pour the sauce into a bowl. Beat in a pinch of salt, the sugar and a pinch of nutmeg. Beat the egg yolks lightly. Beating constantly, pour the yolks into the sauce in a thin stream. Cool to lukewarm.

Beat the egg whites with a pinch of salt until stiff but not dry. Fold one quarter of the whites into the lukewarm sauce. Sift in 2 tablespoons [30 ml.] of flour, followed by a third of the remaining whites. Repeat with the remaining flour and egg whites. Pour the mixture into the prepared pan; level the top with a spatula.

Bake for five minutes, reduce the oven temperature to 300° F. [150° C.] and bake for 50 to 55 minutes, or until the sponge is golden brown and springy. Turn the sponge out onto a damp cloth lined with wax paper. Remove the foil and trim any crusty edges. Starting at one narrow end, roll the sponge loosely with the cloth and wax paper. Cool.

To make the filling, first blend the cream cheese, lemon juice and sour cream together. Season to taste with pepper.

Whip the heavy cream until light and fluffy; fold it into the cream-cheese mixture, followed by the red caviar. Correct the seasoning and chill the mixture until firm.

Unroll the baked sponge; sprinkle it with the chopped chives; spread with the filling and roll it up like a jelly roll. Serve cut into 12 slices, each about ¾ inch [2 cm.] thick. Garnish each portion with a little sour cream and 1 teaspoon [5 ml.] of red caviar.

ROBERT CARRIER
ROBERT CARRIER'S ENTERTAINING

Mushroom Roll

The technique of rolling an egg sponge is shown on pages 28-29. The author suggests that 1 tablespoon [15 ml.] of chopped fresh tarragon, rosemary or parsley may be added to the mushroom mixture.

To make a roll about 10 inches [25 cm.] long

1½ lb.	fresh mushrooms, very finely chopped	¾ kg.
6	eggs, the yolks separated from the whites	6
8 tbsp.	butter, melted	120 ml.
½ tsp.	salt	2 ml.
¼ tsp.	freshly cracked white pepper	1 ml.
2 tbsp.	fresh lemon juice	30 ml.
4 or 5	fluted and sautéed fresh mushrooms	4 or 5
2 tbsp.	chopped fresh parsley	30 ml.
1 lb.	cooked crab meat, broken into small pieces (optional)	½ kg.
1 cup	sour cream (optional)	¼ liter

Brush a jelly-roll pan with vegetable oil, then line it with wax paper, letting the paper extend 4 inches [10 cm.] on each end. Brush the paper with vegetable oil and set aside.

Put the chopped mushrooms in the corner of a tea towel a handful at a time, wring them out to remove excess moisture, and put them in a bowl. Beat the egg yolks until fluffy. Add the yolks, melted butter, salt, pepper and lemon juice to the mushrooms. Beat the egg whites until they form soft peaks and fold them into the mushroom mixture.

Pour the mixture into the prepared pan, spread it evenly, and bake in a preheated 350° F. [180° C.] oven for 15 minutes, or until the sponge starts to pull away from the sides of the pan. Turn the sponge out of the pan onto two overlapping sheets of wax paper and, with the paper to help, roll it up like a jelly roll. Alternatively, spread the surface with a mixture of crab meat and sour cream before rolling up the sponge.

Place the roll on a long narrow platter or board, garnish it with mushroom caps placed down the center, and sprinkle it with parsley.

JULIE DANNENBAUM
JULIE DANNENBAUM'S CREATIVE COOKING SCHOOL

Rolled Spinach Omelet

An alternative filling is the layered combination of flavored, whipped cream cheese and smoked-salmon cream demonstrated on pages 28-29. For the whipped cream cheese (page 13), use ½ pound [¼ kg.] of cheese, ¼ cup [50 ml.] of whipped cream, 2 tablespoons [30 ml.] of sour cream, 2 or 3 tablespoons [30 or 45 ml.] of finely cut fresh dill, 1 crushed garlic clove and pepper to taste. For the salmon cream, grind 1 pound [½ kg.] of smoked salmon through the fine disk of a food grinder or in a food processor, and beat into it ½ cup [125 ml.] of the whipped cream cheese.

	To make a roll about 10 inches [25 cm.] long	
1 lb.	spinach, parboiled for 3 minutes, drained, squeezed dry and chopped	½ kg.
6 tbsp.	butter	90 ml.
½ cup	flour	125 ml.
2 cups	milk	½ liter
	salt and pepper	
5	eggs, the yolks separated from the whites	5
2 tbsp.	freshly grated Parmesan cheese	30 ml.
4	shallots, finely chopped	4
1 cup	chopped fresh mushrooms	¼ liter
4	slices boiled ham, finely diced	4
1 tbsp.	Dijon mustard	15 ml.
¼ tsp.	grated nutmeg	1 ml.
6 oz.	cream cheese, softened	175 g.
1 cup	sour cream	¼ liter
3 or 4 tbsp.	cream	45 or 60 ml.

Preheat the oven to 400° F. [200° C.]. Butter a jelly-roll pan. Line the bottom of the pan with wax or parchment paper, butter the paper and dust it lightly with flour.

To make the omelet, first melt 4 tablespoons [60 ml.] of the butter in a saucepan, blend in the flour and cook until foamy. Slowly stir in the milk, then add ½ teaspoon [2 ml.] of salt and a large pinch of pepper. Cook for one minute. Beat the egg yolks in a small mixing bowl, then, continuing to beat them, add a little of the hot sauce. Add the heated yolks to the sauce in the pan and cook the mixture over medium heat for one minute longer, stirring constantly. Do not allow it to boil. Scrape the sauce into a large mixing bowl and set it aside to cool. Stir the sauce occasionally while it is cooling.

Beat the egg whites until stiff and gently fold them into the sauce. Pour the omelet mixture into the prepared jelly-roll pan and spread it to form an even layer. Sprinkle the omelet with Parmesan cheese. Bake for 20 to 30 minutes, or until the omelet is well puffed and brown.

Meanwhile, prepare the filling in a skillet: First melt the remaining butter, then add the shallots and sauté them for

two minutes. Next, add the mushrooms to the skillet and cook over medium heat until they give up their moisture, about four minutes. Add the spinach, ham, mustard and nutmeg to the skillet. Then stir in the cream cheese and season to taste with salt and pepper. Set the skillet aside.

When the omelet is done, turn it immediately onto a clean towel. Spread the top with the spinach filling. Then, with the aid of the towel, roll the omelet into a long cylinder. Slide the omelet onto a serving platter, seam side down. Serve it hot or cold, sliced and accompanied by a sauceboat of sour cream thinned with cream.

THE GREAT COOKS' GUIDE TO OMELETS FROM AROUND THE WORLD

Stuffed Bread Cases and Loaves

Toast Ramekins with Curried Shrimp Filling

To make 12 shrimp-filled bread cases

12	slices firm-textured white bread, cut no more than ¼ inch [6 mm.] thick	12
2 to 3 tbsp.	butter, melted	30 to 45 ml.
	Curried shrimp filling	
6	medium-sized shrimp (about ¼ lb. [125 g.])	6
	salt	
2 tbsp.	butter	30 ml.
2 tbsp.	finely chopped onion	30 ml.
1½ tsp.	curry powder	7 ml.
2 tbsp.	flour	30 ml.
¾ cup	light cream	175 ml.
	dried thyme	

To make the bread more flexible and less porous, roll a rolling pin backward and forward once over each slice. Use a 3-inch [8-cm.] cookie cutter to cut each slice into a round. Brush melted butter over one side of each round. Press the round, buttered side down, into the cup of a muffin tin with 4-ounce [125-ml.] cups to form a shell ½ inch [1 cm.] deep that will hold about 1 tablespoon [15 ml.] of filling. Mold the bottom and sides of the round to the shape of the cup. Flatten the top edge into a neat rim.

Bake on the middle shelf of a preheated 425° F. [220° C.] oven for 12 minutes, or until the rims are lightly browned.

When the ramekins are cool enough to handle, invert them onto paper towels to drain off any excess butter.

To make the filling, first place the shrimp in a small saucepan and add cold water to cover. Over medium heat, bring the water to a simmer. Cook uncovered for four to six minutes, or until the shrimp turn pink and are firm to the touch. Immediately drain them under cold running water to stop their cooking; keep them under the running water until they are cool. Shell and devein the shrimp. With a sharp knife, cut them lengthwise into halves, then cut them across into slices about ⅛ inch [3 mm.] thick. Sprinkle the shrimp bits lightly with salt, toss thoroughly and set aside. Preheat the oven to 450° F. [230° C.].

Melt the butter in a small, heavy saucepan over low heat. When the butter is hot, add the onion. Increase the heat to medium and cook the onion for two or three minutes, or until transparent. Stirring with a wooden spoon, add the curry powder. Cook for one minute more and remove from the heat. Add the flour, stirring it in with a wire whisk until all of the ingredients are blended. Still stirring, return the pan to medium heat. Stir for two minutes.

Off the heat, whisk constantly while gradually adding the cream, then a pinch of thyme and ½ teaspoon [2 ml.] of salt. Continuing to beat, return the pan to high heat and bring the sauce to a boil. Immediately reduce the heat to low; no longer beating, let the sauce simmer for four minutes. Remove it from the heat. Place a strainer over a small bowl; using the back of a wooden spoon, push the sauce through. Stir the shrimp into the sauce.

To fill and bake the ramekins: Fill each ramekin with 1 tablespoon of the shrimp mixture, mounding it slightly. Arrange the ramekins on a small, ungreased baking sheet. Bake on the middle shelf of the oven for five minutes. With a metal spatula, transfer the ramekins from the baking sheet to a platter. Serve hot.

JOHN CLANCY & FRANCES FIELD
CLANCY'S OVEN COOKERY

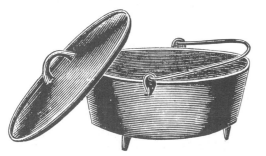

Shrimp Toast à la Rothschild

Toast de Crevettes à la Rothschild

The crème fraîche called for in this recipe may be available at French food markets. If not, make it from the heavy —but not ultrapasteurized —cream usually sold in health-food stores. Add about 1½ teaspoons [7 ml.] of buttermilk to 1 cup [¼ liter] of cream. Stirring, heat to 85° F. [30° C.]. Pour the mixture into a crock, cover, and let it rest in a warm place for six to eight hours, or until it thickens. Refrigerate it until you are ready to use it.

To make 4 filled bread cases

1 lb.	small raw shrimp, the shells removed and reserved	½ kg.
4	slices firm-textured white bread, cut about 1½ inches [4 cm.] thick, and hollowed out to make cases ½ inch [1 cm.] thick	4
4 tbsp.	peanut oil	60 ml.
8 tbsp.	butter	120 ml.
2 tbsp.	finely chopped shallots	30 ml.
1	medium-sized onion, finely chopped	1
1	carrot, finely chopped	1
1 tbsp.	tomato paste	15 ml.
½ cup	dry white wine	125 ml.
¾ cup	fish fumet *(recipe, page 162)*	175 ml.
1	bouquet garni	1
	salt and freshly ground black pepper	
2 tbsp.	*crème fraîche,* or heavy cream	30 ml.
2 tbsp.	Cognac	30 ml.
¼ cup	shredded Swiss cheese	50 ml.
4	thin slices of truffle	4

Sauté the bread cases in 3 tablespoons [45 ml.] each of the oil and butter until they are crisp and golden brown. Drain these croustades on paper towels and place in a baking dish.

Crush the shrimp shells in a mortar with a pestle until they are almost a paste, or blend them in a blender.

Heat the rest of the oil and one more tablespoon [15 ml.] of the butter in a saucepan and cook the shallots, onion and carrot in it until they are golden brown. Add the paste made of the shrimp shells, mix well, and cook over low heat for about three minutes. Add the tomato paste, wine, fish fumet and the bouquet garni. Cover, and simmer over low heat for 20 minutes. Strain the sauce into another saucepan, return it to the stove, and reduce over high heat to about ¾ cup [175 ml.]. Season to taste with salt and pepper.

Cook the shrimp in 3 tablespoons of the remaining butter for four or five minutes (or less if they are tiny), transfer them to the sauce and simmer for another minute, stirring constantly with a wooden spoon. Take out the shrimp with a slotted spoon and place them in the toast shells.

Stir the *crème fraîche* or heavy cream and the Cognac into the reduced sauce and bring to a final boil. Remove from the heat and stir in the remaining butter, cut into pieces.

Spoon some of the sauce over the shrimp into each croustade, sprinkle with some of the shredded cheese and place a truffle slice on top of each. Brown quickly under the broiler.

RAYMOND OLIVER
LA CUISINE

Sardine Bread Cases

If anchovy essence (pure puréed anchovies with oil) is un-available, substitute 1 teaspoon [5 ml.] anchovy paste.

	To make 10 bread cases	
3 or 4	large slices stale white bread	3 or 4
about 6 tbsp.	butter	about 90 ml.
3¾ oz.	canned sardines, drained, skinned and boned	125 g.
1 tbsp.	white sauce or tomato sauce (recipes, page 167)	15 ml.
	anchovy essence (optional)	
	fresh lemon juice	
2 tsp.	freshly grated Parmesan cheese, or 1 tbsp. [15 ml.] grated Cheddar cheese	10 ml.
	watercress sprigs	

Stamp out of the bread slices eight to 10 rounds or ovals, each about 2 inches [5 cm.] in diameter. With a smaller cutter, make a second circle or oval about ⅓ inch [1 cm.] deep and ⅓ inch inside the edge of each round. Fry these croustades in hot butter until lightly browned—about two or three minutes. Drain the croustades, then with the point of a small knife lift out the inner rings and remove any moist crumbs. If wished, place the croustades in a 350° F. [180° C.] oven for a few minutes to crisp the insides. Cool before using.

Mash the sardines and mix in the white sauce or tomato sauce; if using white sauce, add a few drops of anchovy essence. Season, then blend with a few drops of lemon juice and the cheese. Put this sardine filling into the crisp croustades and garnish them with watercress.

IRENE HIRST (EDITOR)
HORS D'OEUVRES & SALADS

Fried Bread "Cushions"

Cuscinetti di Pandorato

	To make 6 bread cases	
1	large unsliced loaf sandwich bread	1
1 lb.	mozzarella cheese, thinly sliced	½ kg.
5 oz.	thinly sliced prosciutto, or 6 oil-packed flat anchovy fillets, rinsed, patted dry and chopped	175 g.
½ cup	flour	125 ml.
1 cup	milk	¼ liter
3	eggs, beaten with a little salt	3
	lard or oil for deep frying	

Slice the loaf into six thick slices, trim off the crusts, and with a sharp knife slit each slice through the middle without cutting it completely through, like a cushion cover. Stuff each slice with slices of cheese and the ham or anchovies. Flour each "cushion" lightly, dip it quickly into the milk and arrange it in a deep dish. Pour the beaten eggs over the top. Leave until the eggs are completely absorbed by the bread.

Heat plenty of lard or oil and deep fry the cushions, two at a time, until golden brown on both sides. Drain on paper towels. Keep hot in a warm oven until all of the cushions are fried. Serve hot.

ADA BONI
ITALIAN REGIONAL COOKING

Meat-filled Bread Cases

Mince Croustades Savoury

	To make 6 filled bread cases	
2	slices bacon	2
3	pork sausages	3
1	loaf stale bread	1
3 tbsp.	tomato sauce (recipe, page 167)	45 ml.
6	fresh button mushrooms, coarsely chopped	6
½ tsp.	finely chopped fresh parsley	2 ml.
	milk	
1	egg	1
	bread crumbs	
	butter or lard	
	salt and pepper	
	parsley sprigs	

Place the bacon in a frying pan and fry until rather crisp; remove it. Prick the sausages and fry them in the bacon fat.

When cool, mince both into small dice, first removing the skins of the sausages. Put the mince and the sauce, mushrooms and parsley in a stewpan, season to taste and reheat.

To make the croustades, cut six 1-inch [2½-cm.] slices from a stale loaf, stamp out round or oval shapes and scoop out the centers, forming hollows to hold the meat mince. Now dip the cases in milk, let them become moistened without being sodden, then coat them with egg and bread crumbs, and fry in ½ inch [1 cm.] butter or lard until nicely browned. Have the mince ready, fill the cases, garnish with parsley sprigs deep fried for a minute or so, and serve.

MRS. BEETON
MRS. BEETON'S HORS D'OEUVRE AND SAVOURIES

Mushrooms in Toast Shells

Champignons en Croustade

The technique of hollowing rolls to make toast shells is demonstrated on page 53.

To make 6 filled toast shells

½ lb.	fresh mushrooms, finely sliced	¼ kg.
12 tbsp.	unsalted sweet butter	180 ml.
2 tbsp.	chopped shallots	30 ml.
1 tbsp.	chopped garlic	15 ml.
1 tsp.	salt	5 ml.
¼ tsp.	cayenne pepper	1 ml.
3 or 4 tbsp.	fresh lemon juice	45 or 60 ml.
1 cup	heavy cream	¼ liter
½ cup	finely chopped smoked beef tongue	125 ml.
2	egg yolks, beaten	2
1 tsp.	Worcestershire sauce	5 ml.
6	soft, round rolls	6

To make the croustades, melt 6 tablespoons [90 ml.] of the butter. Cut off the top of each roll and remove the soft inside crumbs with a sharp knife, leaving just the shell. With a pastry brush, paint the inside and outside of the rolls with the melted butter. Put the rolls into a preheated 450° F. [230° C.] oven until brown and crisp—about five minutes.

Melt the remaining butter in a saucepan. Add the shallots and simmer for five minutes; do not brown. Add the garlic and mushrooms, cover the pan and simmer for three minutes. Stir in the salt, pepper, lemon juice, cream and beef tongue. Simmer for two minutes. Beat a little of this sauce

mixture into the egg yolks so that the yolks will not curdle. Then blend the egg-yolk mixture into the sauce. Add the Worcestershire sauce. Check the seasoning. Mix well. Spoon the sauce mixture into the croustades. Bake the croustades in a preheated 450° F. [230° C.] oven for five minutes, or until the tops are browned.

ANTOINE GILLY AND JACK DENTON SCOTT
ANTOINE GILLY'S FEAST OF FRANCE

Miniature Stuffed Rolls

Canapés da Napoli

To make 36 rolls

1 cup	finely chopped mozzarella cheese (¼ lb. [125 g.])	¼ liter
¼ cup	finely chopped fresh parsley	50 ml.
1 cup	finely chopped prosciutto or boiled ham (¼ lb. [125 g.])	¼ liter
¼ tsp.	freshly ground black pepper	1 ml.
¼ tsp.	grated nutmeg	1 ml.
¼ tsp.	oregano	1 ml.
36	miniature rolls	36
	butter	

In a bowl combine the cheese, parsley, prosciutto or boiled ham, pepper, nutmeg and oregano.

Cut the tops from the miniature rolls; scoop out the bread from the centers, then butter the insides. Spoon 1 tablespoon [15 ml.] of filling into each roll and replace the tops. Wrap the rolls in foil and heat them in a 350° F. [180° C.] oven until the cheese melts—five to 10 minutes. Serve hot.

NANCY FAIR MCINTYRE
COOKING IN CRUST

Stuffed Salmon Rolls

To make 6 stuffed rolls

½ lb.	fresh salmon, poached in lightly salted water for 10 minutes, drained, skinned and boned, and puréed through a sieve	¼ kg.
3 to 4 tbsp.	mayonnaise *(recipe, page 166)*, or stiffly whipped heavy cream flavored with a drop each of Worcestershire sauce and tarragon vinegar	45 to 60 ml.
1	small sour gherkin, finely chopped	1
	salt and pepper	
	butter, softened	
6	soft rolls or scones	6
	lettuce, shredded	

Mix the salmon with a little mayonnaise or the whipped-cream mixture. Add the gherkin and salt and pepper.

Cut off the tops of the rolls or scones, remove the soft insides and butter the shells sparingly. Fill the shells with the salmon mixture, place a little shredded lettuce over it and replace the tops after buttering the bottoms lightly.

LADY JEKYLL, D. B. E.
KITCHEN ESSAYS

Vegetable-stuffed Loaf

Patafla

Always make *patafla* the day before it is needed.

To make 1 large stuffed loaf

4	tomatoes	4
¼ cup	ripe olives	50 ml.
⅓ cup	green olives	75 ml.
2	green peppers	2
1	large onion	1
¼ cup	capers	50 ml.
¼ cup	chopped sour gherkins	50 ml.
	olive oil	
	paprika	
	salt and black pepper	
1	large loaf French bread	1

Peel the tomatoes, pit the olives, take the cores and seeds out of the peppers, and chop them together with all the other ingredients. Cut the loaf in half lengthwise and, with a sharp knife, remove all the crumb, which you mix with the tomato preparation, kneading it all together with a little olive oil, a pinch of paprika, black pepper and salt.

Now fill the two halves of the loaf with the mixture, press them together and put the loaf into the refrigerator.

To serve, cut into slices about ¼ inch [6 mm.] thick, and pile them up on a plate.

ELIZABETH DAVID
A BOOK OF MEDITERRANEAN FOOD

Stuffed Bread

To make 1 long stuffed loaf

1	long loaf French or Italian bread	1
1 lb.	cream cheese, softened	½ kg.
¼ cup	beer	50 ml.
1 tbsp.	dry mustard	15 ml.
¼ cup	chopped fresh watercress	50 ml.
¼ cup	finely chopped onion	50 ml.
¼ cup	finely chopped radish	50 ml.
½ lb.	liver sausage, diced	¼ kg.

Preheat the oven to 350° F. [180° C.]. Slice off the ends of the loaf of bread and discard them. Cut the remaining loaf into three long pieces. Scoop or cut out the doughy center of the bread, leaving crust shells about ¼ inch [6 mm.] thick. Crumble the bread cut from the shells and toast these crumbs on a baking sheet for 15 minutes, or until browned.

Beat the cream cheese with a wooden spoon until it is smooth and soft. Mix the beer and mustard and stir them into the cheese. Add the watercress, onion and radish and mix well. Add the liver sausage and mix lightly. Stir in the crumbs. Pack this stuffing into the bread shells by standing each shell on end and pressing the stuffing in with the spoon.

Wrap each stuffed bread shell in foil and refrigerate for at least four hours, or until the stuffing is firm. To serve, unwrap and cut each chunk into the thinnest possible slices.

ELEANOR GRAVES
GREAT DINNERS FROM LIFE

Pastries

Roquefort-and-Walnut Tarts

Tartelettes au Roquefort

The author suggests that the tarts also may be served without baking the filling. In this case, the egg yolk should be omitted from the Roquefort-cheese mixture. The technique of baking tart shells is demonstrated on pages 66-67.

To make four 3- to 4-inch [8- to 10-cm.] tarts

3½ oz.	Roquefort cheese (about 1 cup [¼ liter])	100 g.
¼ cup	finely chopped walnuts, plus 4 walnut halves	50 ml.
	Cognac	
1	egg yolk	1
1 to 2 tbsp.	cream	15 to 30 ml.
4	baked short-crust pastry tart shells (recipe, page 164)	4
	fresh parsley sprigs	

Rub the Roquefort through a sieve. Blend the Roquefort with the chopped walnuts, a dash of Cognac, the egg yolk and enough cream to form a soft, smooth mixture. Fill the tart shells with the cheese mixture and bake them in a preheated 375° F. [190° C.] oven for 30 minutes, or until they are golden. Garnish the tarts with the walnut halves and parsley.

NANCY EEKHOF-STORK
THE GREAT INTERNATIONAL CHEESE BOARD

Swiss After-Ski Tarts

To make 24 tarts

½ lb.	Swiss cheese, grated (about 2 cups [½ liter])	¼ kg.
¼ cup	grated onion	50 ml.
2 tbsp.	butter	30 ml.
3	eggs, beaten	3
2 cups	heavy cream	½ liter
¼ tsp.	dry mustard	1 ml.
1 tsp.	salt	5 ml.
⅛ tsp.	cayenne pepper	½ ml.
	short-crust pastry (recipe, page 164, but double the quantities called for)	

Sauté the onion in the butter for five minutes. Mix the onion with the cheese. In a bowl, stir together the eggs, cream, mustard, salt and cayenne pepper. Combine the egg mixture with the cheese and onion. Roll out the short-crust pastry ⅛ inch [1 mm.] thick on a floured board. Cut 24 rounds of dough to fit 2-inch [5-cm.] tartlet tins: Press the dough into the tins and pour in the cheese filling. Bake the tarts in a preheated 400° F. [200° C.] oven for 20 minutes, or until they are puffy and golden brown.

NANCY FAIR MCINTYRE
COOKING IN CRUST

Scrambled Eggs

Oeufs Brouillés

To make 1 cup [¼ liter] filling for tart shells

4	eggs	4
	salt and pepper	
6 tbsp.	unsalted butter	90 ml.

To make scrambled eggs properly, it is essential to mix the egg whites and yolks absolutely homogeneously so that they are creamy and have no lumps. This can be done in the following way:

First break the eggs into a bowl, season with salt and pepper, and beat moderately as you would for an omelet. In a saucepan, not too large but big enough for the quantity of eggs used, melt 1 tablespoon [15 ml.] of butter for each egg; add the eggs and cook slowly, stirring continuously with a wooden spoon. It is best to do this in a bain-marie (a saucepan set in a large pan of simmering water). When the eggs are cooked, they should have the consistency of cream; remove from the heat and add, while stirring, 1 tablespoon of butter for every two eggs.

PAUL BOCUSE
PAUL BOCUSE'S FRENCH COOKING

Herb Pasty

To make 4 pasties

1 cup	fresh parsley sprigs	¼ liter
1 cup	fresh watercress leaves	¼ liter
2½ lb.	spinach	1¼ kg.
4	shallots or 1 leek, finely chopped	4
1 or 2	thick slices bacon, finely chopped	1 or 2
	short-crust pastry (recipe, page 164, but double the quantities called for)	
1	egg, beaten	1

Chop and scald a quantity of well-washed parsley, watercress and spinach for one minute. Drain; press out the excess liquid, and chop the mixture fine. Add the shallots or leek and the chopped bacon.

Divide the pastry dough into four pieces. Roll out the pieces and place the vegetable mixture on the rounds of pastry, fold the rounds in half, crimp each pasty except at one point and pour into this a small amount of beaten egg. Seal the pasties and bake in a preheated 450° F. [230° C.] oven until the pastry is pale brown, about 10 minutes. Then reduce the heat to 350° F. [180° C.] for about 40 minutes.

ANN PASCOE
CORNISH RECIPES OLD AND NEW

Potato Pies

The technique of covering potato pies is demonstrated on pages 62-63, and requires twice the quantity of pastry called for in this recipe. To prepare duxelles, simmer ¼ cup [50 ml.] finely chopped shallots or onions in butter until soft; add ½ lb. [¼ kg.] finely chopped mushrooms and cook over medium heat, stirring, until the mushroom liquid evaporates. Season with salt, pepper, tarragon, and Madeira or port.

To make twelve 3-inch [8-cm.] pies

2	large Idaho potatoes, peeled	2
3	large truffles, grated, or 1 cup [¼ liter] *duxelles* or finely cut fresh chives	3
1 cup	heavy cream	¼ liter
	salt and pepper	
	chives (optional)	
	short-crust pastry *(recipe, page 164)*	

Roll out the pastry and fit it into the cups of a 12-cup muffin pan. Parboil the whole potatoes for eight minutes. Grate the potatoes; they will be slightly gummy. Fill each pastry-lined tin half-full with potatoes. Add grated truffles or *duxelles* and top with more grated potato. Fill each pastry with seasoned heavy cream. If you use chives, mix them with the cream. Bake on the lowest rack of a preheated 400° F. [200° C.] oven for five minutes. Then move the muffin pan to the upper middle rack of the oven, and continue baking at 325° F. [160° C.] until the tops of the pies are golden.

MADELEINE KAMMAN
THE MAKING OF A COOK

Meat Patties

To make about 36 patties

¼ lb.	lean beef	125 g.
¼ lb.	lean pork	125 g.
1	slice bacon	1
1	piece fresh hot chili	1
1	onion	1
	thyme and marjoram sprigs	
1 tbsp.	butter	15 ml.
2 tbsp.	flour	30 ml.
½ cup	meat stock *(recipe, page 161)*	125 ml.
½ tsp.	Worcestershire sauce	2 ml.
	short-crust pastry *(recipe, page 164, but triple the quantities called for)*	

Cut the beef and pork into pieces and boil them in lightly salted water until the meat is soft—about 20 to 30 minutes.

Cool the meat and chop it fine with the bacon, chili, onion and herbs. Make a binding sauce by melting the butter in a saucepan, adding the flour gradually, then adding the stock slowly until it is smooth. Add this to the meat mixture and stir in the Worcestershire sauce, making a soft paste.

Cut the rolled dough into 2-inch [5-cm.] rounds with a pastry cutter and place a teaspoon [5 ml.] of the meat mixture on each round. Dampen the edges of each round and cover it with another round of dough. Press the edges together with a fork. With a skewer, make a hole in the top center of each patty; brush the top with beaten egg. Bake the patties on a greased baking sheet in a preheated 450° F. [230° C.] oven for about 15 to 20 minutes, or until very light brown.

RITA G. SPRINGER
CARIBBEAN COOKBOOK

English Cornish Pasties

To make 6 pasties

1 lb.	beef round steak, finely diced	½ kg.
1 cup	finely diced raw potatoes	¼ liter
1 cup	finely chopped onions	¼ liter
½ tsp.	thyme	2 ml.
1 tsp.	salt	5 ml.
¼ tsp.	ground black pepper	1 ml.
	short-crust pastry (recipe, page 164, but double the quantities called for)	
6 tbsp.	butter	90 ml.
6 tbsp.	finely chopped fresh parsley	90 ml.
1	egg yolk, beaten with 1 tbsp. [15 ml.] water	1
½ cup	heavy cream	125 ml.

In a bowl, combine the diced beef and potatoes with the onions. Season with the thyme, salt and pepper.

Roll the pastry ⅛ inch [3 mm.] thick and cut it into 5-inch [13-cm.] rounds.

Spoon 3 tablespoons [45 ml.] of the filling onto one side of each round. Dot with 1 tablespoon [15 ml.] of the butter and sprinkle with 1 tablespoon of the parsley. Moisten the edges of the pastry and fold them over into turnovers. Crimp the dough together with a fork. Prick the tops of the turnovers, and brush them with the diluted egg yolk.

Bake in a preheated 325° F. [160° C.] oven for one hour: 15 minutes before the pasties are done, make a small hole in the top of the crusts and spoon 2 tablespoons [30 ml.] of heavy cream into the holes. (If the crusts brown too quickly during baking, cover the turnovers with foil.)

NANCY FAIR MCINTYRE
COOKING IN CRUST

Lancashire Foot

A Lancashire Foot is similar to a very thick pasty, but was elliptical in shape to fit into the oval tins that miners once used to carry their snappin or snap (snack) down the pit. The name foot was given because of the shape and because the miner's wife or mother would usually make a pair. Apparently the plural was not feet, but foots! The pastry was rolled into a long oval and cut lengthways into two, then the rolling pin was placed halfway along the length and the pastry was just rolled from the center to the further edge. This gave the foot shape, with the heel nearer to the cook and the sole widening out at the top edge. It was a simple but effective way of keeping the base crust thick, and the upper one thin but also larger to cover the filling.

To make 2 pastries

	short-crust pastry (recipe, page 164, but double the quantities called for)	
¾ lb.	lean beef, cut into small pieces	⅓ kg.
2 or 3	medium-sized potatoes, peeled and diced	2 or 3
1	large onion, thinly sliced	1
	salt and pepper	

Make the short-crust pastry. Combine the meat, potatoes and onion, and season to taste. Cook this mixture with a little water in a 350° F. [180° C.] oven until the meat is tender—about one hour. Cool the mixture. When cold, use it to fill the pastry. Bake the foots in a preheated 375° F. [190° C.] oven until brown, about 40 minutes.

JOAN POULSON
OLD LANCASHIRE RECIPES

Creamed Sweetbreads

To make about 8 cups [2 liters] filling for tart shells

4	pairs calf's sweetbreads	4
3 tbsp.	butter	45 ml.
4 tsp.	grated onion	20 ml.
1 tbsp.	flour	15 ml.
2 cups	light cream	½ liter
12	small fresh mushrooms, sliced	12
	salt and pepper	
	paprika	

Soak the sweetbreads in cold water for one hour. Parboil them in fresh water for five minutes, then drain and let them cool. Remove the membranes and cut the sweetbreads into small pieces. Put the butter in a frying pan and heat it until hot and bubbly. Add the sweetbreads and the grated onion. Fry until the sweetbreads are slightly brown, stirring fre-

quently. Sprinkle the flour over the mixture and stir to blend it in. Then add the cream and mushrooms, mixing thoroughly. Cook over low heat for about 10 minutes. Season with salt and pepper to taste. Dust with paprika. Serve over hot toast or in heated patty shells.

NORMA JEAN AND CAROLE DARDEN
SPOONBREAD AND STRAWBERRY WINE

Sausage in Pastry

To make about twenty ½-inch [1-cm.] slices

1	garlic-flavored poaching sausage, 8 to 10 inches [20 to 25 cm.] long and 2 to 2½ inches [5 to 6 cm.] in diameter	1
	short-crust pastry (recipe, page 164)	
	water	
3 tbsp.	Dijon mustard	45 ml.
1	egg, beaten with 1 tbsp. [15 ml.] milk or cream	1

Butter a small baking sheet and set it aside. With the tip of a sharp knife, prick the skin of the sausage in eight to 10 places, and put it into a 3- to 4-quart [3- to 4-liter] pot with water to cover. Bring the water to a boil over high heat. Reduce the heat and simmer the sausage, partially covered, for 45 minutes. Drain the sausage and set it aside. When the sausage is cool enough to handle, skin it with a small knife.

Place the pastry on a lightly floured surface, dust the top with flour, and roll out the pastry into an oval 6 by 12 inches [15 by 20 cm.] and ⅛ inch [3 mm.] thick.

Spread the mustard over the sausage. Place the sausage on the long edge of the pastry nearest you. Roll up the sausage in the pastry, making one complete turn to enclose it. Trim off all but 1 inch [2½ cm.] of the length of the pastry.

With a pastry brush dipped in water, dampen the 1-inch strip of pastry extending beyond the sausage. Fold the dampened strip back onto the pastry, enclosing the sausage, and press it down. Roll the sausage over the seam to make it adhere better. Turn the sausage so the seam faces you. Trim only the rough edges of the side flaps, fold them inward and press the edges firmly toward the seam. Turn the sausage seam side down on the baking sheet; press the flaps again.

To decorate the top of the sausage, roll out the excess pastry and cut out decorative shapes with a cookie cutter. Dampen the underside of each shape with water and press it onto the pastry. Leave the sausage on the baking sheet, and refrigerate it for 15 minutes.

Just before baking, paint a film of the egg mixture on top of the pastry. Place the pastry on the middle shelf of the oven and bake it in a preheated 375° F. [190° C.] oven for 45 minutes, or until the pastry is golden brown. Transfer the sausage to a warm serving dish. Serve it hot, cut into slices ¼ to ½ inch [6 mm. to 1 cm.] thick, with additional mustard.

JOHN CLANCY & FRANCES FIELD
CLANCY'S OVEN COOKERY

Coney Island Filling

*To make enough filling for 26 to 28
2-inch [5-cm.] turnovers*

3	slices lean bacon	3
½ lb.	sauerkraut, washed under cold running water and squeezed dry	¼ kg.
½ cup	finely chopped onion	125 ml.
½ cup	chicken stock *(recipe, page 161)*	125 ml.
3	all-beef frankfurters, cut into ¼-inch [6-mm.] dice	3
1	egg, hard-boiled and chopped	1
2 tbsp.	chopped fresh dill, or 1 tsp. [5 ml.] dried dillweed	30 ml.
¼ tsp.	salt	1 ml.
¼ tsp.	freshly ground black pepper	1 ml.
1 tbsp.	prepared mustard	15 ml.

Cook the bacon over medium heat and place it on paper towels to drain. Measure 4 teaspoons [20 ml.] of the bacon fat into an 8- to 10-inch [20- to 25-cm.] skillet and set over medium heat. When the fat is hot, add the onion and cook until it is transparent. Remove from the heat. Using a wooden spoon, stir in the sauerkraut.

Return the pan to medium heat and add the chicken stock all at once. Flatten the sauerkraut-onion mixture into the broth with a wooden spoon. Reduce the heat to low, cover the pan and cook for 15 minutes.

Remove the cover and turn the heat to high; stirring constantly to prevent scorching, reduce the liquid in the pan until the sauerkraut is dry. Check for residual liquid by tilting the pan and pressing the sauerkraut with a wooden spoon; if liquid flows out, continue to cook until the mixture sticks just slightly to the pan. Remove from the heat. Immediately transfer the sauerkraut to a bowl, stir in the diced frankfurters and set aside.

Chop the bacon into fine pieces and add them to the sauerkraut. Add the chopped egg and dill. Taste for salt. Add the freshly ground pepper and the mustard; with a wooden spoon mix until all of the ingredients are well blended. Taste once more for seasoning, and let cool to room temperature.

JOHN CLANCY & FRANCES FIELD
CLANCY'S OVEN COOKERY

Creamed Shellfish

Skaldjursstuvningar

*To make about 4 cups [1 liter] filling
for tart shells*

½ lb.	cooked lobster or crab meat or cooked and shelled mussels or shrimp, cut into small pieces (about 2 cups [½ liter])	¼ kg.
1½ tbsp.	butter	22 ml.
2 tbsp.	flour	30 ml.
1½ cups	cream or milk	375 ml.
	salt and pepper	
	finely cut fresh dill (optional)	

Make a roux with the butter and flour. Stir in the cream or milk and cook this sauce for three to five minutes, until it is smooth and thickens lightly. Stir in the lobster, crab, mussels or shrimp, and heat through. Season to taste.

J. AUDREY ELLISON
THE GREAT SCANDINAVIAN COOK BOOK

Oysters Ritz Bar

To make 24 small turnovers

24	small live oysters, shucked	24
2 tbsp.	wine vinegar	30 ml.
6 tbsp.	light olive oil	90 ml.
¼ tsp.	salt	1 ml.
⅛ tsp.	ground black pepper	½ ml.
¼ tsp.	dry mustard	1 ml.
1 tbsp.	finely chopped fresh parsley	15 ml.
½ lb.	short-crust pastry *(recipe, page 164)*	¼ kg.

Drain the oysters. In a bowl combine the vinegar, oil, salt, pepper, mustard and parsley. Mix well. Marinate the oysters in this French dressing for three hours in the refrigerator. Drain the oysters and dry them on paper towels.

Roll out the pastry dough on a lightly floured board to a thickness of ⅛ inch [3 mm.]. Cut the dough into rounds 2½ inches [6 cm.] across. Place an oyster on each round. Moisten the edges, fold the dough over the oyster and seal the edges together with a fork. Arrange the turnovers on a baking sheet and cut a small vent in each one.

Bake the turnovers in a preheated 450° F. [230° C.] oven for 15 minutes, or until the pastry is golden.

NANCY FAIR MCINTYRE
COOKING IN CRUST

Shrimp Curry Puffs

Chia Li Chiao

To make about 60 puffs

1 lb.	small shelled raw shrimp	½ kg.
1 cup	finely chopped onions	¼ liter
3 tbsp.	lard	45 ml.
2 tsp.	imported Madras curry powder	10 ml.
1 tbsp.	salt	15 ml.
1 tsp.	sugar	5 ml.
½ cup	mashed potato (about 1 medium-sized potato)	125 ml.
	short-crust pastry (recipe, page 164, but substitute shortening or lard for the butter and double the quantities called for)	
2 to 3	eggs, beaten	2 to 3

Cover the shrimp with water and bring it just to the boiling point. Drain, then grind or chop the shrimp fine. Set them in a mixing bowl. Stir fry the onion with the lard until it wilts, add the curry powder and stir them together for one minute. Pour the onion mixture onto the shrimp and add salt, sugar and mashed potato. Mix and stir thoroughly. Let the mixture cool, then put it in the refrigerator to chill for one hour.

Divide the pastry dough into two balls. Roll out one ball at a time on a lightly floured surface into a sheet about 1⁄16 inch [1 mm.] thick. Using a cookie cutter, cut out circles about 3 inches [8 cm.] in diameter. Knead the scraps into the remaining dough to make more circles. Place about one heaping teaspoon of the shrimp filling in the center of each round, fold over the dough into a half-moon shape and seal the edges tightly, making a scalloped edge. Place the puffs on ungreased baking sheets and prick each puff with a fork. Brush the tops with the beaten egg. Bake the puffs in a preheated 400° F. [200° C.] oven for about 20 minutes, or until they turn golden brown.

FLORENCE LIN
FLORENCE LIN'S CHINESE REGIONAL COOKBOOK

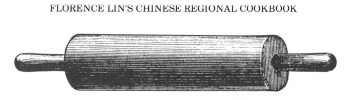

Spinach Cheese Puffs

Spanakopitas

The technique of folding phyllo pastry into triangles is demonstrated on pages 68-69.

To make rolls instead of triangles, cut the sheets of phyllo pastry into quarters crosswise. Brush each quarter sheet as you use it with warm melted butter. Place 1 teaspoon [5 ml.] of filling 1 inch [2½ cm.] from the bottom edge of the sheet, fold the bottom up over the filling, then fold the sides in toward the middle. Brush with warm melted butter and roll the sheet loose. Brush each roll with warm melted butter as you place it, seam side down, in a baking pan.

To make about 80 triangles

2 lb.	spinach	1 kg.
1 lb.	feta cheese	½ kg.
12 oz.	pot cheese or pot-style cottage cheese (about 1½ cups [375 ml.])	⅓ kg.
6 tbsp.	olive oil	90 ml.
6	scallions, including the green tops, finely chopped	6
½ cup	finely chopped fresh parsley	125 ml.
⅛ tsp.	white pepper	½ ml.
1 tsp.	dill	5 ml.
6	eggs, beaten	6
16 tbsp.	unsalted butter (½ lb. [¼ kg.])	240 ml.
1 lb.	phyllo-pastry leaves, at room temperature	½ kg.

Drain and chop the spinach. Heat the oil and sauté the scallions until soft and wilted. Add the spinach and simmer until all of its moisture evaporates. Rinse the feta under cold water, drain, and crumble it into a bowl. Blend in the pot or cottage cheese, parsley, pepper and dill. Add the beaten eggs and mix well. Add the spinach and scallions and mix well.

Melt the butter in a small saucepan over very low heat. Do not let it brown. Set it aside. Gently unfold the phyllo sheets and cut them into thirds lengthwise, using scissors and cutting through the entire stack at one time. Wrap two thirds of the sheets in plastic wrap or wax paper to prevent them from drying out, and refrigerate them until needed. Drape another piece of wrap over the remaining third. Remove one phyllo sheet at a time, lay it on the counter and, with a pastry brush, coat it lightly with melted butter. Fold the two long sides toward the middle, making a strip about 2 inches [5 cm.] wide and 11 inches [28 cm.] long. Brush the strip with melted butter again. Place a teaspoon [5 ml.] of the spinach mixture at the bottom left corner of the strip. Pick up the corner with the filling and fold it over so that the bottom edge meets the adjacent side edge and forms a right-angle triangle. Continue folding over from side to side into neat triangles until you reach the end of the strip. Brush the finished triangle with butter and place it on an ungreased baking sheet. Repeat for each sheet of phyllo. Do not let the triangles touch; they will puff up quite a bit during baking.

Bake in a preheated 425° F. [220° C.] oven for 12 to 14 minutes, or until plump, crisp and golden. Do not turn the triangles over while baking. Arrange the *spanakopitas* on an attractive plate and serve.

ANNE THEOHAROUS
COOKING AND BAKING THE GREEK WAY

Brain and Egg Turnovers

Briks Bil Mohk

The technique of frying these turnovers is shown on page 69.

The author suggests two other pastry fillings: The first alternative is to fill each turnover with 2 tablespoons [30 ml.] of ground beef cooked with a little onion and parsley and seasoned with salt and pepper. Mix in 1 tablespoon [15 ml.] of grated Parmesan cheese and a few drops of lemon juice, and use a sliced hard-boiled egg instead of a raw one. The second alternative is to use six anchovy fillets mixed with 1 tablespoon of chopped onion, cooked in butter and 1 tablespoon of grated Parmesan cheese for each turnover; season with freshly ground black pepper and top with a raw egg.

	To make 4 turnovers	
¾ lb.	lamb's, calf's or beef brains	⅓ kg.
	salt and freshly ground black pepper	
	vinegar	
2 tbsp.	unsalted butter	30 ml.
¼ cup	finely chopped onion	50 ml.
1 tbsp.	finely chopped parsley	15 ml.
1 tbsp.	freshly grated Parmesan cheese	15 ml.
2	phyllo-pastry leaves or 4 Chinese spring-roll skins	2
4	eggs	4
1	egg white, lightly beaten	1
	oil for deep frying	
	lemon quarters	

Soak the brains for 30 minutes in several changes of water. Remove the membranes, then rinse the brains and drain them. In a 2-quart [2-liter] saucepan bring 1½ quarts [1½ liters] of seasoned and acidulated water to a simmer. Slip in the brains, cover, and cook over low heat for 20 minutes. Drain, cool and dice the brains.

Melt the butter in the saucepan and cook the onion over low heat until soft but not browned. Add the brains, parsley, and salt and pepper to taste. Cook gently for 10 minutes, stirring often. Stir in the cheese. Mix and mash, then separate this filling mixture into four equal portions.

Spread out the phyllo leaves and cut them in half crosswise. (Leave spring-roll skins whole.) Fold each of the phyllo leaves in half crosswise and place one portion of the filling 2 inches [5 cm.] away from one corner. Flatten the center of the filling slightly to make a hollow. Break an egg into the hollow. Fold over the pastry to cover the egg; dab the edges with the egg white and press the edges so that they adhere. Then fold each rim over ½ inch [1 cm.] for a secure closing, being careful not to break the egg inside. Repeat with the three remaining phyllo leaves. (If you are using spring-roll skins, fold in the left and right sides in order to make a square, then proceed as directed above.)

Pour oil to a depth of 1 inch [2½ cm.] into a large deep skillet. Heat the oil until hot but not smoking (about 350° F. [180° C.]), then slide in one *brik*. Lightly push it down into the oil, then press one corner in order to make the *brik* swell. When the *brik* is golden brown on both sides (after about two minutes), transfer it to paper towels to drain. Repeat with the three remaining *briks*. Serve hot with lemon quarters.

PAULA WOLFERT
MEDITERRANEAN COOKING

Cheese Pastry Ring

La Gougère

The technique of making gougère is shown on pages 70-71.

With the exception of the delicious cheese of Époisses, in upper Burgundy, there is no notable Burgundian cheese, but the Burgundians are great cheese eaters for the obvious reason that cheese is one of the best accompaniments for wine. *Gougère*, a kind of cheese pastry made with *choux* paste similar to that used for éclairs, is the great cheese dish of the country. It is rather tricky to make, so if it doesn't come right the first time one just has to persevere.

	To make one 8-inch [20-cm.] ring	
¾ cup	finely diced Gruyère cheese (3 oz. [100 g.])	175 ml.
1¼ cups	milk	300 ml.
1 tsp.	salt	5 ml.
	freshly ground pepper	
4 tbsp.	butter, cut into small pieces	60 ml.
1 cup	flour, sifted	¼ liter
4	eggs	4
	salt and pepper	

The paste is made as follows: Bring the milk to a boil and then let it get quite cold. Strain it. Put in the butter, the salt and a little pepper, and bring rapidly to a boil so that the butter and milk amalgamate. Pour in, all at once, the sifted flour. Stir until a thick, smooth paste is obtained; it will come away clean from the sides and bottom of the pan.

Off the heat stir in the eggs one at a time, each egg to be thoroughly incorporated before the next is added. When the paste is shiny and smooth add the cheese, cut into very small dice, reserving about a tablespoon [15 ml.] of the little cubes. Leave to cool a little.

Lightly butter a baking sheet. Take tablespoons of the mixture and arrange them, like so many half-eggs, in a circle about 7 inches [18 cm.] across, the space in the middle being about 2½ inches [6 cm.]. When you have made one circle, put the remaining spoonfuls on top of the first, so that you have quite a high wall round the central well. Pat into an even shape with a palette knife.

Place the little pieces of reserved cheese on top and all around. Brush with milk. Cook in a preheated 375° F. [190° C.] oven for about 45 minutes.

Although the *gougère* begins to smell cooked after the first 20 minutes, do not be taken in; it will have swelled up and turned golden brown, but it is not ready. If you can resist, do not open the oven, because of the risk of the mixture's collapsing. If you feel you have to look, open and shut the door of the oven very gently. To test when the *gougère* is done, press lightly with a finger in the center of the cake; it should be firm to the touch. If it is too soft, it will fall the instant you take it from the oven into a sad, flat pancake.

If you are going to serve the *gougère* hot, transfer it for five minutes to a warm place before transferring it to the serving dish or, if you cook by gas, turn the oven off and leave it five more minutes. If to be served cold, ease the cake off the baking sheet onto a wire cake rack so that there is air all round it, but keep it away from sudden drafts.

ELIZABETH DAVID
FRENCH PROVINCIAL COOKING

Chicken and Mushroom Filling for Cold Choux Puffs

If the mushrooms do not supply enough moisture to bind the ingredients, add 1 to 2 tablespoons [15 to 30 ml.] of mayonnaise (recipe, page 166).

To make about 1 ½ cups [375 ml.] filling

1 cup	finely chopped cooked chicken	¼ liter
½ cup	finely chopped fresh mushrooms, sautéed in butter for about 5 minutes and cooled	125 ml.
¼ cup	chopped blanched almonds	50 ml.
	grated nutmeg	
	salt and white pepper	

Combine the chicken, mushrooms and almonds. Add a pinch of nutmeg, and salt and white pepper to taste. Refrigerate until ready to serve.

CORALIE CASTLE AND BARBARA LAWRENCE
HORS D'OEUVRE ETC.

Small Puffs Filled with Curried Tuna Paté

To make about 36 puffs

36	small *choux* puffs, baked and cooled (recipe, page 163)	36
2 tsp.	curry powder	10 ml.
7 oz.	canned oil-packed tuna, coarsely shredded, with its juices	200 g.
½ cup	coarsely chopped onion	125 ml.
about 2 tsp.	strained fresh lemon juice	about 10 ml.
3 to 4 tbsp.	vegetable oil	45 to 60 ml.
8 tbsp.	butter, softened	120 ml.
	salt	

Empty the tuna and all of its juices into the jar of an electric blender. Add the onions, lemon juice and 3 tablespoons [45 ml.] of the vegetable oil. Cover and blend at high speed for about a minute. Then turn off the blender, scrape down the sides of the jar with a rubber spatula, re-cover it and resume blending at high speed for a few seconds, or until the purée is smooth. (If at any point the blender clogs, stop the machine and add the remaining vegetable oil, then resume blending.)

In a mixing bowl, beat the butter with a wooden spoon until it is creamy. Beat in the curry powder and ½ teaspoon [2 ml.] of salt. Then, spoonful by spoonful, beat in the tuna purée. When the mixture is smooth, taste for seasoning and add more salt and lemon juice if needed. Cover the bowl with plastic wrap and refrigerate the mixture for about two hours, or until it is about the consistency of cream cheese.

Cut the *choux* puffs in half horizontally and use a small spoon to scrape out any moist paste inside. Fill the bottom of each shell with a teaspoon [5 ml.] or more of the paté and set the upper halves in place, allowing a little filling to show.

These puffs are best if served at once. If they must wait, cover them with plastic wrap and refrigerate them for up to six hours. Before serving them, remove the puffs from the refrigerator and let them rest at room temperature for about 10 minutes. This will allow the paté to soften a bit to the velvety consistency it should have.

MICHAEL FIELD
COOKING ADVENTURES WITH MICHAEL FIELD

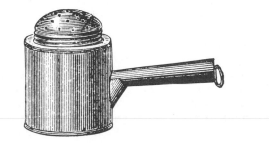

Egg Rolls with Pork Stuffing

To make 20 egg rolls

1 lb.	ground pork	½ kg.
2 tbsp.	vegetable oil	30 ml.
1 to 1¼ lb.	Chinese cabbage, cut into thin shreds, mixed with ⅔ tsp. [3 ml.] salt and left to drain for 15 minutes	½ to ⅔ kg.
4	scallions, cut into thin strips 2 inches [5 cm.] long	4
1 tsp.	finely chopped fresh ginger root, or ½ tsp. [2 ml.] ground ginger	5 ml.
½ cup	bamboo-shoot strips	125 ml.
4 or 5	large dried Chinese mushrooms, soaked in warm water for 30 minutes, drained, the tough stems discarded and the caps cut into strips	4 or 5
3 to 4 tsp.	salt	15 to 20 ml.
½ tsp.	black pepper	2 ml.
1½ tbsp.	soy sauce	22 ml.
½ tsp.	sesame-seed oil	2 ml.
2 tbsp.	cornstarch	30 ml.
20	egg-roll wrappers	20
2 tbsp.	cornstarch, dissolved in ½ cup [125 ml.] water	30 ml.
	oil for deep frying	

Heat a deep pan until very hot. Add the 2 tablespoons [30 ml.] of oil. Heat for a few seconds. Stir in the pork and cook until the meat changes color (about two minutes). Remove the pan from the heat and cool the pork to room temperature.

Squeeze the cabbage dry. Add the cabbage, scallions, ginger, bamboo shoots, mushrooms, salt, pepper, soy sauce, sesame-seed oil and the 2 tablespoons [30 ml.] of cornstarch to the pork. Mix well.

Place one twentieth of the stuffing slightly off the center of each egg-roll wrapper. Roll up the wrapper to enclose the filling. Tuck in the sides neatly. Brush the open edge with the cornstarch-water mixture. Fold and seal. Place each completed egg roll on a platter, sealed edge down.

Heat 1¼ inches [3 cm.] of oil to 400° F. [200° C.] (or until a bread cube browns quickly). Deep fry the egg rolls (sealed side down first) for one and one half to two minutes on each side, or until golden. Drain on paper towels. Serve hot.

EVA LEE JEN
CHINESE COOKING IN THE AMERICAN KITCHEN

Chicken-and-Vegetable Egg Rolls

Packaged egg-roll and spring-roll wrappers, obtainable at Chinese food stores, often may be too stiff to manipulate easily. Before filling them, rub a few drops of water into the surface of each wrapper until it is pliable. After forming each roll, place it seam side down in a covered dish to prevent it from drying out before it is fried; do not allow the filled rolls to touch, lest they stick.

To make 12 to 15 rolls

½ lb.	chicken meat, cooked or uncooked, cut into thin shreds (about ¾ cup [175 ml.] shreds)	¼ kg.
3	Chinese dried mushrooms, soaked in warm water for 30 minutes, stems removed and caps shredded	3
2½ tbsp.	thinly shredded bamboo shoots	37 ml.
½ cup	bean sprouts, blanched in boiling water for 5 seconds and drained	125 ml.
2	scallions, chopped	2
2 tbsp.	vegetable oil	30 ml.
¾ tsp.	salt	4 ml.
3¾ tsp.	soy sauce	19 ml.
1¼ tsp.	sugar	6 ml.
1¼ tsp.	cornstarch	6 ml.
1	egg, beaten	1
12 to 15	egg-roll or spring-roll wrappers	12 to 15
	oil for deep frying	

Heat the 2 tablespoons [30 ml.] of oil in a frying pan. Add the chicken, bamboo shoots and scallions. Stir fry over high heat for one minute; then add the mushrooms and bean sprouts. Stir fry for a further minute. Add all of the other ingredients except the egg, wrappers and remaining oil, and continue to stir fry for one minute. Remove the mixture from the pan and put it in a colander to cool and drain.

Place about 2 tablespoons [30 ml.] of the cooled filling just below the center of an egg-roll or spring-roll wrapper, spreading it crosswise. Fold the edge nearest to you over the filling, then turn in the edges of the two sides. Roll up the filling in the wrapper. Seal the seam with the beaten egg.

Place the filled rolls, four or five at a time, in a wire basket and lower them into oil heated to a temperature of 375° F. [190° C.]. Deep fry for about five minutes, or until they are crisp and brown. Alternatively, egg rolls and spring rolls can be pan fried, just like sausages, in shallow oil, by turning them to fry them on all sides.

KENNETH LO
THE ENCYCLOPEDIA OF CHINESE COOKING

Wheat Starch Dumpling Wrappers

Wheat and tapioca starch are obtainable in Chinese grocery stores. The techniques of rolling and shaping the dough are demonstrated on pages 76-77.

To make 36 to 48 dumpling wrappers

1 cup	wheat starch	¼ liter
⅔ cup	tapioca starch	150 ml.
½ tsp.	salt	2 ml.
2 tsp.	oil	10 ml.
1 cup plus 2 tbsp.	water	280 ml.

In a bowl, mix together the wheat starch, tapioca starch, salt and oil. Bring the water to a rolling boil and immediately pour it into the bowl. Working quickly, use chopsticks or a fork to stir the water into the dry ingredients until the dough coheres. It will have a chalky white appearance.

Cover the bowl and let the dough cool for 15 minutes. Lightly oil the work surface and knead the dough for several minutes, until it is smooth. The dough can be used at once or kept for up to 24 hours if it is tightly covered with plastic wrap and stored at room temperature.

RHODA YEE
DIM SUM

Flour-and-Water Dumpling Wrappers

The techniques of filling and shaping Chinese dumpling wrappers are demonstrated on pages 74-75.

To make about 36 dumpling wrappers

2 cups	flour	½ liter
¾ to 1 cup	boiling water	175 to 250 ml.

Place the flour in a mixing bowl. Make a well in the flour and gradually add the boiling water while stirring with a chop-

stick or fork. Turn the dough out onto a lightly floured board and knead it for five minutes, or until the dough is smooth. Cover the dough with a damp cloth and let it rest for at least 30 minutes. Knead the dough a second time for about three minutes, or until the dough becomes quite elastic.

To make the dumpling wrappers, first divide the dough in half. Put half of the dough under a damp cloth to keep it from drying out. Take the other half of the dough and shape it into a long cylinder. Pinch off enough dough from one end to make a 3-inch [8-cm.] circle. Flour the board if necessary to keep the dough from sticking. Repeat until the dough is used up and you have about 36 wrappers. If your filling is not ready, keep the prepared wrappers covered with a damp cloth until you fill them.

CALVIN B. T. LEE AND AUDREY EVANS LEE
THE GOURMET CHINESE REGIONAL COOKBOOK

Shrimp-and-Bamboo-Shoot Filling

Recipes for dumpling wrappers appear at left. The techniques of filling, shaping and steaming dumplings are demonstrated on pages 76-77.

To make enough filling for about 48 dumplings

1 lb.	raw shrimp, shelled, deveined and finely chopped	½ kg.
1 cup	finely chopped bamboo shoots	¼ liter
2 tbsp.	cornstarch	30 ml.
1 tbsp.	light soy sauce	15 ml.
1 tbsp.	rice wine or dry sherry	15 ml.
½ tsp.	salt	2 ml.
½ tsp.	sesame-seed oil	2 ml.
	peanut oil	

Combine the filling ingredients and let the mixture stand for 20 minutes to blend the flavors. Fill and shape the dumplings, and steam them above boiling water for 15 minutes. Remove the dumplings from the heat and brush them with a little peanut oil to keep the skins from drying out and to give them a shiny appearance. Serve hot.

MARGARET GIN AND ALFRED E. CASTLE
REGIONAL COOKING OF CHINA

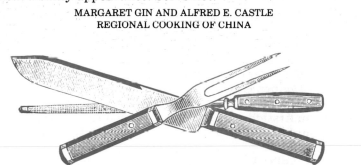

Steamed Dumplings

The techniques for making steamed dumplings are demonstrated on pages 76-77.

To make 30 dumplings

½ lb.	cooked crab meat, the cartilage removed and the meat flaked	¼ kg.
1 lb.	lean ground pork	½ kg.
1	medium-sized onion, finely chopped	1
1 tbsp.	dry sherry, or Chinese rice wine	15 ml.
1 tbsp.	soy sauce	15 ml.
1 tsp.	salt	5 ml.
¼ tsp.	sugar	1 ml.
1 tbsp.	sesame-seed oil	15 ml.
1 tbsp.	cornstarch	15 ml.
1	hard-boiled egg yolk, crumbled	1
1 tbsp.	chopped boiled spinach	15 ml.
1 tbsp.	chopped boiled ham	15 ml.

Flour and boiling-water wrappers

1½ cups	sifted flour	375 ml.
¾ cup	boiling water	175 ml.
1 tbsp.	cornstarch	15 ml.

To prepare the filling, mix together the crab meat, pork, onion, wine, soy sauce, salt, sugar, sesame-seed oil and cornstarch, and let the mixture stand in a bowl while you are preparing the wrappers.

To make the wrappers, first mix the flour with the boiling water, using chopsticks briskly until the dough is cool enough to handle. Knead it well, cover it with a damp cloth and let the dough stand for 20 minutes. Roll the dough into a long sausage form and cut it into 30 pieces. Flatten each piece with the palm of your hand. Sprinkle cornstarch on the edges and use a rolling pin to roll each piece into a thin pancake 3½ inches [9 cm.] in diameter. Place an appropriate amount of filling (about 1½ tablespoons [22 ml.]) on the center of each pancake and wrap, leaving the edges free. Place a pinch of egg yolk, green spinach and ham as garnish on the mouth of the wrapping. Lay a cheesecloth in a steamer tray, or brush the steamer tray with oil, and place the dumplings on it, slightly separated. Steam them for 15 minutes and serve immediately with hot mustard or a mixture of soy sauce and vinegar.

NANCY CHIH MA
COOK CHINESE

Fried Pork Dumplings

Recipes for dumpling wrappers appear on page 143. The techniques of filling and shaping Chinese dumplings are demonstrated on pages 74-75. The filled dumplings—made with either wrapper—may alternatively be boiled in 1½ quarts [1½ liters] of water or stock for about 10 minutes. If wheat-starch wrappers are used, the dumplings may instead be steamed for 20 minutes.

To make about 36 dumplings

¾ lb.	ground lean pork	⅓ kg.
½ cup	finely chopped bamboo shoots	125 ml.
½ cup	finely diced celery cabbage	125 ml.
1½ tbsp.	dark soy sauce	22 ml.
½ tsp.	sugar	2 ml.
1 tbsp.	dry sherry	15 ml.
¾ tsp.	salt	4 ml.
1 tbsp.	sesame-seed oil	15 ml.
2 tsp.	cornstarch	10 ml.
2 tbsp.	chicken stock *(recipe, page 161)*	30 ml.
	wheat-starch or flour-and-water wrappers	
2 tbsp.	peanut oil	30 ml.
¾ cup	water	175 ml.

Mix together the pork, bamboo shoots, cabbage, soy sauce, sugar, sherry, salt, sesame-seed oil, cornstarch and stock, and use the mixture to fill the wrappers, shaping the dumplings as desired.

To pan fry the dumplings, heat a skillet over medium-high heat. Add the peanut oil. When the oil is moderately hot, arrange the dumplings in the skillet. Cook until they are golden brown on the bottom, about two to three minutes. Pour in the water around the edge of the skillet and cover. Cook the dumplings over high heat for about five minutes, until most of the water has boiled away. Turn the heat to low and cook for about seven minutes. Then return the heat to high if all of the water has not evaporated. Transfer the dumplings to a plate and serve them with dipping sauce.

CALVIN B. T. LEE AND AUDREY EVANS LEE
THE GOURMET CHINESE REGIONAL COOKBOOK

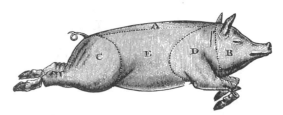

Steamed Beef Dumplings

Recipes for dumpling wrappers and dipping sauce appear on page 143 and below. The techniques of filling, shaping and steaming dumplings are demonstrated on pages 76-77.

	To make about 24 dumplings	
½ lb.	lean ground beef	¼ kg.
1 tsp.	finely chopped fresh ginger root	5 ml.
1 tbsp.	soy sauce	15 ml.
1 tbsp.	dry sherry	15 ml.
4	water chestnuts, finely chopped	4
1	scallion, including the green top, finely chopped	1
2	dried Chinese mushrooms, soaked in warm water for 30 minutes, drained, the tough stems discarded and the caps finely chopped	2
½ tsp.	sugar	2 ml.
24	wheat-starch or flour-and-water dough wrappers	24
	lettuce leaves (optional)	

Mix together the beef, ginger, soy sauce, sherry, water chestnuts, scallion, mushrooms and sugar. Using this mixture, fill the wrappers and shape the dumplings. Place the dumplings on a steamer tray lined, if desired, with lettuce leaves. Steam the dumplings for 20 minutes. Serve the dumplings with a dipping sauce or hot mustard.

JOANNE HUSH AND PETER WONG
CHINESE MENU COOKBOOK

Dipping Sauce for Chinese Dumplings

	To make about 1 cup [¼ liter] sauce	
⅓ cup	soy sauce	75 ml.
⅓ cup	rice vinegar	75 ml.
2 or 3	slices fresh ginger root, finely chopped (optional)	2 or 3
2 or 3	garlic cloves, finely chopped	2 or 3
2 tsp.	sesame-seed oil	10 ml.
1 tsp.	chili oil	5 ml.
½ tsp.	sugar	2 ml.

Combine all of the ingredients and let the mixture stand for 10 minutes to blend the flavors.

MARGARET GIN AND ALFRED E. CASTLE
REGIONAL COOKING OF CHINA

Roquefort Puffs

	To make about 28 puffs	
¾ cup	firmly packed Roquefort cheese (3 oz. [100 g.]), softened	175 ml.
¼ cup	firmly packed cream cheese, softened	50 ml.
1	egg, beaten	1
	Sour-cream pastry	
¾ cup	flour	175 ml.
½ cup	butter	125 ml.
¼ cup	sour cream	50 ml.

Place the flour and butter in a medium-sized mixing bowl; cut in the butter until the particles are tiny. Stir in the sour cream until thoroughly blended. Turn out the soft dough onto a piece of plastic wrap. With a small spatula shape the dough into a rectangle, then wrap it and chill overnight.

Cut the chilled dough into thirds. Work with one third at a time, keeping the remaining dough in the refrigerator. Place scraps left after rolling in the freezer for quick chilling before rerolling them.

Beat the Roquefort and cream cheeses together. On a well-floured pastry cloth, with a floured stockinet-covered rolling pin, roll out the dough to a thickness of 1/16 inch [1½ mm.]. Using a 2-inch [5-cm.] round cookie cutter, cut out the dough. With a small metal spatula, place half of the rounds of dough about 1 inch [2½ cm.] apart on a large baking sheet. Put one level teaspoon [5 ml.] of the Roquefort mixture in the center of each round.

Using a finger or pastry brush, spread beaten egg around the edges of the filled rounds. Cover the filled rounds with plain rounds of dough. Slip the dull edge of a 1½-inch [4-cm.] round cookie cutter (or use a glass about that size) over the puffs and press to seal; seal again with the floured tines of a fork. (If the puffs are not well sealed, the filling will ooze out of them during baking.) Refrigerate the puffs on the baking sheet while you roll, cut and fill the remaining refrigerated portions of dough.

Bake in a preheated 350° F. [180° C.] oven until lightly browned—20 to 25 minutes. Drain the puffs on paper toweling. Cut off any filling that oozes out of the puffs. Transfer the puffs immediately to a serving plate and serve hot.

CECILY BROWNSTONE
CECILY BROWNSTONE'S ASSOCIATED PRESS COOK BOOK

Hot Cheese Crackers

Sajtos Iselitö

To make 30 cracker sandwiches

2 cups	grated Swiss cheese (½ lb. [¼ kg.])	½ liter
¾ cup	flour	175 ml.
16 tbsp.	butter (½ lb. [¼ kg.])	240 ml.
3 tbsp.	sour cream	45 ml.
½ tsp.	paprika	2 ml.
	salt	

Mix the flour and half of the butter until the mixture forms crumbs. Add half of the cheese, 2 tablespoons [30 ml.] of the sour cream, the paprika and a little salt. Knead the dough well, then let it rest in the refrigerator for about two hours.

Stretch the dough into a sheet ¼ inch [6 mm.] thick. Cut the sheet into rounds with a small cookie cutter. Bake in a preheated 350° F. [180° C.] oven for 12 to 15 minutes.

Mix the remaining butter, cheese and sour cream, and spread a ¼-inch layer of the mixture on the cooled crackers. Place a second cracker on top, making little sandwiches.

GEORGE LANG
THE CUISINE OF HUNGARY

Sesame-Seed Corn Crackers

If the crackers are not crisp after cooling, put them back in the oven for a few minutes.

To make about 20 to 30

½ cup plus 1 tbsp.	boiling water	140 ml.
½ cup	cornmeal	125 ml.
2 tbsp.	butter, melted	30 ml.
	salt	
¼ cup	sesame seeds	50 ml.

Add the boiling water gradually to the cornmeal. Add the melted butter and ½ teaspoon [2 ml.] of salt. To make sure the batter is the right consistency, place one teaspoonful on a baking sheet. The batter should keep its round shape and spread to make a cracker about 2 inches [5 cm.] in diameter. If the batter spreads more than this, add an extra teaspoon [5 ml.] of cornmeal.

Drop the batter by teaspoonfuls onto buttered nonstick baking sheets, spacing the rounds 2 to 3 inches [5 to 8 cm.] apart. Sprinkle the top generously with sesame seeds and additional salt, using approximately ⅓ teaspoon [1½ ml.] of sesame seeds for each cracker.

Bake in a preheated 425° F. [220° C.] oven for eight to 12 minutes. The crackers should be brown around the edges and beginning to harden in the center. Remove the crackers from the sheets at once. The crackers will get crisper as they cool. Store in an airtight container.

JANET KAPLAN
CRACKERS AND SNACKERS

Herbed Cocktail Wafers

To make about 36 cocktail wafers

1½ cups	flour	375 ml.
½ tsp.	salt	2 ml.
6 tbsp. plus 2 tsp.	unsalted butter, 6 tbsp. [90 ml.] chilled and cut into small bits and 2 tsp. [10 ml.] softened	100 ml.
6 tbsp.	cream cheese (3 oz. [100 g.])	90 ml.
2 tbsp.	finely cut fresh chives	30 ml.
2 tbsp.	finely chopped fresh chervil, or 1 tsp. [5 ml.] dried chervil	30 ml.
1 tbsp.	finely chopped fresh tarragon, or 1 tsp. [5 ml.] dried tarragon	15 ml.
1	egg	1
2 tbsp.	cream or milk	30 ml.
	coarse salt	

Place the flour in a medium-sized bowl. Scatter the salt over the flour. Add the chilled butter bits and the cream cheese. With your hands, combine the ingredients by kneading them until thoroughly blended. Shape the pastry into a ball. Wrap it, and refrigerate for one hour before using.

Lightly grease a 14-by-16-inch [35-by-40-cm.] baking sheet with the softened butter and set aside.

Remove the chilled pastry from the refrigerator, unwrap and place it in a bowl. Add the chives, chervil and tarragon. With your hands, combine the ingredients until they are thoroughly blended and can be shaped into a ball.

Place the pastry on a lightly floured surface. With the flat of your hand, press it into a thick cake. Shape it into a round, and dust it lightly with flour. Lightly flour your rolling pin. Roll the pastry from the center outward, ending each stroke just short of the edge. From time to time, lift the edge and turn the pastry clockwise. Continue rolling out the pastry, turning it clockwise, until it is ⅛ inch [3 mm.] thick.

With a 2- to 2½-inch [5- to 6-cm.] cookie cutter, press out circles of the pastry as close together as you can. Distribute the cutout wafers evenly on the baking sheet.

Place the baking sheet in the refrigerator and chill the wafers for 20 minutes. Just before baking the wafers, beat the egg and cream or milk together well. With a pastry brush, paint a film of the mixture on top of each wafer, then sprinkle each one generously with coarse salt.

Place the baking sheet on the middle shelf of an oven preheated to 375° F. [190° C.] and bake the wafers for 10 minutes. Remove them from the oven. Transfer the wafers from the baking sheet to a wire rack with a metal spatula. Let them cool to room temperature before serving.

JOHN CLANCY & FRANCES FIELD
CLANCY'S OVEN COOKERY

Cheddar Pennies

Variations on this theme are legion. Before baking, brush the pennies with slightly beaten egg, and sprinkle them with chopped nuts or with sesame, poppy, caraway or dill seeds. Or mix a little oregano or some chili powder in when you knead. Or roll the dough into a cylinder, then chill, slice and bake at once.

To make about 24 rounds

2 cups	grated aged Cheddar cheese (about ½ lb. [¼ kg.])	½ liter
8 tbsp.	butter	120 ml.
½ tsp.	salt	2 ml.
	cayenne pepper	
1¼ cups	flour	300 ml.

Combine the cheese with the butter, salt, a dash of cayenne and the flour. Work all together with your hands, and chill for at least two hours. Roll the mixture about ¼ inch [6 mm.] thick, cut it in 1¼-inch [3-cm.] rounds, arrange the rounds on baking sheets and chill again. Bake at 350° F. [180° C.] for 10 minutes, or until a pale, pale gold.

HELEN EVANS BROWN
A BOOK OF APPETIZERS

Liver Knishes

To make about 48 small knishes

1 lb.	beef liver	½ kg.
4	eggs, at room temperature	4
5 to 8 tbsp.	rendered chicken fat	75 to 120 ml.
1	medium-sized onion, roughly chopped	1
	salt and pepper	

Shortening pastry

⅔ cup	shortening	150 ml.
2 cups	flour	½ liter
about ⅓ cup	cold water	about 75 ml.

Broil the beef liver until well done (about seven to 10 minutes). Rare liver will not do.

Bring to a boil enough water to cover the eggs. Add the eggs and simmer them for 10 minutes. Plunge the eggs into cold water. Remove the shells.

Heat 2 tablespoons [30 ml.] of the chicken fat in a skillet and sauté the onion until golden brown. In a meat grinder, not a blender, grind together the liver, eggs and onions. Grind the mixture twice, first through the medium disk, then through the fine. Put the liver filling in a bowl and mix in enough chicken fat to reach the desired smoothness. It is hard to use too much chicken fat. Three tablespoons [45 ml.] is the minimum. Add salt and pepper to taste. Refrigerate the filling until chilled—about two hours.

To prepare the pastry dough, first cut the shortening into the flour with two knives or a pastry blender until the dough has the consistency of cornmeal. Add the water one tablespoon [15 ml.] at a time, mixing it in with a wooden spoon, until the dough can be pressed into a ball. Chill for a minimum of one hour.

Preheat the oven to 375° F. [190° C.]. On a lightly floured board or marble, roll out the dough into a rectangle slightly larger than 16 by 12 inches [40 by 30 cm.]. Cut the rectangle into four strips, each 4 by 12 inches [10 by 30 cm.]. Spread about ¾ cup [175 ml.] of the liver filling evenly down the center of each strip. There will probably be some filling left over. If you think you can accommodate it and still seal the strips into tubes, add this excess. Otherwise, reserve the filling for another snack.

To roll the strips into tubes, flour your fingers and pull one side of the strip over the other. Moisten the edges and press them gently together until sealed. Seal the ends. Make a series of crosswise cuts an inch [2½ cm.] or so apart and halfway through each tube along the entire length of each tube to facilitate serving. Set the tubes on a baking sheet greased with shortening and bake them for 45 minutes, or until golden brown.

RAYMOND A. SOKOLOV
GREAT RECIPES FROM THE NEW YORK TIMES

Karelian Pasties

Karjalan Piirakat

To make 25 pasties

¾ cup	raw unprocessed medium-grain rice (about 5 oz. [150 g.])	175 ml.
1½ cups	boiling water	375 ml.
½ tsp.	salt	2 ml.
¾ cup	milk	175 ml.
8 tbsp.	butter	120 ml.
1	egg, lightly beaten	1
¼ tsp.	pepper	1 ml.
½ cup	water	125 ml.

Pasty dough

½ cup	rye flour	125 ml.
½ cup	all-purpose flour	125 ml.
¼ tsp.	salt	1 ml.
9 tbsp.	water	135 ml.
	flour	

Egg butter

4	eggs, hard-boiled	4
4 tbsp.	butter, softened	60 ml.
¼ tsp.	salt	1 ml.
¼ tsp.	pepper	1 ml.

Preheat the oven to 475° F. [250° C.].

Cook the rice in the boiling salted water until the water has been absorbed—about 20 minutes. Add the milk and simmer until the milk is absorbed. Add 4 tablespoons [60 ml.] of the butter, the egg and pepper, and stir. Adjust the seasonings to taste.

While the rice is cooking, mix the rye and all-purpose flours and ¼ tsp. [1 ml.] salt in a bowl, and stir in the water gradually to make a stiff dough. Flour the work surface well. Roll the dough by hand into a bar 15 inches [38 cm.] long. Cut the bar into 25 pieces. Roll out the pieces into thin circles. Sprinkle flour on the circles; brush off the excess flour.

Place 1½ tablespoons [22 ml.] of the rice mixture lengthwise down the center of each dough circle, leaving the sides empty. Crimp the edges together with your finger tips, both sides at the same time, starting at the center. The final shape should be oval. Place the pasties on an ungreased baking sheet and bake them for 15 minutes. Meanwhile, make a butter dip by heating 4 tablespoons of butter and ½ cup [125 ml.] of water until the butter is melted. Set aside.

To make the egg butter, mash the still-warm, hard-boiled eggs roughly together with the softened butter. Blend in the salt and pepper. The texture should be like scrambled eggs. Refrigerate it only long enough to chill it; in other words, make the egg butter shortly before serving.

Line a platter with cloth and wax paper. As the pasties are taken out of the oven, dip them in the butter dip and place them on the wax paper. Cover them with a cloth until ready to serve.

Serve the pasties with the egg butter on the side.

RAYMOND A. SOKOLOV
GREAT RECIPES FROM THE NEW YORK TIMES

Scallion Pancakes

Ts'ung Yu Ping

The techniques of rolling and coiling scallion pancakes are demonstrated on pages 72-73.

To make 4 pancakes

4 tsp.	finely chopped scallions	20 ml.
2 cups	flour	½ liter
about ⅔ cup	water	about 150 ml.
2 tsp.	salt	10 ml.
4 tbsp.	lard, softened	60 ml.
8 tsp.	vegetable oil	40 ml.

Put the flour into a large bowl and make a well in the center of the flour. Gradually add the water, stirring with your fingers to make a soft but not sticky dough (if it is too dry, add more water). Knead the dough until it feels smooth. Put the dough back into the bowl, cover it with a damp cloth and let it rest for about 15 minutes.

Turn the dough out onto a lightly floured surface and knead it again for two minutes. Divide the dough into four pieces. Roll out one piece of the dough into a 10-by-6-inch [25-by-15-cm.] rectangle about ⅛ inch [3 mm.] thick. Sprinkle ½ teaspoon [2 ml.] of the salt on the dough and, with a rolling pin, roll the salted dough once. Spread 1 tablespoon [15 ml.] of the lard on the dough and sprinkle it evenly with 1 teaspoon [5 ml.] of the scallion. From one long side, roll the dough loosely into a 10-inch [25-cm.] sausage shape and pinch the dough to seal the open edge. Coil the sausage into a circle and tuck the ends underneath. Gently press the circle with your hand and roll it into a flat pancake about ¼ inch [6 mm.] thick and 6 inches [15 cm.] in diameter. Cover the pancake with a dry cloth. Repeat the procedure with the other pieces of dough.

Heat a frying pan. Add 2 teaspoons [10 ml.] of the oil and fry the pancakes one at a time over medium heat, turning them once, for about five minutes, or until both sides are browned and crisp. Shake the pan occasionally during the frying. Cut each pancake into four wedges and serve hot.

FLORENCE LIN
FLORENCE LIN'S CHINESE REGIONAL COOKBOOK

Deep-fried Filled Pastries

Samosas

To make ghee (the Indian version of clarified butter), start with at least one third more butter than the amount specified in the recipe. Melt the butter over low heat without browning it, then bring the butter to a boil. When it foams, reduce the heat to very low. Simmer the butter, uncovered, for 45 minutes. Strain the clear liquid ghee through a sieve lined with four layers of dampened cheesecloth. Discard the milk solids.

Garam masala is an Indian spice mixture that is available at stores that sell Indian food.

To make about 60 small, triangular pastries

3 cups	flour	¾ liter
1 tsp.	salt	5 ml.
3 to 4 tbsp.	ghee	45 to 60 ml.
¾ to 1 cup	cold water	175 ml. to ¼ liter
	vegetable oil	
	chutney	

Potato filling

2	small potatoes, boiled, peeled and cut into ½-inch [1-cm.] cubes (about 2 cups [½ liter] cubes)	2
2 tbsp.	vegetable oil	30 ml.
½ tsp.	black mustard seeds	2 ml.
½ cup	finely chopped onions	125 ml.
2 tsp.	finely chopped fresh ginger root	10 ml.
1 tsp.	fennel seeds	5 ml.
¼ tsp.	cumin seeds	1 ml.
¼ tsp.	ground turmeric	1 ml.
½ cup	freshly shelled peas (about ½ lb. [¼ kg.] before shelling)	125 ml.
½ tsp.	salt	2 ml.
1 tbsp.	water	15 ml.
1 tbsp.	finely chopped fresh coriander	15 ml.
½ tsp.	*garam masala*	2 ml.
⅛ tsp.	cayenne pepper	½ ml.

In a deep bowl, combine the flour, salt and 3 tablespoons [45 ml.] of the ghee. With your finger tips, rub the flour and ghee together until they look like flakes of coarse meal. Pour ¾ cup [175 ml.] of water over the mixture all at once, knead together vigorously and gather the dough into a ball. If the dough crumbles, add up to ¼ cup [50 ml.] more water, a tablespoon [15 ml.] at a time, until the particles adhere.

On a lightly floured surface, knead the dough for about 10 minutes, or until it is smooth and elastic. Again gather it into a ball, brush lightly with ghee or vegetable oil and set it in a bowl. Drape a damp kitchen towel over the top to keep the dough moist. (Covered with the towel, it can remain at room temperature for four or five hours.)

To prepare the potato filling, first heat the vegetable oil over medium heat in a heavy 10- to 12-inch [25- to 30-cm.] skillet until a drop of water flicked into it splutters instantly. Add the mustard seeds and when they crackle and begin to burst, immediately add the onions and ginger. Stirring almost constantly, fry for seven or eight minutes, until the onions are soft and golden brown. Stir in the fennel, cumin and turmeric, then add the potatoes, peas, salt and water.

Reduce the heat to low, cover the skillet tightly, and cook for five minutes. Then stir in the coriander, cover, and continue to cook for at least 10 minutes longer, or until the peas are tender. Remove the skillet from the heat and stir in the *garam masala* and cayenne pepper. Taste for seasoning.

Transfer the entire contents of the skillet to a bowl and cool the filling to room temperature before using it.

Shape and fill the *samosas* two at a time in the following fashion: Pinch off a small piece of dough and roll it into a ball about 1 inch [2½ cm.] in diameter. (Keep the remaining dough covered with the towel.) On a lightly floured surface, roll the ball into a circle about 3½ inches [9 cm.] in diameter. With a pastry wheel or small knife, cut the circle in half. Moisten the straight edge with a finger dipped in water. Then shape each semicircle into a cone, fill it with about 1½ teaspoons [7 ml.] of the potato mixture, and moisten and press the top edges closed. (Covered with foil or plastic wrap and refrigerated, the pastries may be kept for two or three hours before they are fried.)

To deep fry the pastries, pour 3 cups [¾ liter] of vegetable oil into a 12-inch [30-cm.] wok, or pour 2 to 3 inches [5 to 8 cm.] of oil into a deep fryer. Heat the oil until it reaches a temperature of 375° F. [190° C.] on a deep-frying thermometer. Deep fry the *samosas,* four or five at a time, for two to three minutes, or until golden brown on all sides. As they brown, transfer them to a baking dish lined with paper towels and keep the *samosas* warm in the oven.

To serve, mound the *samosas* on a heated platter, and accompany them with chutney presented in a bowl.

FOODS OF THE WORLD: THE COOKING OF INDIA

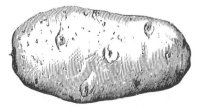

Ham Turnovers

Grind the ham and onion through a food grinder, using the medium disk, or purée them coarse in a food processor.

	To make about 18 turnovers	
2 cups	freshly ground cooked ham	½ liter
2 tbsp.	butter	30 ml.
2 tbsp.	flour	30 ml.
1 cup	hot milk	¼ liter
1	small onion, ground	1
	pepper	

Lard pastry

8 tbsp.	lard, softened	120 ml.
1½ cups	flour	375 ml.
½ tsp.	salt	2 ml.
1 tsp.	baking powder	5 ml.
3 to 4 tbsp.	cold water	45 to 60 ml.

Sift the flour, salt and baking powder together. Cut in the lard and add enough cold water to make the dough stick together. Roll out this extra-rich biscuit dough on a floured board to a thickness of about ¼ inch [6 mm.] and cut it into 3-inch [8-cm.] squares.

To make the ham filling, make a white sauce by melting the butter, stirring in the flour until smooth, then adding the milk, stirring constantly as it thickens. Add the ham, onion and a pinch of pepper.

Put a heaping spoonful of filling in the center of each square, fold it into a triangle and pinch the edges together. Cut a slit in the top of each turnover. Bake on an ungreased baking sheet in a preheated 400° F. [200° C.] oven for about 15 minutes, or until the turnovers are puffed and golden brown. Serve hot.

BEATRICE VAUGHAN
YANKEE HILL-COUNTRY COOKING

Special Containers and Bases

Batter Cases

Krustader

These batter cases, or croustades, are fried on decorative molds that screw onto the tips of long-handled rosette irons,

as demonstrated on pages 80-81. Among the suitable fillings for these cases are scrambled eggs (page 135), creamed sweetbreads (page 137) and creamed shellfish (page 138).

	To make 20 cases	
1 cup	flour	¼ liter
¼ tsp.	salt	1 ml.
1	egg yolk	1
½ cup	cream	125 ml.
	oil for deep frying	

Beat the flour, salt, egg yolk and cream together to a smooth batter. Pour the batter into a cup or bowl just large enough to hold the croustade mold.

Heat the oil to 375° F. [190° C.]. Heat a croustade mold in the oil. Lift out the mold and let it drain briefly. Dip the mold into the batter. Hold the mold above the hot oil until the batter sets and is firm. Lower the mold into the oil and fry the croustade until golden brown—about one minute.

Detach the croustade from the mold with a fork and let the croustade drain on paper toweling. Reheat the mold before frying each successive croustade.

J. AUDREY ELLISON
THE GREAT SCANDINAVIAN COOK BOOK

Blini

	To make about 10 blini	
1 tbsp.	dry yeast, dissolved in ½ cup [125 ml.] tepid water for 5 minutes	15 ml.
1 cup	milk, at room temperature	¼ liter
1½ cups	sifted flour	375 ml.
3	eggs, the yolks separated from the whites	3
½ tsp.	salt	2 ml.
¼ tsp.	sugar	1 ml.
6 tbsp.	butter, melted and cooled	90 ml.
1 cup	butter (½ lb. [¼ kg.]), clarified and warm	¼ liter
2 cups	sour cream	½ liter
8 oz.	red or black caviar	¼ kg.

Prepare the batter about two and a half hours before you plan to serve the blini: Pour the dissolved yeast into the blender jar and add the milk, flour, egg yolks, salt, sugar and the 6 tablespoons [90 ml.] of melted butter. Blend at high speed for about 40 seconds; turn off the machine and, with a rubber spatula, scrape down the flour clinging to the sides of the jar. Blend a few seconds longer, then pour the batter into a mixing bowl and cover it loosely with a kitchen towel. Let it rest for two hours at room temperature. If your kitchen seems cool, place the bowl near a warm stove or radiator.

To make the batter by hand, sift the flour into a large mixing bowl and, with a large spoon, rub into it the egg yolks and the salt and sugar. Beat in the dissolved yeast and the milk a few drops at a time. Beat in the melted butter and continue to beat until the mixture becomes a fairly smooth cream. Strain this through a fine-meshed sieve, rubbing any undissolved bits of flour through with the back of the spoon. Cover the bowl loosely with a towel and let the batter rise.

At the end of two hours the batter will have risen considerably and bubbled at the top. Now beat the egg whites with a pinch of salt until they are stiff, then gently but thoroughly fold them into the batter.

The most reliable way to cook blini is on an automatic electric griddle. Not only is it large enough to cook at least a dozen blini simultaneously but, because the temperature remains constant, each batch is entirely predictable.

Preheat an electric griddle to 400° F. [200° C.], then brush it lightly with a little clarified butter. Ladle out enough batter to make blini about 3 inches [8 cm.] in diameter, leaving enough space between them so that they can be turned easily. Cook until lightly browned on each side— about one minute—turning them only once. Or preheat a *plättlagg*, or Swedish cast-iron pancake pan, until water flicked onto the surface evaporates at once; then butter each circular section of the pan before you pour in the batter.

To serve, arrange three blini on each plate and bathe them with a little of the clarified butter. Drop a small mound of sour cream on each pancake and top with a spoonful of caviar. Serve at once.

MICHAEL FIELD
MICHAEL FIELD'S COOKING SCHOOL

Buckwheat Blini

To make about 36 blini

2 cups	sifted buckwheat flour	½ liter
2 cups	tepid milk	½ liter
¾ cup	tepid water	175 ml.
1 tbsp.	dry yeast, dissolved in ¼ cup [50 ml.] tepid water for 5 minutes	15 ml.
3	eggs, the yolks separated from the whites	3
2 tbsp.	butter, softened	30 ml.
1 tsp.	sugar	5 ml.
1 tsp.	salt	5 ml.

In a bowl, combine half of the milk with the water. Add the dissolved yeast to the milk mixture. Stir in about 1 cup [¼ liter] of the flour to make a thick batter. Beat well. Cover

and set in a warm place until this yeast sponge mixture is doubled in volume—about two and a half to three hours.

Beat the egg yolks. Gradually beat in the remaining cup of milk, the butter, sugar and salt. Stir into the yeast mixture along with the remaining flour.

Beat the egg whites until stiff but not dry, and fold them into the batter. Cover and let stand at room temperature without stirring for 45 minutes.

Ladle the mixture onto a hot greased griddle, or heavy skillet, to make 3-inch [8-cm.] pancakes. It will take about ¼ cup [50 ml.] of batter for each blini. Cook until lightly browned on the bottom, turn, and brown the second side. Keep the blini warm while cooking the remaining batter.

RAYMOND A. SOKOLOV
GREAT RECIPES FROM THE NEW YORK TIMES

Yeast Dough for Steamed Buns

When doubling this recipe, you must allow the dough to rise for an extra hour.

To make enough dough for about 20 buns

3½ cups	flour	875 ml.
1½ tsp.	dry yeast	7 ml.
¼ cup	tepid water	50 ml.
1 cup	milk	¼ liter
2 tbsp.	sugar	30 ml.
½ tsp.	baking powder	2 ml.

Place the flour in a large mixing bowl. Sprinkle the yeast over the tepid water and leave it for two minutes. Heat the milk to warm, add the sugar and dissolve it. Stir the yeast mixture well and combine it with the milk, then slowly stir this mixture into the flour to form a soft, firm dough. Knead the dough until smooth—about 15 to 20 minutes—and return it to the bowl. (With an electric mixer with a dough hook, use speed number 2 for 10 minutes. Leave the dough in the bowl to rise.) Cover the bowl with a damp towel and let the dough rise in a warm place for about one and one half to two hours, or until doubled in bulk.

Punch the risen dough down and turn it out onto a lightly floured surface. Add the baking powder and knead for 10 minutes, or until the dough is smooth, sprinkling flour onto the dough from time to time while kneading.

FLORENCE LIN
FLORENCE LIN'S REGIONAL CHINESE COOKING

Chicken Filling for Steamed Buns

A recipe for steamed-bun dough appears on page 151.

To make enough filling for about 20 buns

½ lb.	boned chicken breast	¼ kg.
1	egg white	1
2 tbsp.	finely chopped water chestnut	30 ml.
2 tbsp.	finely chopped bamboo shoot	30 ml.
2 tbsp.	finely chopped scallion	30 ml.
1 tbsp.	sesame-seed oil	15 ml.
1 tsp.	sugar	5 ml.
1 tbsp.	light soy sauce	15 ml.
2 tbsp.	dry sherry	30 ml.
1 tbsp.	peanut oil	15 ml.
½ tsp.	salt	2 ml.

Chop the chicken fine and mix it with the egg white. Combine the water chestnut, bamboo shoot and scallion; set aside. Combine the sesame-seed oil, sugar, soy sauce and sherry, and set aside.

Heat a wok or a skillet over high heat until a drop of water immediately sizzles into steam. Maintain high heat throughout the cooking process. Add the peanut oil and salt to the pan and rotate the pan to spread the oil around. Just before the oil begins to smoke, add the chicken and stir fry it for one minute. Add the vegetables and stir for a second before adding the sesame-seed-oil mixture. Stir fry for about two minutes. Remove from the heat, transfer the mixture to a bowl and allow it to cool to room temperature before using it to fill the buns.

CALVIN B. T. LEE AND AUDREY EVANS LEE
THE GOURMET CHINESE REGIONAL COOKBOOK

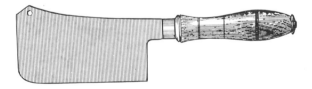

Steamed Buns with Roast Pork Filling

A recipe for steamed-bread dough appears on page 151.

Brown bean sauce is a thick condiment made from fermented yellow beans, flour and salt. It is available in cans where Chinese foods are sold. The technique of shaping

steamed buns and an alternative way to hang the pork strips in the oven for roasting are shown on pages 84-85.

To make about 24 buns

1 lb.	boneless pork, preferably Boston shoulder	½ kg.
1 tbsp.	chicken stock *(recipe, page 161)*	15 ml.
3 tbsp.	soy sauce	45 ml.
½ tbsp.	mashed brown bean sauce	7 ml.
½ tbsp.	Chinese rice wine or pale dry sherry	7 ml.
4 tsp.	sugar	20 ml.
¼ tsp.	salt	1 ml.
½ tsp.	chopped garlic	2 ml.
2 tbsp.	peanut oil	30 ml.
2 tbsp.	cornstarch, diluted in 3 tbsp. [45 ml.] cold chicken stock	30 ml.
	steamed-bread dough	

With a cleaver or a large, sharp knife, cut the pork into strips 1½ to 2 inches [4 to 5 cm.] wide. Cut the strips in half lengthwise. Lay the strips flat in one or two layers in a large, shallow dish or pan.

In a small bowl, combine the chicken stock with 1 tablespoon [15 ml.] of the soy sauce, the brown bean sauce and the wine. Add 1 teaspoon [5 ml.] of the sugar, the salt and the garlic, and stir until the ingredients are well mixed. Pour the sauce over the pork strips, baste them thoroughly and let them marinate for at least three hours at room temperature or for at least six hours in the refrigerator. Turn the strips over in the marinade every hour or so.

Preheat the oven to 350° F. [180° C.]. To catch the drippings of the pork strips as they roast and to prevent the oven from smoking, fill a large, shallow roasting pan with water and place it on the lowest rack of the oven. Insert one curved tip of an S-shaped hook at the end of each strip of pork. (Any hook will do: a curtain hook, S hook, even a 5- or 6-inch [13- or 15-cm.] length of heavy-duty wire or unpainted wire coat hanger bent into that shape.) Hang the hooks from the uppermost rack of the oven, directly above the pan of water.

Roast the pork undisturbed for 45 minutes. Then increase the oven heat to 450° F. [230° C.] and roast it for an additional 15 minutes, or until the pork strips are crisp and a rich, golden brown. Remove the pork from the oven and dice the strips.

Set a wok or large skillet over high heat for about 30 seconds. Pour in 1 tablespoon [15 ml.] of the oil, swirl it about in the pan and heat for 30 seconds, turning the heat down to medium if the oil begins to smoke. Add the chopped pork and stir fry for one minute. Then stir in the remaining 3 teaspoons [15 ml.] of the sugar and 2 tablespoons [30 ml.] of the soy sauce.

Give the cornstarch mixture a quick stir to recombine it, and add it to the pan. Cook, stirring constantly, for another 10 seconds, or until the mixture thickens and the pork is covered with a clear glaze. Immediately transfer the contents of the pan to a bowl and cool to room temperature. On a lightly floured surface, form the dough with your hands into a long roll 2 inches [5 cm.] in diameter. Slice the roll into 1-inch [2½-cm.] rounds. Flatten each round with the palm of your hand; then, with a rolling pin, roll out each round into a disk 4 inches [10 cm.] in diameter, turning the round counterclockwise as you roll it to help keep its circular shape.

Place 1 or 2 tablespoons [15 or 30 ml.] of filling in the center of each round. With your fingers, gather the edges of the round up around the filling in loose folds meeting at the top. Then twist or press the dough firmly closed. Place the buns on 2-inch [5-cm.] squares of wax paper, cover them with a dry kitchen towel and let the rolls rise again for 30 minutes, or until the dough springs back slowly when poked gently with a finger.

Pour enough boiling water into the lowest part of a steamer to come within an inch of the cooking rack. Arrange the buns an inch apart on two trays and set them in the steamer. Over high heat, bring the water in the steamer to a boil, cover the pan tightly and steam for about 20 minutes. Arrange the buns on a heated platter and serve them hot.

FOODS OF THE WORLD/THE COOKING OF CHINA

Small Breads with Cabbage Filling

Pyriszhky

To make about 48 filled breads

3 to 3½ cups	sifted flour	750 to 875 ml.
1 tbsp.	dry yeast	15 ml.
¾ cup	tepid water	175 ml.
½ tsp.	sugar	2 ml.
1 tsp.	salt	5 ml.
3 tbsp.	unsalted butter, softened	45 ml.
3	eggs, lightly beaten	3
1	egg, mixed with 2 tbsp. [30 ml.] milk	1

Cabbage filling

1½ lb.	coarsely chopped cabbage	¾ kg.
3 tbsp.	unsalted butter	45 ml.
1 cup	finely chopped onions	¼ liter
1 tsp.	sugar	5 ml.
1½ tsp.	salt	7 ml.
¼ tsp.	freshly ground black pepper	1 ml.
½ cup	water	125 ml.

In a small bowl, sprinkle the tepid water with the yeast and sugar, and let the mixture rest for two or three minutes. Stir to dissolve the yeast, then set the bowl aside in a warm, draft-free place (such as an unlighted oven) for 10 to 15 minutes, or until the yeast bubbles and the mixture almost doubles in volume.

Place 3 cups of the flour and the salt in a large mixing bowl and make a well in the center. Drop in the yeast mixture, 2 tablespoons of the butter and the three eggs. With a large spoon, gradually incorporate the flour into the liquid ingredients. Stir until the ingredients can be gathered into a ball, then transfer the ball to a lightly floured surface. Knead the dough, pressing it down, pushing it forward with the heel of your hand and folding it back on itself, until you have a smooth, medium-soft dough. Add up to ½ cup of the flour by the tablespoonful if the dough sticks to your hands or to the work surface.

Coat the bottom and sides of a large mixing bowl with the remaining tablespoon of softened butter and place the dough in the bowl. Drape the bowl with a kitchen towel and set it aside in the warm, draft-free place for 45 minutes, or until the dough almost doubles in volume. Punch it down with a blow of your fist and set it aside to double again in volume.

To make the cabbage filling, first melt the butter in a 10- to 12-inch [25- to 30-cm.] skillet over medium heat. Stir in the onions and, stirring frequently, cook for four to six minutes, or until they are soft and translucent. Add the cabbage, sugar, salt and black pepper, then pour in the water. Bring to a boil over high heat, then reduce the heat, cover the skillet and simmer for 45 minutes. Uncover the pan, increase the heat to high and boil briskly until the liquid in the pan evaporates. Put the contents of the skillet through the finest disk of a food grinder, or chop them as fine as possible with a large, heavy knife. Adjust the seasoning, if necessary, and cool to room temperature.

Preheat the oven to 325° F. [160° C.]. Place the dough on a large surface and pull off pieces equal to about 2 tablespoons [30 ml.]. Flatten the pieces, one at a time, into oval shapes about ¼ inch [6 mm.] thick. Place 2 teaspoons [10 ml.] of filling in the center of each dough oval and pull one side of the dough over the filling. Press the edges together.

Set the *pyriszhky* an inch [2½ cm.] apart on a baking sheet and, with a pastry brush, coat them with the egg-and-milk mixture. Bake in the center of the oven for 10 to 12 minutes, or until they are golden brown. Serve hot.

FOODS OF THE WORLD/AMERICAN COOKING: THE MELTING POT

Thick-Crust Pizza

To make three 7-by-11-inch [18-by-28-cm.] thick-crust pizzas

2½ cups	milk	625 ml.
8 tbsp.	butter	120 ml.
about 8 cups	flour	about 2 liters
about ¾ cup	yellow cornmeal	about 175 ml.
1 tbsp.	dry yeast, or ⅗ oz. [30 g.] compressed fresh yeast	15 ml.
3 tbsp.	sugar	45 ml.
1 tsp.	salt	5 ml.
4	eggs, beaten	4
	olive oil	
2 cups	tomato sauce *(recipe, page 167)*	½ liter
1 lb.	mozzarella cheese, grated	½ kg.
½ cup	freshly grated Parmesan cheese	125 ml.

Heat the milk and butter to scalding, stirring occasionally. Cool to 115° F. [46° C.].

Combine 5½ cups [about 1⅓ liters] of the flour, ½ cup [125 ml.] of the cornmeal, the yeast, sugar and salt in a large bowl. Stir in the cooled milk, add the eggs and then enough of the remaining flour to make a dough that is easy to handle. Knead the dough on a floured surface for about 15 minutes, or until smooth and elastic. Put the dough in a greased bowl, turn it over and cover it. Let the dough rise in a warm place until it has doubled in volume, about one and one half hours. Punch down and let the dough rise again for about one hour, or until again doubled in volume.

Grease three pans, each 7 by 11 by 2 inches [18 by 28 by 5 cm.], with olive oil; sprinkle the pans lightly with cornmeal. Divide the dough into three parts and roll each to a rectangle measuring about 9 by 13 inches [23 by 32½ cm.]. Transfer the dough to the pans; the edges of the dough will stand against the sides of the pans to form rims.

Spoon the tomato sauce over the dough, spreading it evenly; top with the cheeses. Bake in a preheated 400° F. [200° C.] oven for about 25 minutes, or until the crust is browned and the cheeses have melted.

LYDIA SAIGER
THE JUNK FOOD COOKBOOK

Pizza Margherita

This is a pizza for those who love the semisharp flavor of Parmesan cheese that, blended with tomatoes, is a pleasant contrast to the mozzarella.

To make four 12-inch [30-cm.] pizzas

	basic bread dough *(recipe, page 164)*	
	olive oil	
3 to 4 cups	peeled plum tomatoes	¾ to 1 liter
1 lb.	whole-milk mozzarella, grated	½ kg.
¾ cup	freshly grated Parmesan cheese	175 ml.
	salt	
	freshly ground pepper (optional)	

Preheat the oven to 450° F. [230° C.] and prepare the dough, brushing it lightly with olive oil.

Cut the tomatoes into chunks and spread them around on top of the dough. Top the tomatoes with the mozzarella. Sprinkle the pizza as evenly as possible with the Parmesan cheese. Salt (and pepper, if you wish) very lightly. Sprinkle the pizza with olive oil.

Bake the pizza for 20 to 25 minutes, or until it is golden, the cheeses having melted and blended with the tomatoes.

MARGARET AND G. FRANCO ROMAGNOLI
THE ROMAGNOLIS' TABLE

Rustic Pizza

To make one 12-inch [30-cm.] pizza

3⅛ cups	flour	775 ml.
1½ tbsp.	lard	22 ml.
¼ tsp.	salt	1 ml.
¼ tsp.	pepper	1 ml.
1 tbsp.	dry yeast, dissolved in 1 cup [¼ liter] tepid water	15 ml.
3 cups	ricotta cheese (1½ lb. [¾ kg.])	¾ liter
2	small eggs, beaten	2
2 tbsp.	freshly grated Parmesan cheese	30 ml.
¼ lb.	thinly sliced prosciutto, cut into slivers	125 g.

Place the flour in a mound on a pastry board. Make a well in the center and add the lard, ⅛ teaspoon [½ ml.] each of the salt and pepper, and the dissolved yeast. Work the ingredients together well and knead until the dough is elastic and smooth—about 10 minutes. Place the dough in a bowl, cover, and let it stand in a warm place for two hours, or until it has doubled in volume.

In a bowl, combine the ricotta, eggs, Parmesan cheese and the remaining salt and pepper. Mix together well with a wooden spoon.

When the dough is ready, cut it into two pieces and roll out each piece into a circle about 12 inches [30 cm.] across. Stretch one piece over the bottom of a shallow, greased, 12-inch casserole dish. Spread the ricotta mixture over this, leaving a 1-inch [2½-cm.] border around the edge. Spread the prosciutto over the ricotta mixture and place the second circle of dough over the first, pressing the edge closed carefully and cutting off any excess dough around the outside. Bake the pizza in a preheated 375° F. [190° C.] oven for 45 minutes, or until it is golden brown. Serve cool.

ADA BONI
THE TALISMAN ITALIAN COOKBOOK

Pizza Neapolitan-Style

Pizza alla Napoletana

The technique of making pizza is shown on pages 86-87.

To serve 4

	basic bread dough made with olive oil (recipe, page 164, but use only one third of the quantities called for)	
Neapolitan-style topping		
2½ tbsp.	olive oil	37 ml.
6	canned plum tomatoes, drained and puréed through a food mill (about 10 tbsp. [150 ml.] purée)	6
1 cup	coarsely grated mozzarella cheese	¼ liter
6	oil-packed flat anchovy fillets, or 6 salt anchovies, filleted under cold running water and patted dry	6
1 tsp.	capers, packed in wine vinegar	5 ml.
	salt and freshly ground pepper	
	oregano	

Prepare the dough and let it rest until doubled in size—about one hour at room temperature, away from drafts.

Preheat the oven to 450° F. [230° C.].

When the dough is ready, place on a board a sheet of heavy aluminum foil about 16 by 18 inches [40 by 46 cm.].

Oil the foil with 1 tablespoon [15 ml.] of the olive oil, then place the dough on the foil. Spread the dough (using the tips of your fingers, not a rolling pin) until you have a sheet of dough about 16½ by 14 inches [41 by 36 cm.].

Spread the puréed tomatoes over the surface of the dough. Distribute the grated mozzarella evenly over the tomatoes, then distribute the anchovy fillets and capers. Add salt, pepper and oregano to taste and pour the remaining 1½ tablespoons [22 ml.] of olive oil over everything. Slide the pizza and the foil directly onto the middle shelf of the oven and bake in the preheated oven for about 35 minutes, or until crisp. Remove the pizza, slice and serve.

GIULIANO BUGIALLI
THE FINE ART OF ITALIAN COOKING

Wheat Flour Tortillas

To make about 12 tortillas, each 12 inches [30 cm.] across

4 cups	all-purpose flour	1 liter
about 1 cup	water	about ¼ liter
8 tbsp.	lard, cut into small pieces	120 ml.
1½ tsp.	salt	7 ml.

Mix the flour and the salt, then cut in the lard as in making piecrust. Add enough water to make a pliable dough. Knead the dough until it is soft; it should be soft and elastic enough so that it will stretch. Grease your hands and form the dough into small balls about the size of eggs. Cover with a dry cloth, and let the dough stand for half an hour.

Roll or pat the balls of dough paper-thin until they are each about 12 inches [30 cm.] across. Bake one at a time in a medium-hot ungreased skillet or on a griddle. When the tortillas start to bubble, flip them like pancakes and bake them for a few seconds longer. Experiment with a few to get the time right. A few burned spots do not hurt a bit.

Serve immediately, folded in quarters, each on a hot bread-and-butter plate with a big pat of soft butter.

GEORGE E. SANDOVAL
SANDOVAL'S MEXICAN COOKBOOK

Corn Tortillas

The techniques of making corn tortillas are shown on page 88.

You can make tortillas about two hours ahead of time. Wrap the package of tortillas in foil and reheat in a 275° F. [140° C.] oven before serving.

To make 16 tortillas, each about 5 inches [13 cm.] across

2 cups	masa harina	½ liter
about 1⅓ cups	cold water	about 325 ml.
	lard	

Add the water all at once to the flour and mix quickly and lightly. Do not compress the dough into hard pieces. Set the dough aside for about 20 minutes, then try it for consistency by making a tortilla. Set two heavy griddles or frying pans over medium heat and let them heat up; the dough should sizzle just faintly as it touches the pan. Lightly grease the griddles with lard before you start making the tortillas.

Open up a tortilla press. Place a polyethylene bag on the bottom plate. Take a piece of the tortilla dough and roll it into a ball about 1½ inches [4 cm.] across. Flatten the ball slightly and set it on the bag, a little more toward the hinge than the handle of the press, then smooth a second bag over the dough. Close the press and push the handle down hard. Open it up and peel off the top bag. Lift the second bag with the flattened tortilla on it, and invert it dough side down onto your hand, more on the fingers than the palm. Peel the bag from the dough—do not attempt to peel the dough from the bag—and lay the tortilla carefully on the hot griddle. Do not slam it down, or you will get air bubbles in the dough.

Pause at this stage and consider the dough. If the tortilla is rather thick, with a grainy edge, then the dough is too dry. Work a little more water into it. Be careful not to add too much water, or the dough will become unmanageable—it may be impossible to peel the bag off, leaving the dough in one piece—or, even if it is not quite as bad as that, your tortillas will be sodden and will not rise nicely.

If the griddles are at the right heat, the tortilla should take no more than two minutes to cook.

Assuming that the dough is now the right consistency, press out the next tortilla and place it on the griddle. When it has just begun to dry out around the edges (do not wait for the dough to dry out completely and curl up, or your tortilla will be tough), flip it over and cook for a slightly longer time on the second side, or until it just begins to color. Flip it back onto the first side and finish cooking through. If the dough is right and the heat of the pan is right, the tortilla should puff up invitingly. (This is the "face" of the tortilla, and this is the side the filling goes on when you are making tacos or enchiladas.) Remove the tortilla from the griddle and keep it warm in a thick napkin. As each tortilla is cooked, stack one on top of the other in the napkin and cover. In this way the tortillas will retain their heat and flexibility.

DIANA KENNEDY
THE TORTILLA BOOK

Fried Tortillas with Avocado Dip

Tostadas Guacamole

To make 6 tortillas

½ cup	yellow cornmeal	125 ml.
¾ cup	flour	175 ml.
¼ tsp.	salt	1 ml.
2 tbsp.	olive oil	30 ml.
⅓ cup	warm water	75 ml.
	oil for frying	

Avocado dip		
2	large ripe avocados	2
2 tbsp.	fresh lemon juice	30 ml.
1	tomato, peeled	1
4 to 6	scallions, white parts only	4 to 6
½ tsp.	salt	2 ml.
½ tsp.	coriander seeds	2 ml.
	fresh parsley sprigs	

Sift the cornmeal, flour and salt into a mixing bowl and make a well in the center. Pour in the olive oil and the water and mix to a soft dough. Turn out onto a floured surface, knead for four or five minutes, then cover and set this dough to one side for 15 minutes.

Divide the dough into six pieces and roll these into balls between your hands. On a floured surface, with a rolling pin, roll each ball into a paper-thin 6-inch [15-cm.] round and cut it to an even shape, using an upturned plate as a guide.

Put a heavy skillet or frying pan over medium heat and add a tablespoon [15 ml.] of oil, tilting the pan to cover the surface. As soon as the oil is hot, slide in one tortilla and cook for about 20 seconds, pressing down with the back of a pancake turner until the tortilla puffs up. Turn once or twice until dry but not brown. Add more oil as needed before cooking each tortilla. Wrap the tortillas in a clean, warm cloth.

After all the tortillas have been fried, cut each one into six wedges. Pour about 1 inch [2½ cm.] of oil into a deep skillet and bring to a temperature of 360° F. [180° C.]. Fry the tortilla wedges a few at a time until golden brown—about 30 seconds on each side. Drain on paper towels, keeping the wedges apart.

To make the *guacamole,* halve the avocados, remove the pits, then scoop out the flesh, mash it and beat in the lemon juice. Chop the tomato and scallions fine and blend them into the avocado with the salt and coriander.

To serve the *guacamole* as a dip for the tortillas, first pile it into a round bowl and garnish with the parsley. Stand the bowl in the center of a serving dish and arrange the *tostadas* in a circle around the edge of the dish.

CECILIA NORMAN
THE CRÊPE AND PANCAKE COOKBOOK

Chicken Flutes

Flautas de Pollo

A recipe for corn tortillas appears on page 156.

The technique of shredding meat with a fork is demonstrated on page 89. Husk tomatoes are green ground cherries, marketed in cans as tomatillos. Serrano chilies are very hot small, green chilies; if fresh serrano chilies are unavailable, you can substitute fresh cayenne chilies. Husk tomatoes and chilies are obtainable where Latin American foods are sold. For a milder tomato sauce, the authors suggest substituting one large poblano chili, broiled, peeled, seeded and deribbed, for the three serrano chilies.

The volatile oils in chilies may irritate your skin. Wear rubber gloves when handling them.

	To make 24 flutes	
2½ lb.	chicken, cut into serving pieces	1¼ kg.
4 cups	chicken stock *(recipe, page 161)*	1 liter
24	corn tortillas, each 4 inches [10 cm.] in diameter	24
	melted lard, or corn or safflower oil	
	shredded Monterey Jack cheese (optional)	
	sour cream (optional)	

Cooked husk-tomato sauce

1 lb.	fresh husk tomatoes, husked, or 2 cups [½ liter] tomatillos, drained	½ kg.
3	serrano chilies, seeded, deveined and chopped	3
1	small onion, chopped	1
2	garlic cloves	2
1 tbsp.	finely chopped fresh coriander	15 ml.
2 tbsp.	lard, or corn or safflower oil	30 ml.
	sugar	
	salt	

To make the sauce with fresh husk tomatoes, cook them with the chilies in a small amount of boiling salted water until they become tender, about 10 minutes; drain them. If you are using canned tomatillos, cook the chilies alone in a small amount of boiling salted water until tender, then drain. Purée the tomatillos and chilies with the onion, garlic and coriander in a blender or food mill.

In a heavy skillet, heat the lard or corn or safflower oil. Add the purée and, stirring constantly, cook it for three to four minutes, until it becomes slightly thickened. Then add a pinch of sugar and salt to taste. Set aside.

Place the chicken in a saucepan with the chicken stock. Bring the stock to a boil, then reduce the heat, partially cover the pan and simmer until the chicken becomes tender,

30 to 45 minutes. Allow the chicken to cool in its stock, then skin, bone and shred it with a fork.

Heat each tortilla briefly on a lightly greased griddle or in a lightly greased skillet. Place a spoonful of chicken along one edge of the tortilla and roll it up very tightly. Fasten each rolled tortilla with a toothpick.

In a heavy skillet, heat ¼ inch [6 mm.] of lard or oil to the smoking point. Fry the rolled tortillas until they turn crisp and golden, then drain them briefly on absorbent paper. Place the *flautas* on a heated serving dish, cover with the sauce, add cheese and/or sour cream if you like, and serve.

ANGELES DE LA ROSA AND C. GANDIA DE FERNANDEZ
FLAVORS OF MEXICO

Tacos

A recipe for making corn tortillas appears on page 156.

	To make 12 tacos	
2	onions, finely chopped	2
1	garlic clove, crushed to a paste	1
	lard or vegetable oil	
1 lb.	lean ground beef	½ kg.
1 tsp.	salt	5 ml.
2 tsp.	chili powder	10 ml.
¼ cup	chili sauce	50 ml.
½ tsp.	ground cumin	2 ml.
12	corn tortillas, each about 7 inches [18 cm.] across	12
2 cups	grated Cheddar cheese (½ lb. [¼ kg.])	½ liter
1 cup	shredded lettuce	¼ liter
1 or 2	tomatoes, chopped	1 or 2

Sauté half of the chopped onion and the garlic in 1 tablespoon [15 ml.] of the lard or oil until they turn translucent. Stir in the beef, salt and chili powder; sauté until the beef is brown. Add the cumin and chili sauce. In a skillet, heat the tortillas in hot lard or oil until they become limp; fold them in half and continue to fry them until they turn crisp. Spoon the beef mixture into each shell and top the taco with the cheese, the remaining chopped onion, the lettuce and the chopped tomato.

THE JUNIOR LEAGUE OF CORPUS CHRISTI
FIESTA

Beef Tacos

A recipe for corn tortillas appears on page 156. The technique of shredding meat with a fork is demonstrated on page 89.

To make the prepared sour cream called for in this recipe, blend 2 cups [½ liter] sour cream with ⅓ cup [75 ml.] milk and 1 teaspoon [5 ml.] salt in a blender. In the refrigerator, the mixture will stabilize and become a little thicker. It will keep well for several days.

Ideally, tacos should be slightly crisp on the outside and slightly doughy inside, so you can still taste the corn and the texture of the tortilla. If you are not serving pickled chilies with the tacos and want a *picante* sauce, blend two fresh serrano chilies with the tomatoes.

To make 12 tacos		
12	corn tortillas, each about 7 inches [18 cm.] across	12
	lard	
¾ cup	prepared sour cream	175 ml.
½ cup	crumbled farmer cheese	125 ml.
Shredded beef filling		
2 lb.	boneless beef	1 kg.
¼	medium-sized onion, roughly sliced, plus ½ medium-sized onion, thinly sliced	¼
1	garlic clove	1
	salt	
5	peppercorns	5
1½ tbsp.	peanut or safflower oil	22 ml.
Cooked tomato sauce		
2	medium-sized tomatoes, broiled for about 20 minutes or until lightly colored on all sides, then peeled and puréed in a blender or food mill; or 1½ cups [375 ml.] drained, canned tomatoes	2
¼	medium-sized onion	¼
1	garlic clove	1
¼ tsp.	salt	1 ml.
1½ tbsp.	peanut or safflower oil	22 ml.

To prepare the shredded beef, cut the meat into large cubes, put it into a saucepan with the roughly sliced onion, the garlic, salt and peppercorns, and cover with cold water. Bring the water to a boil, then reduce the heat and simmer the meat until just tender—about 45 minutes. Remove from the heat and let the meat cool in the broth. When the meat is cool enough to handle, drain it, reserving the broth. Shred

the meat and add more salt if necessary. Heat the peanut or safflower oil in a pan and fry the thinly sliced onion gently until soft but not brown. Add the meat and cook over medium heat, stirring from time to time, until it is lightly browned. Set aside to cool a little.

To make the tomato sauce, blend the ingredients together until smooth. Heat the oil and cook the purée over high heat for three minutes, stirring almost all of the time. Season the sauce and keep it warm.

To fill the tortillas, put a little of the prepared filling across—but slightly to one side—the face of each tortilla. Start from that side and roll up the tortilla fairly firmly but not too tightly, then secure it with a wooden pick so that this taco does not become unrolled. Providing the filling is not so hot that it will make the taco turn soggy, this can be done ahead of time.

Heat lard in a heavy pan until it is very hot. There should be no more than ¼ inch [6 mm.] of lard, so that it will not seep into the filling. Fry the taco for a minute or so with the open edge on top. As it becomes golden underneath—not too hard—roll it, removing the wooden pick, so that the open edge is underneath (you may need to press the taco down a little at this point to prevent it from opening up). Continue frying until it is slightly crisp and golden all the way around. Drain well on paper toweling, then serve immediately with the sauce, sour cream and cheese as a garnish.

DIANA KENNEDY
THE TORTILLA BOOK

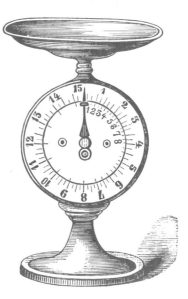

Green Enchiladas

Enchiladas Verdes

Jalapeña sauce is a hot, bottled relish containing green jalapeño peppers and both red and green tomatoes. Tomatillos are canned green ground cherries. They are both available in Latin American food stores.

These enchiladas are always made with pork, but they could be made with cooked cubed chicken, moistened with a little of the sauce.

	To make 12 enchiladas	
12	corn tortillas, each about 8 inches [20 cm.] across	12
	oil for frying	
	Green enchilada sauce	
½ cup	canned peeled green chilies, seeded and cut into strips	125 ml.
1	medium-sized green pepper, seeded and cut into strips	1
2½ cups	drained tomatillos, with 1 cup [¼ liter] of their juice reserved	625 ml.
1	medium-sized onion, peeled	1
2	garlic cloves, peeled	2
1	large tomato, peeled, or ¾ cup [175 ml.] canned tomatoes	1
¼ cup	oil	50 ml.
	salt	
	jalapeña sauce	
½ cup	finely chopped parsley	125 ml.
	Pork filling	
2 lb.	boneless lean pork, cut into small pieces	1 kg.
2	garlic cloves, peeled	2
¼ cup	water	50 ml.
	salt	
1	medium-sized onion, chopped	1
1	large tomato, peeled and chopped, or ¾ cup [175 ml.] canned tomatoes	1
3 tbsp.	freshly grated Parmesan or Romano cheese	45 ml.

To prepare the green sauce, lightly blend the chilies, green pepper strips, tomatillos and tomatillo juice, onion, garlic and tomato in an electric blender, using about one third of these ingredients at a time, or put them through the fine blade of a food mill. Heat the oil, add the blended mixture and salt to taste, then simmer for about five or 10 minutes. Add jalapeña sauce to taste and simmer a few minutes longer. Add the chopped parsley.

Make the filling by putting the pork, garlic, water and salt to taste in a skillet. Cover, and simmer for half an hour. Uncover and cook until the meat starts to brown, stirring occasionally. Add the chopped onion and tomato, and simmer until almost all liquid is absorbed—about 15 or 20 minutes. Now dip the tortillas, one at a time, into the green sauce and fry each lightly in oil. Put about ⅓ cup [75 ml.] filling on the face of each tortilla, roll them up and place them in a shallow glass baking dish. Pour the remaining sauce over the enchiladas. Sprinkle them generously with grated cheese. Keep them warm until serving.

ELENA ZELAYETA
ELENA'S SECRETS OF MEXICAN COOKING

━━━━━━━◆━━━━━━━

Swiss Enchiladas
Enchiladas Suizas

The technique of shredding meat with a fork is demonstrated on page 89. A recipe for corn tortillas appears on page 156.

A mild dish, without chilies, using fresh heavy cream rather than sour cream.

	To make 12 enchiladas	
4	chicken breasts	4
8	tomatoes, peeled, seeded and coarsely chopped (2 lb. [1 kg.])	8
1	small onion, quartered	1
1	garlic clove	1
	salt	
½ cup	corn oil or safflower oil	125 ml.
12	corn tortillas, each 6 inches [15 cm.] across	12
1 cup	heavy cream	¼ liter

Place the chicken breasts in a saucepan with salted water to cover and simmer, partially covered, until tender. Allow the chicken to cool in its broth, then skin, bone and shred it with a fork. Set the chicken aside.

In a blender or a food mill, purée the tomatoes, onion and garlic; add salt to taste. In a heavy skillet, heat 2 tablespoons [30 ml.] of the oil, and cook and stir the tomato mixture over medium heat until it has thickened slightly, about five to 10 minutes. Taste and adjust the seasoning. Set aside and keep warm. In another large skillet, heat the remaining oil almost to the smoking point and cook the tortillas one at a time until they are softened but not browned. Drain the tortillas on absorbent paper very briefly, then fill each with a spoonful of shredded chicken, roll them up and place them in a heated serving dish, seam sides down. When all of the tortillas are filled and rolled, pour the tomato sauce over them. Pour the heavy cream over the tortillas and serve at once.

ANGELES DE LA ROSA AND C. GANDIA DE FERNANDEZ
FLAVORS OF MEXICO

Burritos

Recipes for wheat-flour tortillas and refried beans appear on page 155 and below.

	To make 12 burritos	
1½ lb.	lean ground beef	¾ kg.
¼ cup	chopped onion	50 ml.
1	garlic clove, finely chopped	1
1 tsp.	salt	5 ml.
¼ tsp.	pepper	1 ml.
1 tsp.	chili powder	5 ml.
½ tsp.	ground cumin (optional)	2 ml.
1 cup	tomato sauce *(recipe, page 167)*	¼ liter
12	wheat-flour tortillas, each 7 inches [18 cm.] across	12
1½ cups	hot refried beans	375 ml.
	oil for frying (optional)	

Crumble the beef into a skillet and brown it well; pour off the excess fat. Add the onion and garlic and cook for about five minutes, stirring frequently, until the onion is soft. Stir in the salt, pepper, chili powder and the cumin, if using. Then add the tomato sauce. Continue cooking the mixture for about 15 minutes longer.

Spread each tortilla with about 1 tablespoon [15 ml.] of refried beans, spreading the beans to within about ½ inch [1 cm.] of the edge. Spoon a heaping tablespoon of the ground-beef mixture along one side of the tortilla. Fold in the ends about 1 inch [2½ cm.] to cover the ends of the beef filling, then roll up the tortilla, starting with the side on which the beef has been placed. Serve at once.

Or, fry in about 1 inch of hot oil until crisp, placing each *burrito* in the skillet with the open flap on the bottom, then turning to fry the top and sides—about two minutes in all. Drain the fried *burritos* on absorbent paper. Serve hot.

THE CULINARY ARTS INSTITUTE STAFF
MEXICAN COOKBOOK

Refried Beans

This bean paste is traditionally used as a topping for tostadas and as a condiment for tacos and burritos. The author recommends cooking the beans in water to cover for about one and one half hours, or until tender. The beans should be flavored at the start of cooking with 1 tablespoon [15 ml.] of lard and a little chopped onion. When tender, they are salted, then simmered for an additional 30 minutes, or until very soft.

To get the very best flavored beans, fry them with good-quality lard, but do not use bacon fat, which is too strong. A word of caution: Blend the beans in two or three lots and, if the mixture in the blender is hot, keep your hand firmly on the lid when the machine is switched on.

	To make about 2 ½ cups [625 ml.] bean paste	
½ lb.	dried pinto or pink beans, freshly cooked (beans and cooking broth together should measure about 4 cups [1 liter])	¼ kg.
5 tbsp.	lard (2½ oz. [100 g.]) or vegetable oil	75 ml.
¼	medium-sized onion, finely chopped	¼

Put about half of the beans and broth (about 2 cups [½ liter]) into a blender and blend for a few seconds until you have a rough purée. Blend the rest in the same way.

Heat the lard in a heavy frying pan and cook the onion gently until it is soft but not brown. Add the bean purée, little by little, and cook it over a fairly high flame until it starts to dry out to a thick consistency. Keep scraping the bottom and sides of the pan as the beans cook so that the crusty bits are well incorporated and do not stick and burn. The beans are now ready to be used, or stored or frozen.

DIANA KENNEDY
THE TORTILLA BOOK

Chili-Tomato Sauce for Tacos

Salsa de Jitomate

Serrano chilies are very hot small green chilies obtainable fresh or canned where Latin American foods are sold. A milder sauce can be made by substituting one jalapeño chili for the serrano chilies.

	To make about 2 cups [½ liter] sauce	
2 or 3	fresh or canned serrano chilies, finely chopped	2 or 3
2	large tomatoes, peeled, seeded and chopped	2
2 tbsp.	vegetable oil	30 ml.
1	onion, finely chopped	1
1	garlic clove, finely chopped	1
½ tsp.	sugar	2 ml.
	salt and freshly ground pepper	
1 tbsp.	chopped fresh coriander	15 ml.

Heat the oil and fry the onion and garlic until limp. Add all of the other ingredients except the coriander, and cook gently for 15 minutes. Add the coriander and cook for a minute or two longer. Serve either hot or cold.

ELISABETH LAMBERT ORTIZ
THE COMPLETE BOOK OF MEXICAN COOKING

Red-Chili Sauce

Salsa de Chile Colorado

The chilies called for in this recipe are obtainable where Latin American foods are sold. If the chilies specified are not available, four each of ancho and mulato chilies may be substituted. The sauce can be enriched by adding 1 cup [¼ liter] of milk during the last stage of cooking, as shown on page 88.

Since some chilies are not as hot as others, the author suggests adding tepín, or pequín, chilies for a hotter sauce.

My personal touch is adding the tomato sauce, but it is not the Mexican custom to do so. This sauce may be used for enchiladas, cooked chicken, beef or pork.

To make about 1 quart [1 liter] sauce

6	fresh *pasilla* chilies, each about 6 inches [15 cm.] long	6
6	fresh *colorado* chilies, each about 4½ to 5 inches [11 to 13 cm.] long	6
3 cups	hot water or stock *(recipe, below)*	¾ liter
2	garlic cloves	2
1 tsp.	oregano	5 ml.
¼ tsp.	ground cumin	1 ml.
1 tbsp.	vinegar	15 ml.
	salt	
1 cup	tomato sauce *(recipe, page 167)*	¼ liter
2 tbsp.	oil	30 ml.

Fry the chilies in a hot, dry skillet until they are parched on all sides. Pull out the stems and remove the seeds. Wash and soak the chilies in the hot water or stock for 15 to 20 minutes, or until they are soft. Add to them all of the remaining ingredients except the tomato sauce and oil, and mix in a blender or grind until very smooth; strain if necessary. Heat the oil in a pan, add the chili mixture and the tomato sauce, and simmer for about 10 minutes.

ELENA ZELAYETA
ELENA'S SECRETS OF MEXICAN COOKING

Standard Preparations

Basic Meat Stock

This stock may be made, according to your taste and recipe needs, from beef, veal, pork or chicken—or a combination of these meats. For the beef, use such cuts as shank, short ribs, chuck and oxtail; for the veal, use neck, shank and rib tips; for the pork, use hocks, Boston shoulder and back ribs; for the chicken, use backs, necks, wings and carcasses. Adding gelatinous elements such as calf's feet, pig's feet or pork rind will make the finished stock set to a clear, firm jelly that can serve as an aspic if prepared carefully enough.

To make about 2 quarts [2 liters] stock

4 to 5 lb.	meat, bones and trimmings of beef, veal, pork and/or chicken	2 to 2½ kg.
1 lb.	pig's, calf's or chicken feet, pig's ears or fresh pork rind (optional)	½ kg.
3 to 4 quarts	water	3 to 4 liters
4	carrots	4
2	large onions, 1 stuck with 2 or 3 whole cloves	2
1	celery rib	1
1	leek, split and washed	1
1	large bouquet garni	1

Put the pieces of bone on a rack in the bottom of a heavy stockpot, and place the meat and trimmings on top of them. Add cold water to cover by 2 inches [5 cm.]. Bring to a boil over low heat, starting to skim before the liquid reaches the boil. Keep skimming, occasionally adding a glass of cold water, until no scum rises—this may take up to 30 minutes. Do not stir, lest you cloud the stock.

Add the vegetables and bouquet garni to the pot, pushing them down into the liquid so that everything is submerged. Continue skimming until a boil is reached again. Reduce the heat to very low, partially cover the pan, and cook at a bare simmer for two hours if you are using only chicken trimmings, otherwise for five hours—skimming off the surface fat three or four times during the cooking period.

Strain the stock by pouring the contents of the pot into a large bowl through a colander lined with a double layer of cheesecloth or muslin. Discard the bones and meat trimmings, vegetables and bouquet garni. Cool the strained stock and remove the last traces of fat from the surface with a folded paper towel. If there is any residue at the bottom of the container after the stock cools, pour the clear liquid slowly into another container and discard the sediment.

Refrigerate the stock if you do not plan to use it immediately; it will keep safely for three to four days. To preserve the stock longer, refrigerate it for only 12 hours—or until the last bits of fat solidify on the top—then scrape off the fat and warm the stock enough so that it may be poured into four or five pint-sized freezer containers. Be sure to leave room in the containers to allow for expansion, and cover the containers tightly. The freezer stock will keep for six months while you draw on the supply as necessary.

Fish Fumet

To make about 1 quart [1 liter] fumet

1 lb.	fish heads, bones and trimmings, rinsed and broken into convenient sizes	½ kg.
1	small onion, sliced	1
1	carrot, sliced	1
1	leek, sliced	1
1	rib celery, diced	1
1	bouquet garni	1
1 quart	water	1 liter
	salt	
1 cup	dry white wine	¼ liter

Place the fish, vegetables and herbs in a large pan. Add the water and season lightly with salt. Bring to a boil over low heat. With a large, shallow spoon, skim off the scum that rises to the surface as the liquid reaches a simmer. Keep skimming until no more scum rises, then cover the pan and simmer for 15 minutes. Add the wine and simmer, covered, for another 15 minutes.

Strain the fumet through a colander placed over a deep bowl. If the fumet is to be used for a sauce or for aspic, do not press the solids when straining lest they cloud the liquid.

Fish Aspic

To make about 1 quart [1 liter] aspic

1 quart	fish fumet *(recipe, above)*	1 liter
2	egg whites	2
2	eggshells, finely crushed	2
2 to 4 tbsp.	Madeira or other fortified wine	30 to 60 ml.
3 to 4 tbsp.	powdered gelatin	45 to 60 ml.

Strain the fumet into a bowl through a fine sieve lined with three or four layers of dampened cheesecloth or one layer of muslin. Place the bowl in the refrigerator for several hours in order to allow the fine solids in the fumet to form a sediment. Decant the clear liquid into a large saucepan and warm it over low heat.

In a small bowl soften 3 tablespoons [45 ml.] of the gelatin with 6 or 8 tablespoons [90 or 120 ml.] of cold water. Add a little of the warm fumet, then stir the softened gelatin into the fumet in the saucepan. When the gelatin is completely dissolved, remove the pan from the heat. Refrigerate a spoonful of the fumet. If the fumet does not set within 10

minutes, soften the remaining gelatin in 4 tablespoons [60 ml.] of water, warm the fumet again and stir in the gelatin.

To clarify the fumet, beat the egg whites until they form soft peaks, and add them to the saucepan with the crushed eggshells. Place the pan over high heat and whisk the fumet to incorporate the egg whites thoroughly. Cook without stirring so that the whites will separate from the fumet and rise to form a curdlike layer on its surface. When a few bubbles begin to break the egg-white layer, remove the pan from the heat and set it aside for 10 minutes. Bring the fumet to a boil two more times, letting it stand off the heat for 10 minutes between each boil.

Strain the fumet into a bowl through a fine sieve lined with three or four layers of dampened cheesecloth or one layer of muslin. When all of the fumet has dripped through the cloth, test another spoonful in the refrigerator, and add more softened gelatin if necessary. Leave the fumet in the bowl to cool to room temperature. Taste the cooled aspic for salt and add the Madeira. The aspic is now ready for use.

Aspic Cream

Sauce Chaud-Froid

The technique for preparing aspic cream is demonstrated on pages 42-43.

To make about 2 cups [½ liter] aspic

1½ cups	gelatinous veal or chicken stock *(recipe, page 161)* or fish aspic *(recipe, left)*	375 ml.
1 cup	heavy cream	¼ liter
¼ cup	dry white wine or vermouth	50 ml.
1	small onion, sliced	1
1	small carrot, diced	1
1 tsp.	chopped fresh thyme or tarragon, or substitute ¼ tsp. [1 ml.] dried thyme or tarragon	5 ml.
	salt and white pepper	

Combine the stock, cream, wine, onion, carrot and thyme or tarragon in a small, heavy saucepan. Bring to a boil over medium heat, stirring frequently. Reduce the heat to low and simmer, uncovered, until the liquid has reduced to about half of its original volume—20 to 30 minutes. Add salt and pepper to taste. Strain the mixture through a fine-meshed sieve into a bowl, letting it drain naturally without pressing on the vegetables. Cool the aspic cream over ice before using.

Green aspic cream. Blanch 1 cup [¼ liter] of fresh herbs—chervil, parsley, tarragon or thyme—in boiling water for one minute. Drain the herbs, then squeeze them dry. Chop the herbs fine and stir them into the aspic mixture before straining it.

Yellow aspic cream. Beat three egg yolks with 1 tablespoon [15 ml.] of heavy cream. Warm the yolks by whisking in a little of the simmering but reduced aspic mixture, then stir them into the remaining aspic. Strain immediately.

Orange aspic cream. Stir a dash of cayenne pepper and 2 teaspoons [10 ml.] of paprika into the aspic mixture before straining it into a bowl.

Pink aspic cream. Reduce tomato sauce *(recipe, page 167)* to a thick purée, and stir 3 to 4 tablespoons [45 to 60 ml.] of the purée into the aspic mixture before straining it.

Compound Butter

To produce a fluffy but not greasy mixture, the butter must be chilled in advance and worked quickly. The technique of making compound butter is demonstrated on pages 10-11.

To make about 1 ¼ cups [300 ml.] butter

16 tbsp.	unsalted butter, chilled in 1 or 2 pieces (½ lb. [¼ kg.])	240 ml.
2 cups	mixed fresh herbs: parsley, chervil, watercress, tarragon and/or savory	½ liter
	salt and white pepper	
	fresh lemon juice (optional)	

Blanch the herbs by plunging them into boiling water for one minute. Drain the herbs, dry them on paper towels and chop them very fine.

Set the butter on a smooth work surface—preferably marble—and use a rolling pin or kitchen mallet to pound the butter until it softens enough to be easily dented with a finger. Transfer the butter to a bowl and beat it with a wooden spoon or whisk until it is light and fluffy.

Beat the herbs into the butter. Then force the flavored mixture through a fine-meshed sieve or strainer into a clean bowl with a pestle or wooden spoon. Season the butter to taste with salt, pepper and lemon juice. Covered, the butter will keep in the refrigerator for seven to 10 days.

Cheese butter. Crumble, grate or shred ½ pound [¼ kg.] of cheese—blue, Cheddar, Edam, Parmesan, Romano and goat cheeses are all possibilities. Beat the cheese into the whisked butter and force the mixture through a sieve. Season the cheese butter to taste.

Horseradish butter. Peel and grate 2 ounces [75 g.] of fresh horseradish. Mix the horseradish with the whisked butter and force the mixture through a sieve. Season.

Liver butter. Sauté ½ pound [¼ kg.] of fresh goose, chicken or duck livers in butter for one or two minutes, or until they are lightly browned but still pink inside. Drain the livers on paper towels, pound them to a paste and beat the paste into the whisked butter. Force the mixture through a sieve. Season to taste.

Mushroom butter. Chop ½ pound [¼ kg.] of fresh mushrooms coarse and stew them with a little butter, stirring frequently, until they have given up all their liquid and are lightly colored—about five minutes. Pound the mushrooms to a paste, beat them into the whisked butter and force the mixture through a sieve. Season to taste.

Nut butter. Chop ½ pound [¼ kg.] of blanched nuts—pistachios, walnuts, hazelnuts, almonds—and pound them to a paste in a mortar. Mix the nuts with the whisked butter and season to taste.

Anchovy butter. Drain eight or nine oil-packed flat anchovy fillets and pound them to a paste. Press the paste through a fine sieve into the whisked butter a little at a time; taste often and use only as much paste as liked. Season.

Tomato butter. Cook tomato sauce *(recipe, page 167)* to a thick purée. Force the purée through a sieve into the whisked butter, tasting frequently and using only enough purée to flavor and color the butter without making it too fluid. Season to taste.

Shrimp butter. Poach ½ pound [¼ kg.] of fresh unpeeled shrimp in lightly salted water for three or four minutes, or until they are pink and firm. Drain the shrimp, chop them coarse and then pound the chopped shrimp with their shells in a mortar. Add the whisked butter and continue pounding to make a fine paste. Force the flavored butter through a fine-meshed sieve into a bowl. Season to taste.

Choux Pastry

To form *choux* puffs, pipe or spoon small mounds of this pastry on a baking sheet that has been buttered and floured or lined with parchment paper. Bake in a preheated 375° F. [190° C.] oven for 20 minutes, or until the pastry is puffed and lightly browned. Cool on a rack.

To make forty 1-inch [2 ½-cm.] choux puffs

1 cup	water	¼ liter
8 tbsp.	unsalted butter	120 ml.
1 cup	flour	¼ liter
⅛ tsp.	salt	½ ml.
4	eggs	4

Put the water in a heavy saucepan over medium heat. Add the butter. Sift the flour and salt into a bowl.

When the butter has melted, increase the heat to bring the water to a boil. Turn the heat to low, and pour the flour all at once into the water. Stir the mixture until thoroughly combined, then stir over medium heat until the mixture forms a solid mass that comes away cleanly from the sides of the pan. Remove the pan from the heat and cool the mixture for a few minutes.

Break one egg into a bowl and add it to the contents of the pan, beating with a spoon to incorporate the egg thoroughly. Repeat with the other eggs. Continue beating until the ingredients are smoothly blended.

Short-Crust and Rough Puff Pastry

When baking small tart shells blind, you can make a firmer pastry that is less likely to shrink by substituting one beaten egg for 4 tablespoons [60 ml.] of the butter called for in this recipe. The techniques of shaping tarts and baking them unfilled are demonstrated on pages 66-67.

One simple formula produces dough both for plain short-crust pastry and for rough puff pastry. The difference is in how you roll it out.

To make enough pastry for 12 short-crust or 8 rough puff tarts —each about 3 inches [8 cm.] across		
1 cup	flour	¼ liter
¼ tsp.	salt	1 ml.
8 tbsp.	cold unsalted butter, cut into small pieces	120 ml.
3 to 4 tbsp.	cold water	45 to 60 ml.

Mix the flour and salt in a bowl. Add the butter and cut it into the flour rapidly, using two table knives, until the mixture resembles fine crumbs. Do not work for more than a few minutes. Add half of the water and, with a fork, quickly blend it into the flour-and-butter mixture. Add just enough of the rest of the water to allow you to form the dough into a firm ball with your hands. Wrap the dough in plastic wrap or wax paper and refrigerate it for two or three hours.

To roll out short-crust pastry. Remove the ball of pastry dough from the refrigerator and put it on a cool, floured surface (a marble slab is ideal). Press the dough out partially with your hand, then give it a few gentle smacks with the rolling pin to flatten it and render it more supple. Roll out the dough from the center until the pastry forms a circle about ½ inch [1 cm.] thick. Turn the pastry over to flour both sides, and continue rolling it until the circle is approximately ⅛ inch [3 mm.] thick.

To roll out rough puff pastry. Place the dough on a cool, floured surface and smack it flat with the rolling pin. Turn the dough over to make sure that both sides are well floured. Roll out the pastry rapidly into a rectangle about 1 foot [30 cm.] long and 5 to 6 inches [13 to 15 cm.] wide. Fold the two short ends to meet each other in the center, then fold again to align the folded edges with each other. Following the direction of the fold lines, roll the pastry into a rectangle again, fold again in the same way, and refrigerate for at least 30 minutes. Repeat this process two or three more times before using the pastry. Always let the pastry dough rest in the refrigerator between rollings.

Basic White Bread

This recipe is for a crusty loaf similar to French country bread *(pain de campagne)*. It can be varied by including dark flour (for example, one part whole-wheat and one part rye to two parts all-purpose or bread flour) and by allowing the yeast to ferment for 24 hours before making the bread. For a sourdough sponge, dissolve the yeast in 1 cup [¼ liter] of warm water and stir in 2 cups [½ liter] of the flour, beat the mixture until smooth, cover tightly with plastic wrap and leave the bowl in a warm place overnight. Add the remaining ingredients and continue with the recipe.

When using this dough for pizza, you can enrich its flavor by adding 1 to 2 tablespoons [15 to 30 ml.] of olive oil to the yeast mixture along with the flour and salt.

To make 1 large loaf or 2 small ones — about 1½ pounds [¾ kg.] in all		
1 tbsp.	dry yeast, or ⅗ oz. [30 g.] compressed fresh yeast	15 ml.
2 cups	tepid water	½ liter
	salt	
about 6 cups	flour, preferably bread flour	about 1½ liters
	farina, cornmeal or cracked wheat (optional)	

In a large bowl, dissolve the yeast in ½ cup [125 ml.] of the water and leave for about 15 minutes, or until foamy. Add the remaining water and the salt, and begin stirring in the flour. When the dough is stiff and starts to pull away from the sides of the bowl, turn it out onto a floured work surface. Knead by folding the dough toward you, pushing it away with the heels of your hands and giving it a quarter turn. Continue kneading until the dough is smooth and shiny and not sticky—at least 10 minutes. Sprinkle the dough with more flour as necessary during kneading. Gather the dough into a ball, dust it with flour and place the dough in a clean bowl. Cover with a cloth and leave in a warm place until the dough has more than doubled in bulk—one to two hours.

Turn out the dough onto the floured surface and punch the ball down to expel all of the air. Knead again briefly and form the dough on a lightly floured baking sheet into a large round loaf or two long, tapered, cylindrical French loaves. Or form one large or two small cylinders and put them into buttered loaf pans. Leave the bread to rise, covered loosely with a towel, until it doubles in volume—about one hour. (If you are baking a large round loaf, you may let it rise for a second time on a work surface generously sprinkled with farina, cornmeal or cracked wheat.)

Preheat the oven to 400° F. [200° C.]. If you are not baking the bread in pans, place a baking sheet in the oven while it preheats. To create steam, put a baking pan containing about 1 inch [2½ cm.] of hot water on the floor of the oven or the lowest shelf.

To bake the bread, slash the surface of each loaf in three or four places with a razor blade or razor-sharp knife, and transfer the loaf with a rapid jerk to the heated baking sheet. After the first 20 minutes of baking, remove the pan of water and turn the oven down to 350° F. [180° C.]. The bread will take about one hour to bake, depending on the size and shape of the loaves. When it is done, it will be golden brown all over and the bottom crust will sound hollow when you rap it with your knuckles. Cool the bread on a wire rack.

Sandwich Bread

Pain de Mie

The technique of shaping sandwich bread is demonstrated on pages 6-7.

To make one 10-by-4-inch [25-by-10-cm.] loaf		
about 4 cups	flour	about 1 liter
1 tbsp.	dry yeast, or ⅗ oz. [30 g.] compressed fresh yeast	15 ml.
2 tsp.	salt	10 ml.
1½ cups	tepid milk	375 ml.
7 tbsp.	butter, softened	105 ml.

Sift 4 cups [1 liter] of the flour with the salt into a bowl. Dissolve the yeast in ½ cup [125 ml.] of the milk and leave it in a warm place for about 10 minutes, or until the mixture is foamy. Pour the yeast mixture and the remaining milk into the flour and salt, and work in the softened butter until a sticky dough is obtained. Turn the dough out onto a lightly floured work surface and knead it vigorously for 10 to 15 minutes, or until the dough is elastic, smooth and glossy. The dough should be fairly firm; add more flour if necessary.

Gather the dough into a ball, put the ball in a clean, buttered bowl and turn it to coat all sides. Cover the bowl with a towel or plastic wrap and let the dough rise in a warm, draft-free place such as an unlighted oven until it has doubled in volume—about one and a half to two and a half hours, depending on the temperature and humidity. The dough is ready when a finger pressed into it leaves a dent that does not immediately smooth itself out.

Turn the dough out onto a work surface, punch it down, and knead it again for three or four minutes. Shape the dough into a flat rectangle and fold it in thirds—bringing one third up over the center and then covering it with the other third. Place the dough on a floured surface and cover it with a towel until doubled in volume—about 45 minutes.

Punch the dough down, knead it for another three or four minutes, and shape it into a rectangle again. Fold the rectangle in half lengthwise, seal the edges, roll the dough forward until the long seam is underneath, and place the dough in a loaf pan equipped with a cover. Cover the pan with a towel and let the bread rise until it doubles in volume again, or rises to fill the pan—about 45 minutes to one hour.

Slide the cover onto the pan and set the bread in a preheated 400° F. [200° C.] oven; immediately reduce the heat to 375° F. [190° C.] and bake for 45 minutes to one hour. The bread is ready when it has turned golden brown and when, turned out of the pan, it sounds hollow when the base is rapped with the knuckles. Cool the bread on a wire rack before slicing or storing it.

Vinaigrette

The proportion of vinegar to oil may be varied according to the acidity of the vinegar used and the tartness of the food to be dressed, but one part of vinegar to four or five parts of oil is a good mean ratio. Despite its name, this dressing may be made, if desired, with lemon juice instead of vinegar or with a combination of the two.

To make about ½ cup [125 ml.] vinaigrette		
1 tsp.	salt	5 ml.
¼ tsp.	freshly ground pepper	1 ml.
2 tbsp.	wine vinegar	30 ml.
½ cup	oil	125 ml.

Put the salt and **pepper** into a small bowl. Add the vinegar and stir until the salt dissolves. Finally, stir in the oil.

Garlic vinaigrette. In a mortar or small bowl, pound half of a garlic clove to a purée with the salt and **pepper** before adding the vinegar and oil.

Mustard vinaigrette. Mix about 1 teaspoon [5 ml.] of Dijon mustard or ¼ teaspoon [1 ml.] dry mustard with the salt and **pepper**. Add the vinegar and stir until the mustard dissolves before adding the oil.

Handmade Mayonnaise

To prevent curdling, the egg yolks, oil, and vinegar or lemon juice should be at room temperature and the oil should be added very gradually at first. The ratio of egg yolks to oil may be varied according to taste. The prepared mayonnaise will keep for several days in a covered container in the refrigerator. Stir it well before use.

To make about 1 ½ cups [375 ml.]
mayonnaise

2	egg yolks	2
	salt and white pepper	
2 tsp.	vinegar or fresh lemon juice	10 ml.
1 to 1½ cups	oil	250 to 375 ml.

Put the egg yolks in a warmed, dry bowl. Season with a little salt and pepper and whisk for about a minute, or until the yolks become slightly paler in color. Add the vinegar or lemon juice and whisk until thoroughly mixed.

Whisking constantly, add the oil, drop by drop to begin with. When the sauce starts to thicken, pour the remaining oil in a thin, steady stream, whisking rhythmically. Add only enough oil to give the mayonnaise a soft but firm consistency. It should just hold its shape when lifted in a spoon. If the mayonnaise is too thick, add 1 to 2 teaspoons [5 to 10 ml.] of additional vinegar or lemon juice, or of warm water.

Green mayonnaise. Parboil ¼ pound [125 g.] of spinach leaves for one to two minutes; drain the spinach in a strainer, plunge it into cold water to stop the cooking, and squeeze the spinach dry with your hands. Chop the spinach fine, then purée it through a food mill or in a food processor. Stir the purée into the prepared mayonnaise, along with 1 tablespoon [15 ml.] of fines herbes.

Garlic mayonnaise. In a mortar, pound one or two garlic cloves to a paste with coarse salt. Mix thoroughly with the egg yolks and vinegar or lemon juice before adding the oil.

Mustard mayonnaise. Add 1 teaspoon [5 ml.] of Dijon mustard or ¼ teaspoon [1 ml.] of dry mustard to the egg yolks, along with the vinegar or lemon juice.

Herb mayonnaise. Stir about 1 teaspoon [5 ml.] each of finely chopped fresh chives, chervil, tarragon and parsley into the prepared mayonnaise.

Scandinavian sweet mayonnaise. Add 1 tablespoon [15 ml.] of sugar and ¼ teaspoon [1 ml.] of dry mustard to the egg yolk, along with the salt and pepper.

Tartar sauce. Add 1 tablespoon [15 ml.] each (or more to taste) of finely chopped sour gherkins, capers and fines herbes to 1½ cups [375 ml.] of prepared mayonnaise.

Russian dressing. Stir about ¼ cup [50 ml.] of ketchup, 1½ tablespoons [22 ml.] of grated horseradish and 1 teaspoon [5 ml.] of grated onion into the prepared mayonnaise; then add Worcestershire sauce to taste.

Blender or Processor Mayonnaise

To form an emulsion, the egg, the vinegar or lemon juice, and the oil must be at room temperature. The basic mayonnaise may be colored or flavored as described for Handmade Mayonnaise *(left).*

To make about 1 ½ cups [375 ml.]
mayonnaise

1	egg	1
2 tsp.	vinegar or fresh lemon juice	10 ml.
	salt and white pepper	
1 to 1½ cups	oil	250 to 375 ml.

Combine the egg, vinegar or lemon juice, salt and pepper in the jar of an electric blender or the bowl of a food processor equipped with a steel blade. Cover and blend for a few seconds to mix the ingredients thoroughly. Without stopping the machine, pour the oil in a slow stream through the hole in the cover of the blender or through the tube of the processor. Add 1 cup [¼ liter] of oil for a soft mayonnaise, up to 1½ cups [375 ml.] for a firm one. Taste and add more seasonings, vinegar or lemon juice if desired. Turn off the machine and use a rubber spatula to transfer the mayonnaise to a bowl.

Olive and Anchovy Sauce

Tapenade

This highly flavored mixture has many variations. If you wish, you can pound in thyme, ground bay leaf, garlic cloves or tuna, or stir in Cognac. If desired, the mixture may be prepared in a food processor as shown on pages 14-15.

To make about 1 cup [¼ liter] sauce

½ cup	pitted ripe oil-packed olives, coarsely chopped	125 ml.
2	salt anchovies, soaked in water for 30 minutes, filleted, patted dry and coarsely chopped	2
¼ cup	capers, rinsed and drained	50 ml.
about ¼ cup	olive oil	about 50 ml.
2 to 3 tsp.	fresh lemon juice	10 to 15 ml.
	freshly ground pepper	
1 tsp.	dry mustard (optional)	5 ml.

In a large mortar, pound together the olives, anchovies and capers until they form a paste. Little by little, stir in enough oil to make a sauce of rather firm consistency. Then season the mixture with the lemon juice, pepper to taste, and dry mustard if you are using it.

Basic White Sauce

Use this recipe whenever béchamel sauce is required.

To make about 1 ½ cups [375 ml.] sauce

2 tbsp.	butter	30 ml.
2 tbsp.	flour	30 ml.
2 cups	milk	½ liter
	salt	
	white pepper	
	grated nutmeg (optional)	
	heavy cream (optional)	

Melt the butter in a heavy saucepan. Stir in the flour and cook, stirring over low heat, for two to five minutes. Pour in all of the milk at once, whisking constantly to blend the mixture smoothly. Raise the heat and continue whisking while the sauce comes to a boil. Season with a very little salt. Reduce the heat to very low and simmer for about 40 minutes, stirring every so often to prevent the sauce from sticking to the bottom of the pan.

When the sauce thickens to the desired consistency, add white pepper and a pinch of nutmeg if you like; taste for seasoning. Whisk again until the sauce is perfectly smoooth, then add cream if you prefer a richer and whiter sauce.

Tomato Sauce

When fresh ripe tomatoes are not available, use 3 cups [¾ liter] of drained, canned Italian plum tomatoes.

To make about 1 cup [¼ liter] sauce

6	medium-sized ripe tomatoes, chopped	6
1	onion, diced	1
1 tbsp.	olive oil	15 ml.
1	garlic clove (optional)	1
1 tsp.	chopped fresh parsley	5 ml.
1 tsp.	mixed dried basil, marjoram and thyme	5 ml.
1 to 2 tbsp.	sugar (optional)	15 to 30 ml.
	salt and freshly ground pepper	

In a large enameled or stainless-steel saucepan, gently fry the diced onion in the oil until soft, but not brown. Add the other ingredients and simmer for 20 to 30 minutes, or until the tomatoes have been reduced to a thick pulp. Sieve the mixture, using a wooden pestle or spoon. Reduce the sauce further, if necessary, to reach the desired consistency. Adjust the seasoning.

Tomato Ketchup

To make about 3 pints [1 ½ liters] ketchup

6 lb.	firm ripe tomatoes, peeled, cored, seeded and coarsely chopped (about 4 quarts [4 liters] chopped)	3 kg.
1 cup	chopped onions	¼ liter
½ cup	sweet red pepper	125 ml.
1 ½ tsp.	celery seeds	7 ml.
1 tsp.	allspice berries	5 ml.
1 tsp.	mustard seeds	5 ml.
1	stick cinnamon	1
1 cup	sugar	¼ liter
1 tbsp.	salt	15 ml.
1 ½ cups	vinegar	375 ml.

In a heavy enameled or stainless-steel pan, combine the tomatoes, onions and sweet pepper. Bring to a boil, stirring constantly, then reduce the heat to low and simmer for 20 to 30 minutes, or until the vegetables are soft. Purée the vegetables, a small batch at a time, through a food mill or strainer into a clean pan. Cook over medium heat, stirring frequently, until the mixture thickens and is reduced to about half of its original volume—about one hour. Tie the whole spices in a cheesecloth bag and add them to the tomato mixture together with the sugar and salt. Stirring frequently, simmer gently for about 30 minutes. Then stir in the vinegar and continue to simmer until the ketchup reaches the desired consistency—about 10 minutes. Remove the spice bag; taste the ketchup and adjust the seasoning.

Pour the ketchup boiling hot into hot, sterilized jars, leaving a ¼-inch [6-mm.] headspace. Seal each jar quickly and tightly with its lid. Set the jars on a rack in a canner or other deep pot, pour in enough hot (not boiling) water to cover the jars by 1 inch [2½ cm.], tightly cover the pot and bring to a boil over medium heat. Boil for 10 minutes. Remove the jars with tongs and cool them at room temperature.

Recipe Index

All recipes in the index that follows are listed by their English titles except in cases where a snack of foreign origin, such as guacamole, is universally recognized by its source name. Entries are organized by the type of snack or sandwich and also by the major ingredients specified in the recipe titles. Foreign recipes are listed by country or region of origin. Recipe credits appear on pages 174-176.

General Index/Glossary

Included in this index to the cooking demonstrations are definitions, in italics, of special culinary terms not explained elsewhere in this volume. The Recipe Index begins on page 168.

Allspice: *the dried berry, used whole or ground, of a member of the myrtle family. Called allspice because it has something of the aroma of clove, cinnamon and nutmeg combined.*
Anchovies: adding to creamed butter, 11; in *bagna cauda,* 20; boning, 14; sauce for *mozzarella in carrozza,* 55; puréeing, 11, 15; reducing saltiness of, 14; sieving, 11; in *tapenade,* 14-15; with turnips, 24
Anchovy, salt: *not to be confused with oil-packed anchovy fillets, a salt anchovy is a whole cleaned fish with the head removed. Obtainable in cans or sold by weight at markets specializing in Mediterranean foods.*
Aromatic leaves: lining Chinese steamer with, 76
Aromatic vegetables: in aspic cream, 42
Asparagus: arranging cut stalks on canapés, 39; in ribbon cake, 44-45
Aspic: diced, with pork-liver paté sandwich, 46, 47; glazing open-faced sandwiches with, 34, 35, 40-41; made from fish fumet, 40; made from veal stock, 40-41; toppings not to glaze with, 40. *See also* Fish fumet; Veal stock
Aspic cream, 42-43; adding egg yolks to, 42; coating canapé toppings with, 43; coloring with herbs, 42; reducing, 42; setting, 43; straining, 43
Avocado: mashing for *guacamole,* 17
Baba ghanoush: baking eggplant for, 15; puréeing, 15
Bagna cauda: preparing, 20; serving with raw vegetables, 21
Baking: bread, 6-7; *choux paste,* 8; *choux* puffs, 70; eggplant, 15; filled whole loaf of bread, 57; *gougère,* 70-71; lining baking pan with parchment, 28, 29, 60, 71; Melba toast, 36, 37; mushroom caps, 24; phyllo, 68-69; pizza on tiles, 86; rough-puff rolled cylinder, 65; sandwich bread, 6-7; sheets used for small pastries, 60; shells, 52; short-crust crescents, 60-61; small pies, 62-63; souffléed omelet, 28-29; square turnovers, 64; tarts, on inverted pan, 66-67; tarts, in stacks, 66-67; toasting bread and rolls, 52; triangular turnovers, 64; turnovers (Cornish pasties), 62-63; vegetables before hollowing, 24
Bamboo shoots: *the ivory-colored, cone-shaped shoots of tropical bamboo; available in cans from Oriental*

shops; 76
Barquettes, 66-67. *See also* Tarts
Basil: in vinaigrette, 50; with zucchini, 24
Batter: deep-fried container *(krustader),* 79, 80-81; leavened with yeast *(blini),* 78, 79, 82-83
Beef: fat content of ground, 50; with sweet mayonnaise, 46, 48
Beets: as containers, 24-25; with herring and egg, in sandwich, 46, 48; parboiling, 24
Beurre en pommade (creamed butter), 10
Beverages: served with snacks, 5
Black mustard seed: *the tiny, reddish-brown to black seed of a variety of the mustard plant, smaller than the common yellow mustard seed and much less pungent in flavor. Available where Indian foods are sold.*
Blanch: *to plunge food into boiling water for a short period. Done to facilitate the removal of skins or shells, or to soften vegetables or fruits before further cooking. Another meaning is "to whiten";* 10
Blini, 78, 79, 82-83; accompaniments for, 82; adding yeast to batter, 82; clarifying butter for, 82; cooking in Swedish pancake pan *(plättlagg),* 82, 83
Bouquet garni: *a bunch of mixed herbs — the classic three being parsley, thyme and bay leaf — tied together or wrapped in cheesecloth and used for flavoring stocks, sauces, braises and stews.*
Bread: baking shells, 52; basic dough, 6-7; brushing with olive oil, 53; canapé base, 35, 36, 56; contrasting layers in ribbon sandwiches, 44; firming for canapés, 36; flat, 35, 46; hero, 50; hollowing out loaves of, 56; kneading, 6-7; Melba toast, 36-37; punching down, 7; shaping dough for sandwich bread, 6-7; slicing loaf horizontally, 36, 44; slicing loaf for mass-produced canapés, 36; in *smorrebrod,* 46; stuffing long loaf, 56; stuffing round loaf, 56-57; in *taramosalata,* 16. *See also* Dough; Sandwich; Smorrebrod sandwiches
Broiling: shredded cheese on toasted bread, 53
Brussels sprouts: as containers, 24-25; parboiling, 24; peeling, 24
Butter: adding herbs to make compound butter, 10; clarifying, 82; controlling development of gluten in pastry, 8; cutting into short-crust pastry, 8; in *smorrebrod* sandwiches, 46. *See also* Compound butter
Cabbage: sandwich with stuffed pork, 46, 47
Camembert: coating with pistachios and bread crumbs, 33; marinating in wine, 32; sousing underripe, 32-33
Canapé garnishes, 38-39;

anchoring garnish with mayonnaise, 38; applying in geometric patterns, 38; asparagus stalks, 39; compound butter cut-outs, 39; decorating with aspic cutters, 43; decorating canapés, 37, 38-39, 41, 43; egg yolk, 38; foods to use for, 38; fresh herbs, 38; onion, 38; parsley, 38; for ribbon cake, 44
Canapés: checkerboard sandwiches, 44-45; choosing bread for base, 36; coating with aspic cream, 42-43; decorating, 36, 37, 38-39, 43; firming bread, 36; glazing with aspic, 34, 40-41; Melba-toast rounds, 36-37; multilayered ribbon sandwiches, 44; piping compound butter, 36; producing large numbers of bread-based canapés, 36-37; ribbon cake, 44-45; *smorrebrod* sandwiches, 46-49; topping bread-based, 36. *See also* Open-faced sandwiches; Sandwiches; Smorrebrod sandwiches
Carrots: cutting curls, 23; filling coils with *tapenade,* 23; serving raw, 21; slicing partway, 20
Cauliflower: coring and serving raw, 21
Caviar: as canapé topping, 38; in fillings, 26, 28; and raw egg-yolk sandwich, 46, 49; and shrimp sandwich, 46, 47
Celeriac: parboiling, 24
Celery cabbage: *a variety of Chinese cabbage that grows like celery but has crisp, tightly packed, yellow-white stalks 14 to 16 inches [35 to 40 cm.] long and 4 to 5 inches [10 to 13 cm.] wide. Sold fresh by the bunch or by weight in Oriental specialty stores and in some vegetable stores and supermarkets. Store, refrigerated, for about two weeks. Substitute Savoy cabbage.*
Cheese: adding to *choux* paste to make *gougère,* 70; cheese block, 31; coating with fresh herbs, 31; coating with paprika, 31; coating with peppercorns, 32; combining sharp cheese with cream cheese, 13; in *croque-monsieur,* 54; deep frying cheese sandwiches, 54-55; flavoring and molding Cheddar, 31; in grilled-cheese sandwich, 54; in *mozzarella in carrozza,* 54-55; pan frying cheese sandwiches, 54; potted, 30; rolling log of Liptauer, 31; shredded, in broiled open-faced sandwich, 53; sousing underripe Camembert, 30, 32-33; spreads and molds, 30-33; spreads made with scraps of hard Cheddar, 30, 31; wrapping in vine leaves, 33. *See also* Camembert; Cream cheese
Cheeseburger: fat content of beef, 50; methods of cooking, 50, 51
Chicken: in enchiladas, 89; shredding, 89; in tacos, 90
Chick-peas: puréeing, for *hummus,* 14
Chili dog, 50, 51

Chili oil (hot-pepper oil): *a pungent flavoring oil made by frying hot chilies in oil to extract their capsicin flavoring. When the oil turns red, the fried chilies are removed; they may be used in other dishes. The flavored oil can be stored in a bottle in the refrigerator. Also obtainable ready-made in bottles from Oriental food stores;* 76
Chilies: *ancho* and *mulato,* 88; in enchilada sauce, 88; *salsa,* 90; seeding, 17, 88; *serrano,* 17
Chinese dumplings, 74-77; basket filled with shrimp and bamboo shoots, 76-77; bonnet with ground-beef filling, 74-75; dipping sauces for, 74, 75, 76; fillings for, 74, 76; handling pastry for, 74; pan frying, 74; pastry for, 72, 74; pleating, 75, 77; steaming, 74, 76-77; wheat-starch pastry, 76
Chinese pancakes: coating with scallions, 73; coiling cylinder, 72; fillings, 72; frying, 73; handling, 59, 72; kneading, 72; oil for frying, 72; rolling coil into pancake, 72
Choux paste: baking, 8, 70; enriching with eggs, 9; in *gougère,* 70-71; preparing, 8-9; puffs, 70; qualities of, 8
Clarified butter: *butter with its easily burned milk solids removed. To make, melt butter over low heat, spoon off the foam, and let stand off the heat until the milk solids settle. Then decant the clear yellow liquid on top, discarding the milk solids;* 82
Club sandwich: preparing, 50, 51
Compound butter: adding crushed shrimp, 11; adding flavorings, 10; canapé spreads, 44; creaming butter for, 10; cutting shapes for canapés, 39; farmer's wife, 44; in hard-boiled-egg fillings, 26-27; horseradish, 10, 38; made with anchovies, 11; made with fresh herbs, 10, 24, 38; piping, 36; in zucchini sandwiches, 23
Coriander leaves: in *guacamole,* 17; in tacos, 90
Cornish pasties. *See* Turnovers
Croque-monsieur, 54
Cream cheese: adding herbs and chopped vegetables, 13; blending and molding with other cheeses, 30-33; canapé spreads, 44; coating with peppercorns, 32; fillings, 13, 22, 24, 25, 28; in Liptauer cheese log, 31; in souffléed omelet, 28; thinning with cream, 13; whipping, 13; wrapping molded cheese in vine leaves, 33
Crudités, 20-21
Cucumbers: cups, 22; fluting with mandolin, 22; grating, 14; in *tzatziki,* 14, 17
Deep frying: *krustader,* 80-81; *mozzarella in carrozza,* 54-55; phyllo square, 69; with rosette irons, 80-81; *samosas,* 65; tacos, 90; testing oil for, 80
Dijon mustard: *a mild prepared*

Recipe Credits

The sources for the recipes in this volume are listed below. Page references in parentheses indicate where the recipes appear in the anthology.

Ackart, Robert, *The Cheese Cookbook.* Copyright © 1978 by Robert Ackart. Used by permission of Grosset & Dunlap, Inc.(119).

Adams, Charlotte, *The Four Seasons Cookbook.* Copyright 1971 in all countries of the International Copyright Union by The Ridge Press, Inc. Used by permission of The Ridge Press, Inc. and Crown Publishers, Inc.(107).

Allen, Ida Bailey, *Best Loved Recipes of the American People.* Copyright © 1973 by Ruth Allen Castelli. Reprinted by permission of Doubleday & Company, Inc.(102, 109).

Allen, Lucy G., *A Book of Hors d'Oeuvre.* © Copyright 1925, 1941 by Little, Brown and Company. Reprinted by permission of Little, Brown and Company(109, 126).

Asselin, E. Donald, M.D., *Scandinavian Cookbook.* Copyright in Japan, 1970, by The Charles E. Tuttle Company, Inc. Published by The Charles E. Tuttle Company, Inc., Tokyo. Reprinted by permission of The Charles E. Tuttle Company, Inc.(111).

Beard, James, *Hors d'Oeuvre and Canapés.* Copyright © 1940, 1963 by James Beard. Reprinted by permission of John Schaffner Associates, Inc.(103, 106). *The James Beard Cookbook.* Copyright © 1959 by James Beard. Reprinted by permission of Dell Publishing Co., Inc.(119). *James Beard's New Fish Cookery.* Copyright 1954, © 1976 by James A. Beard. Reprinted by permission of Little, Brown and Company(105).

Mrs. Beeton, *Mrs. Beeton's Hors d'Oeuvre and Savouries.* © Ward Lock Limited. Published by Ward, Lock & Co. Limited, London. Reprinted by permission of Ward Lock Limited(133).

Benell, Julie, *Kitchen Magic.* Copyright © 1973 by Julie Benell. Published by Shoal Creek Publishers, Inc., Austin, Texas. Reprinted by permission of Shoal Creek Publishers, Inc.(126).

Berjane, J., *French Dishes for English Tables.* © Copyright Frederick Warne (Publishers) Limited, London. Published by Frederick Warne & Co. Ltd., London. Reprinted by Frederick Warne (Publishers) Limited, London(128).

Berolzheimer, Ruth (Editor), *The American Woman's Cook Book.* Copyright © 1942 by Delair Publishing Co., Inc., New York. Reprinted by permission of Delair Publishing Co., Inc.(104).

Bocuse, Paul, *Paul Bocuse's French Cooking.* Copyright © 1977 by Random House, Inc. Reprinted by permission of Pantheon Books, a division of Random House, Inc.(93, 135).

Boni, Ada, *Italian Regional Cooking.* English translation copyright © 1969 by Thomas Nelson & Sons, and E. P. Dutton & Co. By permission of Bonanza Books, a division of Crown Publishers, Inc.(132). *The Talisman Italian Cookbook.* Translated by Matilde La Rosa. Copyright 1950, 1977 by Crown Publishers, Inc. Used by permission of Crown Publishers, Inc.(154).

Borghese, Anita, *The Great Sandwich Book.* Copyright © 1978 by Anita Borghese. Reprinted by permission of Rawson, Wade Publishers, Inc.(115, 116, 119, 120).

Boulestin, X. Marcel, *Boulestin's Round-the-Year Cookbook.* Published by Dover Publications, Inc., 1975. Reprinted by permission of Dover Publications, Inc.(95).

Brobeck, Florence, *The Lunchbox and Every Kind of Sandwich.* Copyright 1946 by Florence Brobeck. Published by M. Barrows & Company, Inc., Publishers, New York (99, 112).

Brobeck, Florence and Monika B. Kjellberg, *Smörgasbord and Scandinavian Cookery.* Copyright 1948 by Little, Brown and Company. Reprinted by permission of Little, Brown and Company(110).

Brown, Cora, Rose and Bob, *10,000 Snacks.* Copyright 1937 by Cora Brown, Rose Brown and Robert Carlton Brown. Copyright © 1964 by Cora Brown, Rose Brown and Eleanor Wilson Parker Brown. Published by Garden City Publishing Co., Inc. Reprinted by permission of Carlton Brown(113).

Brown, Helen Evans, *A Book of Appetizers.* Copyright 1958 by Helen Evans Brown. Published by The Ward Ritchie Press, Los Angeles. Reprinted with permission of The Ward Ritchie Press(147).

Brownstone, Cecily, *Cecily Brownstone's Associated Press Cook Book.* © Copyright 1972 by The Associated Press. Published by David McKay Company, Inc., New York. Reprinted by permission of David McKay Company, Inc.(145).

Bugialli, Giuliano, *The Fine Art of Italian Cooking.* Copyright © 1977 by Giuliano Bugialli. Reprinted by permission of Times Books, a division of Quadrangle/The New York Times Book Co., Inc.(155).

Burros, Marian Fox and Lois Levine, *The Elegant But Easy Cookbook.* Copyright © 1960, 1963, 1967 by Marian F. Burros and Lois L. Levine. Reprinted with permission of Macmillan Publishing Co., Inc.(107).

Cadwallader, Sharon, *Sharon Cadwallader's Complete Cookbook.* Copyright © 1977 by Sharon Cadwallader. Reprinted by permission of San Francisco Book Company, Inc.(105).

Capon, Robert Farrar, *Party Spirit.* Copyright © 1979 by Robert Farrar Capon. By permission of William Morrow & Company(104).

Carrier, Robert, *Robert Carrier's Entertaining.* Copyright © 1977, 1978 by Robert Carrier. Reprinted by permission of A & W Publishers, Inc.(93, 106, 129).

Cass, Elizabeth, *Spanish Cooking.* Copyright © Elizabeth Cass, 1957. First published by André Deutsch Ltd., 1957. Also published by Mayflower Books Ltd., 1970. By permission of André Deutsch Ltd., London(113).

Castle, Coralie and Barbara Lawrence, *Hors d'Oeuvre Etc.* Copyright © 1973 Coralie Castle and Barbara Lawrence. Published by 101 Productions, San Francisco. Reprinted by permission of 101 Productions(141).

Chamberlain, Narcissa G. and Narcisse Chamberlain, *The Flavor of France in Recipes and Pictures, Volume II.* Copyright © 1978 by Hastings House, Publishers, Inc. By permission of Hastings House, Publishers(94). *The Flavor of Italy in Recipes and Pictures.* Copyright © 1965 by Hastings House, Publishers, Inc. By permission of Hastings House, Publishers(116).

Chamberlain, Narcisse, *French Menus for Parties.* Recipes by Narcissa G. Chamberlain. Copyright © 1968 by Hastings House, Publishers, Inc. By permission of Hastings House, Publishers(125).

Chantiles, Vilma Liacouras, *The Food of Greece.* Copyright © 1975 by Vilma Liacouras Chantiles. Published by Atheneum, New York. By permission of Vilma Liacouras Chantiles(102).

Clancy, John & Frances Field, *Clancy's Oven Cookery.* Copyright © 1976 by John Clancy and Frances Field. Reprinted by permission of Delacorte Press/Eleanor Friede(130, 137, 138, 146).

Cowles, Florence, *1001 Sandwiches.* Copyright 1936 by Florence A. Cowles. Reprinted by permission of the Estate of Miss Florence A. Cowles(103, 117, 122).

La Cuisine Lyonnaise. Published by Éditions Gutenberg, 1947(110).

The Culinary Arts Institute Staff, *Mexican Cookbook.* Copyright © 1976 by Delair Publishing Co., Inc., New York. Reprinted by permission of Delair Publishing Co., Inc.(160).

Cutler, Carol, *The Six-Minute Soufflé and Other Culinary Delights.* Copyright © 1976 by Carol Cutler. Used by permission of Clarkson N. Potter, Inc.(101).

Dannenbaum, Julie, *Julie Dannenbaum's Creative Cooking School.* Copyright © 1971 by Julie Dannenbaum. Reprinted by permission of Edward Acton, Inc.(95, 129).

Darden, Norma Jean and Carole Darden, *Spoonbread and Strawberry Wine.* Copyright © 1978 by Norma Jean Darden and Carole Darden. Reprinted by permission of Doubleday & Company, Inc.(137).

David, Elizabeth, *A Book of Mediterranean Food.* Copyright © Elizabeth David, 1958, 1965, 1980. Published by Jill Norman Ltd., London. Reprinted by permission of Jill Norman Ltd.(99, 134). *French Provincial Cooking.* Copyright © Elizabeth David, 1960, 1962, 1967, 1970. Published by Penguin Books Ltd., in association with Michael Joseph. By permission of Elizabeth David(141).

De Andrade, Margarette, *Brazilian Cookery.* Copyright in Japan, 1965, by The Charles E. Tuttle Company, Inc. Published by The Charles E. Tuttle Company, Inc., Tokyo. Reprinted by permission of The Charles E. Tuttle Company, Inc.(99).

De la Rosa, Angeles and C. Gandia de Fernández, *Flavors of Mexico.* Copyright © 1978 by 101 Productions. Adapted from *Cocina Mexicana,* copyright © 1972 Editores Mexicanos Unidos, S.A., Mexico, D.F. and *Especialidades de la Cocina Mexicana,* copyright © 1975 Editores Mexicanos Unidos, S.A., Mexico, D.F. By permission of 101 Productions(157, 159).

Mrs. de Salis, *Savouries à la Mode.* Published by Longmans, Green, and Co., London, 1900(109).

Eekhof-Stork, Nancy, *The Great International Cheese Board.* Edited by Adrian Bailey. Based on selections from the *Spectrum Kaasatlas.* © 1976, 1979 by Het Spectrum B.V., Utrecht. Reprinted by permission of Het Spectrum B.V., Utrecht(135).

Ellison, J. Audrey, B.S., *The Great Scandinavian Cook Book.* © Wezäta Förlag, Göteborg, Sweden, 1963. English translation © J. Audrey Ellison, 1966. Reprinted by permission of Crown Publishers, Inc.(105, 111, 138, 150).

Field, Michael, *Cooking Adventures with Michael Field: Pies, Tarts and Chou Puffs.* Copyright © 1971 by Frances Field. Published by Nelson Doubleday, Inc. Reprinted by permission of Jonathan Rude-Field(141). *Michael Field's Cooking School.* Copyright © 1956 by Michael Field. Reprinted by permission of Jonathan Rude-Field(150).

Foods of the World, *American Cooking: Creole and Acadian; American Cooking: The Melting Pot; The Cooking of China; The Cooking of India.* © 1971 Time Inc.; © 1971 Time Inc.; © 1968 Time Inc.; © 1969 Time Inc. Published by Time-Life Books, Alexandria, Virginia(122; 153; 152; 149).

Ghedini, Francesco, *Northern Italian Cooking.* Copyright © 1973 by Paola Schiavina Ghedini, Gabriella Martelli Ghedini and Anita Ghedini Gardini. By permission of Hawthorn Books, a division of Elsevier-Dutton Publishing Co., Inc.(113).

Gill, Janice Murray, *Nova Scotia Down-Home Cooking.* Copyright © Janice Murray Gill, 1978. Reprinted by permission of McGraw-Hill Ryerson, Toronto(113).

Gilly, Antoine and Jack Denton Scott, *Antoine Gilly's Feast of France.* Copyright © 1971 by Antoine Gilly and Jack Denton Scott. Reprinted by permission of Harper & Row, Publishers, Inc.(133).

Gin, Margaret and Alfred E. Castle, *Regional Cooking of China.* © 1975 Margaret Gin and Alfred Castle. Published by 101 Productions, San Francisco, California. Reprinted by permission of 101 Productions(143, 145).

Graves, Eleanor, *Great Dinners from Life.* Copyright © 1969 Time Inc. Published by Time-Life Books, Alexandria, Virginia(134).

The Great Cooks' Guide to Omelets from Around the World. Copyright © 1977 by Laura Sloate. Published by Beard Glaser Wolf Ltd. Reprinted by permission of Carol Cutler(130 — Carol Cutler).

Guérard, Michel, *Michel Guérard's Cuisine Gourmande.* English translation copyright © 1979 by William Morrow & Company, Inc. Originally published in French under the title *La Cuisine Gourmande,* © 1978 by Editions Robert Laffont, S.A. By permission of William Morrow & Company, Inc.(108).

Harrington, Geri, *The Salad Book.* Copyright © 1977 by Geri Harrington. Used by permission of Atheneum Publishers(97).

Hazelton, Nika, *The Picnic Book.* © 1969 by Nika Hazelton. Published by Atheneum, New York. Reprinted by permission of Curtis Brown, Ltd.(105, 125).

Herisko, Clarence, *Drinks and Snacks for All Occasions.* Copyright 1960 by Imperial Publishing Co. Published by Imperial Publishing Co., New York(107).

Hewitt, Jean, *The New York Times Large-Type Cook-*

book. Copyright © 1969 by Jean Hewitt. Reprinted by permission of Times Books, a division of Quadrangle/The New York Times Book Co., Inc.(123). *The New York Times Weekend Cookbook.* Copyright © 1975 by Jean Hewitt. Reprinted by permission of Times Books, a division of Quadrangle/The New York Times Book Co., Inc.(109).

Hill, Janet McKenzie, *Salads, Sandwiches and Chafing-Dish Dainties.* Copyright 1899, 1903, 1914 by Janet M. Hill. Published by Little, Brown and Company, Boston, 1925(116, 123).

Hirst, Irene (Editor), *The Beeton Homebooks: Hors d'Oeuvres and Salads (Volume 6).* © Ward, Lock & Co. Limited 1964. Published by Ward, Lock & Co. Limited, London. Reprinted by permission of Ward Lock Limited (128, 132).

Hush, Joanne and Peter Wong, *The Chinese Menu Cookbook.* Copyright © 1976 by Joanne Hush and Peter Wong. Reprinted by permission of Holt, Rinehart and Winston, Publishers(145).

Lady Jekyll, D.B.E., *Kitchen Essays.* © Copyright Lady Freyburg. Published by Collins Publishers, London. Reprinted by permission of Collins Publishers(134).

Jen, Eva Lee, *Chinese Cooking in the American Kitchen.* Copyright © 1978 by Kodansha International Ltd. Reprinted by permission of Kodansha International Ltd. (128, 142).

Johnson, Alice B., *The Complete Scandinavian Cookbook.* Copyright © Alice B. Johnson 1964. Reprinted with permission of Macmillan Publishing Co., Inc.(110).

The Junior League of the City of New York, *New York Entertains.* Copyright © 1974 by The Junior League of the City of New York, Inc. Reprinted by permission of Doubleday & Company, Inc.(107, 126).

The Junior League of Corpus Christi, *Fiesta: Favorite Recipes of South Texas.* © Junior League of Corpus Christi, Inc., 1973. Reprinted by permission of The Junior League of Corpus Christi, Inc.(157—Mrs. John Charles Abbott).

Junior League of Houston, *Houston Junior League Cook Book.* © Junior League of Houston, Inc., 1968. Reprinted by permission of Junior League of Houston, Inc.(118—Mrs. James H. Weyland).

Kamman, Madeleine, *The Making of a Cook.* Copyright © 1971 by Madeleine Kamman. Used by permission of Atheneum Publishers(136). *When French Women Cook.* Copyright © 1976 by Madeleine M. Kamman. Used by permission of Atheneum Publishers(96, 112).

Kaplan, Janet, *Crackers and Snackers.* Copyright © 1976 by Janet Kaplan. Reprinted by permission of Janet Kaplan, 46 Rodeo Avenue, Sausalito, California 94965(146).

Kennedy, Diana, *Recipes from the Regional Cooks of Mexico.* Copyright © 1978 by Diana Kennedy. Reprinted by permission of Harper & Row, Publishers, Inc.(98). *The Tortilla Book.* Copyright © 1975 by Diana Kennedy. Reprinted by permission of Harper & Row, Publishers, Inc.(156, 158, 160).

Kenney-Herbert, Col. A. F. (Wyvern), *Commonsense Cookery for English Households.* Published by Edward Arnold, London, 1894(92).

Koehler, Margaret H., *Recipes from the Portuguese of Provincetown.* Copyright © 1973 by Margaret H. Koehler. Reprinted by permission of The Chatham Press, Inc., Old Greenwich, Connecticut(120).

Kolatch, David (Editor), *Completely Cheese: The Cheese Lover's Companion,* by Anita May Pearl, Constance Cuttle and Barbara B. Deskins. Copyright © 1978 by Jonathan David Publishers, Inc., Middle Village, New York. Reprinted by permission of Jonathan David Publishers, Inc.(95).

Lang, George, *The Cuisine of Hungary.* Copyright © 1971 by George Lang. Used by permission of Atheneum Publishers(96, 146).

Langseth-Christensen, Lillian, *Cold Foods for Summer and Winter.* Copyright © 1974 by Lillian Langseth-Christensen. Reprinted by permission of Doubleday & Company, Inc.(124, 127, 128).

Lau, Mary Louise, *The Delicious World of Raw Foods.* Copyright © 1977 by Mary Louise Lau. Reprinted by permission of Rawson, Wade Publishers, Inc.(114).

Lee, Calvin B. T. and Audrey Evans Lee, *The Gourmet Chinese Regional Cookbook.* Copyright © 1976 by Calvin B. T. Lee and Audrey Evans Lee. Reprinted by permission of G. P. Putnam's Sons(143, 144, 152).

Lin, Florence, *Florence Lin's Chinese Regional Cookbook.* Copyright © 1975 by Florence Lin. Reprinted by permission of Hawthorn Books, a division of Elsevier-Dutton Publishing Co., Inc.(139, 148, 151).

Lo, Kenneth, *The Encyclopedia of Chinese Cooking.* Copyright © 1979, 1974 by Kenneth Lo. Reprinted by permission of A & W Publishers, Inc.(142).

Lucas, Dione and Marion Gorman, *The Dione Lucas Book of French Cooking.* Copyright 1947 by Dione Lucas. Copyright © 1973 by Mark Lucas and Marion F. Gorman. Reprinted by permission of Little, Brown and Company (93).

Ma, Nancy Chih, *Cook Chinese.* Copyright © 1964 by Kodansha International Ltd. Used by permission of Kodansha International Ltd.(144).

McIntyre, Nancy Fair, *Cooking in Crust.* Copyright © 1974 by Gala Books. Published by Gala Books, Laguna Beach, California. Reprinted by permission of Nancy Fair McIntyre(133, 135, 136, 138).

MacMillan, Diane, *The Portable Feast.* Copyright © 1973 Diane MacMillan. Published by 101 Productions, San Francisco. Reprinted by permission of 101 Productions (105, 120).

Marcus, Melanie, *Cooking with a Harvard Accent.* Copyright © 1979 by Melanie Marcus. Reprinted by permission of Houghton-Mifflin Company(103, 126).

Marty, Albin, *Fourmiguetto: Souvenirs, Contes et Recettes du Languedoc.* Published by Éditions CREER, Nonette, France, 1978. Translated by permission of Éditions CREER(96).

Mayer, Paul, *Paris . . . and then some.* © 1971 Nitty Gritty Productions, Concord, California. Used by permission of Nitty Gritty Productions(114).

Meighn, Moira, M.C.A., *Simplified Cooking and Invalid Diet.* First published in 1939 by Faber and Faber Limited, London. Reprinted by permission of Faber and Faber Limited(106).

Meyers, Perla, *The Peasant Kitchen.* Copyright © 1975 by Perla Meyers. Reprinted by permission of Harper & Row, Publishers, Inc.(115, 121, 125).

Muffoletto, Anna, *The Art of Sicilian Cooking.* Copyright © 1971 by Anna Muffoletto. Reprinted by permission of Doubleday & Company, Inc.(112).

El Mundo Gastronómico. Published by Damas Grises, La Cruz Roja Colombiana, Cali, Colombia(100).

Nilson, Bee (Editor), *The WI Diamond Jubilee Cookbook.* © 1975 A. R. Nilson and National Federation of Women's Institutes. Published by William Heinemann Ltd., London. Reprinted by permission of William Heinemann Ltd.(95).

Norman, Cecilia, *The Crêpe and Pancake Cookbook.* © Cecilia Norman 1979. First published in 1979 by Barrie and Jenkins Ltd., London. Reprinted by permission of Hutchinson Publishing Group Limited(156).

Oliver, Raymond, *La Cuisine: Secrets of Modern French Cooking.* Translated and edited by Nika Standen Hazelton with Jack Van Bibber. French copyright © 1967 by Éditions Bordas. Copyright © 1969 by Leon Amiel, Publisher, New York. Used by permission of Leon Amiel, Publisher (131).

Ortiz, Elisabeth Lambert, *The Complete Book of Mexican Cooking.* Copyright © 1967 by Elisabeth Lambert Ortiz. Reprinted by permission of the publisher, M. Evans and Company, Inc., New York(160).

Pascoe, Ann, *Cornish Recipes, Old and New.* Copyright © by Tor Mark Press. Published by Tor Mark Press, Truro, Cornwall, England. Reprinted by permission of Tor Mark Press(135).

Pellaprat, Henri Paul, *The Great Book of French Cuisine.* Copyright © 1966, 1971 by René Kramer, Publisher, Castagnola/Lugano, Switzerland. Reprinted by permission of Harper & Row, Publishers, Inc.(92).

Petersen, Bengt, *Delicious Fish Dishes.* © Bengt Petersen/Wezäta Förlag 1976. Published by Wezäta Förlag, Göteborg, Sweden. By permission of Wezäta Förlag (115).

Pezzini, Wilma, *The Tuscan Cookbook.* Copyright ©

1978 by Wilma Pezzini. Used by permission of Atheneum Publishers(127).

Poulson, Joan, *Old Lancashire Recipes.* © Joan Poulson 1973. Published by Hendon Publishing Company Limited, Nelson, Lancashire, England. Reprinted by permission of Hendon Publishing Company Limited(137).

Price, Mary and Vincent, *A Treasury of Great Recipes.* Copyright © 1965 by Mary and Vincent Price. Used by permission of Grosset & Dunlap, Inc.(118).

Rhode, Irma, *Cool Entertaining.* Copyright © 1976 by Irma Rhode. Used by permission of Atheneum Publishers(117, 127).

Robbins, Ann Roe, *Treadway Inns Cookbook.* Copyright © 1958 by Ann Roe Robbins. Reprinted by permission of Little, Brown and Company(124).

Robertson, Alden, *The No Baloney Sandwich Book.* Copyright © 1978 by Alden Robertson. Reprinted by permission of Doubleday & Company, Inc.(117).

Romagnoli, Margaret and G. Franco, *The Romagnolis' Table.* Copyright © 1974, 1975 by Margaret and G. Franco Romagnoli. Reprinted by permission of Little, Brown and Company in association with the Atlantic Monthly Press(154).

Rombauer, Irma S. and Marion Rombauer Becker, *Joy of Cooking.* Copyright © 1931, 1936, 1941, 1942, 1943, 1946, 1951, 1952, 1953, 1962, 1963, 1964, 1975 by The Bobbs-Merrill Company, Inc. Reprinted by permission of The Bobbs-Merrill Company, Inc.(94, 101, 102).

Rosen, Ruth Chier, *Just Between Us.* Copyright 1955, Richards Rosen Associates, Inc., New York. Reprinted by permission of Richards Rosen Press, Inc.(116).

Saiger, Lydia, *The Junk Food Cookbook.* Copyright © 1979 by Lydia Saiger. Published by Jove Publications, Inc. Reprinted by permission of Jove Publications, Inc.(118, 120, 154).

St. Paul's Greek Orthodox Church, The Women of, *The Art of Greek Cookery.* Copyright © 1961, 1963 by St. Paul's Greek Orthodox Church of Hempstead, New York. Reprinted by permission of Doubleday & Company, Inc.(101, 103).

St. Stephen's Episcopal Church, *Bayou Cuisine: Its Tradition and Transition.* Edited by Mrs. Arthur B. Clark Jr. Copyright 1970 St. Stephen's Episcopal Church. Published by St. Stephen's Episcopal Church, Indianola, Mississippi. Reprinted by permission of St. Stephen's Episcopal Church(104).

Salta, Romeo, *The Pleasures of Italian Cooking.* © Romeo Salta 1962. Reprinted with permission of Macmillan Publishing Co., Inc.(104).

Sandoval, George E., *Sandoval's Mexican Cookbook.* © 1966 by George E. Sandoval. Published by George E. Sandoval, Publisher, Tucson, Arizona. Reprinted by permission of George E. Sandoval(155).

Schryver, Alice and Francille Wallace, *The Complete Hors d'Oeuvres Book.* © 1957, 1958 by Alice Schryver and Francille Wallace. Reprinted by permission of Curtis Brown, Ltd.(123, 124).

Schultz, Sigrid, *Overseas Press Club Cookbook.* Copyright © 1962 by Overseas Press Club of America, Inc. Reprinted by permission of Doubleday & Company, Inc.(114).

Shircliffe, Arnold, *The Edgewater Sandwich and Hors d'Oeuvres Book.* First published in 1930 by the Hotel Monthly Press under the title *The Edgewater Sandwich Book.* Reprinted by permission of Dover Publications, Inc.(92, 121, 123).

Shulman, Martha Rose, *The Vegetarian Feast.* Copyright © 1979 by Martha Rose Shulman. Reprinted by permission of Harper & Row, Publishers, Inc.(94, 101).

Sokolov, Raymond A., *Great Recipes from the New York Times.* Copyright © 1973 by Raymond A. Sokolov. By permission of Times Books, a division of Quadrangle/The New York Times Book Co., Inc.(147, 148, 151).

Springer, Rita G., *Caribbean Cookbook.* © Rita G. Springer 1968. First published 1968 by Evans Brothers Limited, London. Reprinted by permission of Evans Brothers Limited(136).

Stechishin, Savella, *Traditional Ukrainian Cookery.*

Copyright 1957, 1959 by Savella Stechisin. Published by Trident Press Limited, Winnipeg, Canada. Reprinted by permission of Trident Press Limited(118).
Theoharous, Anne, *Cooking and Baking the Greek Way.* Copyright © 1977 by Anne Theoharous. Reprinted by permission of Holt, Rinehart and Winston, Publishers (99, 139).
Toklas, Alice B., *The Alice B. Toklas Cook Book.* Copyright 1954 by Alice B. Toklas. Reprinted by permission of Harper & Row, Publishers, Inc.(117).
Tschirky, Oscar, *The Cook Book by "Oscar" of the Waldorf.* Published by The Werner Company, New York, 1896(108, 121).
Uvezian, Sonia, *The Book of Yogurt.* Copyright © 1978 Sonia Uvezian. Published by 101 Productions, San Francisco. Reprinted by permission of 101 Productions(97).
Vaughan, Beatrice, *Yankee Hill-Country Cooking.* Copyright © 1963 by Beatrice Vaughan. Published by The Stephen Greene Press, Brattleboro, Vermont. Reprinted by permission of The Stephen Greene Press(150).
Verdon, René, *The White House Chef Cookbook.* Copy-right © 1967 by René Verdon. Reprinted by permission of Doubleday & Company, Inc.(124).
Vergé, Roger, *Roger Vergé's Cuisine of the South of France.* English translation © 1980 by William Morrow & Company, Inc. Originally published in French under the title *Ma Cuisine du Soleil.* © 1978 by Éditions Robert Laffont, S.A. Reprinted by permission of William Morrow & Company, Inc.(111).
Wagner, Bonita, *Nibblers and Munchers.* © 1972 by Westover. Used by permission of Crown Publishers, Inc.(108).
Waldo, Myra, *The Complete Round-the-World Cookbook.* Copyright 1954 by Myra Waldo Schwartz. Reprinted by permission of the author(98).
Willinsky, Grete, *Kulinarische Weltreise.* © 1961 by Mary Hahns Kochbuchverlag, West Berlin. Published by Büchergilde Gutenberg, Frankfurt am Main. Reprinted by permission of Mary Hahns Kochbuchverlag(92).
Witty, Helen and Elizabeth Schneider Colchie, *Better Than Store-Bought.* Copyright © 1979 by Helen Witty and Elizabeth Schneider Colchie. Reprinted by permission of Harper & Row, Publishers, Inc.(100, 106).
Wolfert, Paula, *Mediterranean Cooking.* Copyright © 1977 by Paula Wolfert. By permission of Times Books, a division of Quadrangle/The New York Times Book Co., Inc.(140).
Wolf Trap Associates, *Wolf Trap Picnic Cookbook.* © 1976 by Wolf Trap Associates. Reprinted by permission of Wolf Trap Associates, Vienna, Virginia(102).
Woman's Day Collector's Cook Book. Copyright © 1975 Woman's Day. Reprinted by permission of Woman's Day, a division of CBS Publications(111).
Woman's World Book of Salads & Sandwiches, copyright 1927, Woman's World Magazine Co., Inc., Chicago(98).
Yee, Rhoda, *Dim Sum.* Copyright © 1977 Rhoda Yee. Published by Taylor & NG Press, San Francisco. Reprinted by permission of Taylor & NG Press(143).
Zelayeta, Elena, *Elena's Secrets of Mexican Cooking.* © 1958 by Prentice-Hall, Inc. Published by Prentice-Hall, Inc., Englewood Cliffs, New Jersey. Reprinted by permission of Prentice-Hall, Inc.(97, 100, 158, 161).

Acknowledgments

The indexes for this book were prepared by Louise W. Hedberg. The editors are particularly indebted to Pierre Olaf Fahlman, chef for the Embassy of Sweden, Washington, D.C.; Lydia Jasso, Rio Grande Restaurant, Rockville, Maryland; Elizabeth Moy, Washington, D.C.; and Stacy Zacharias, Alexandria, Virginia (all of whom demonstrated cooking techniques for this book). Special thanks are also due to Elna de Barros, Embassy of Chile, Washington, D.C.; Bruce Bolton, New York, New York;

Katherine Boulukos, St. Paul's Greek Orthodox Church, Hempstead, New York; Gene Cope, U.S. Department of Commerce, Washington, D.C.; Jean S. Danes, L'Estaminet Restaurant, Alexandria, Virginia; Dr. George Flick, Virginia Polytechnic Institute and State University, Blacksburg; Florence Lin, China Institute, New York, New York; Robert Rodriguez, American Institute of Baking, Manhattan, Kansas; Donald Bruce White, New York, New York.

The editors also wish to thank: Sara Beck, U.S. Department of Agriculture; The Bread Oven Restaurant, Washington, D.C.; The British Information Service, New York, New York;

Diane Creedon, Food and Wine from France, Inc., New York, New York; Bertha Fontaine, National Marine Fisheries Service, Pascagoula, Mississippi; Nancy Purves Pollard, Leslie Barnes Hagan, Dorothy Pollard Lagemann, La Cuisine, Alexandria, Virginia; Joan Reynolds, The Wheat Flour Institute, Washington, D.C.; Lois Ross, The Quaker Oats Company, Chicago, Illinois; Dr. Malcolm Ross, U.S. Geological Survey, Reston, Virginia; Ann Seranne, Newton, New Jersey; Cathy Sharpe, Springfield, Virginia; Gay Starrak, National Live Stock and Meat Board, Chicago, Illinois; Ella R. Udall, Washington, D.C.; José Wilson, Rockport, Massachusetts.

Picture Credits

The sources for the pictures in this book are listed below. Credits for the photographers and illustrators are listed by page number with successive pages indicated by hyphens; where necessary, the locations of pictures within pages also are indicated — separated from page numbers by dashes.

Photographs by Aldo Tutino: cover, 4-13, 16-90.

Other photographs (alphabetically): Tom Belshaw, 14-15 — bottom. Louis Klein, 2. Bob Komar, 14-15 — top.

Illustrations (alphabetically): From the Mary Evans Picture Library and private sources and *Food & Drink: A Pictorial Archive from Nineteenth Century Sources* by Jim Harter, published by Dover Publications, Inc., 1979, 93-167.
Endpapers: Designed by John Pack.

Library of Congress Cataloguing in Publication Data
Time-Life Books.
  Snacks and sandwiches.
  (The Good cook, techniques and recipes)
  Includes index.
  1. Snack foods. 2. Sandwiches. I. Title.
  II. Series: Good cook, techniques and recipes.
TX740.T46   1980a   641.5'3   80-13557
ISBN 0-8094-2885-7
ISBN 0-8094-2884-9 lib. bdg.
ISBN 0-8094-2883-0 ret. ed.